SIMPLE
HOMEBREWING

GREAT BEER. LESS WORK. MORE FUN.

By Drew Beechum & Denny Conn

BREWERS
PUBLICATIONS.

Brewers Publications®
A Division of the Brewers Association
PO Box 1679, Boulder, Colorado 80306-1679
BrewersAssociation.org
BrewersPublications.com

Proudly printed in the United States of America

10 9 8 7 6 5 4 3 2 1
ISBN-13: 978-1-938469-59-6
Ebook ISBN-13: 978-1-938469-62-6

Library of Congress Cataloging-in-Publication Data
Names: Beechum, Drew, author. | Conn, Denny, author.
Title: Simple homebrewing : great beer, less work, more fun / by Drew Beechum
  and Denny Conn.
Description: Boulder, Colorado : Brewers Publications, a Division of the
  Brewers Association, [2019] | Includes bibliographical references and
  index.
Identifiers: LCCN 2018056032 | ISBN 9781938469596 (pbk.) | ISBN 9781938469626
  (ebook)
Subjects: LCSH: Brewing--Amateurs' manuals. | Beer. | LCGFT: Cookbooks.
Classification: LCC TP577 .B365 2019 | DDC 641.87/3--dc23 LC record available at https://lccn.loc.gov/2018056032

Publisher: Kristi Switzer
Technical Editor: John Palmer
Copyediting: Iain Cox
Indexing: Doug Easton
Art Direction: Jason Smith, Danny Harms
Cover Design: Danny Harms
Production and Interior Design: Justin Petersen
Cover Photo: Aaron Colussi
Interior photos: Authors unless otherwise noted.

For all the homebrewers striving one pot, one pitch, one pint at a time to find their magic in a glass of beer. We hope this helps you find your way to a moment of simplicity.

TABLE OF CONTENTS

LIST OF RECIPES

FOREWORD

This book is exactly what the homebrewing world needs today. Well, at the very least, this book is exactly what I need, but I know that I'm not the only homebrewer who can't find the time to brew as often as I'd like to. I started homebrewing 25 years ago, a time when all but the geekiest of homebrewers were brewing with extracts and most of us relied on the mantra, "Relax, don't worry, have a homebrew." That mantra was taught to us in *The Complete Joy of Home Brewing*, written by the founder of the American Homebrewers Association (AHA) and godfather of homebrewing, Charlie Papazian. Back in the early days, my homebrewing was quite simple: extract batches, brewed on the stove top, fermented with direct-pitched dried yeast in a single plastic bucket fermentor. I made tasty beers with that simple set-up (at least that's what my friends and family told me).

In 2000, I got hired as the AHA administrator. Suddenly, I was exposed to a deluge of information from *Zymurgy* magazine and Brewers Publications books, but the most direct exposure came from active discussions on the AHA TechTalk and Home Brew Digest email forums. All that information helped me make the leap to all-grain brewing and added new techniques to my repertoire. I built my own brewing equipment, which I felt the need to constantly tweak to gain a tiny bit of improvement in my brewing. In fact, I'm quite sure I spent more time in those days working on my equipment than I did on brewing beer.

When I became a father, I found it much harder to carve out enough hours on the weekends when I wasn't traveling for work, and so my brewing became much less frequent. I'm also terrible at planning ahead in my personal life, so even when I do find time to brew I may not have the ingredients together so that I actually can brew.

I know I'm not alone in my struggles to find time to brew. Surveys of homebrewers conducted at the AHA show that many homebrewers are brewing less frequently or have given up entirely due to the increasingly busy pace of life. In addition, the internet has evolved from the email forums of my early AHA days to a vast proliferation of information (much of which is inaccurate) provided by websites, podcasts, YouTube, and social media. The inundation of information can make it easy to get into brewing, but it can also make homebrewing seem more complicated than it should be, and thus less approachable.

Now, thanks to my friends Drew Beechum and Denny Conn, we have a solution to this problem: the book you hold right now, *Simple Homebrewing*.

Denny and Drew are the perfect authors for this book. They are both extremely accomplished homebrewers. I've been a homebrewer longer than either of those two, and have actually made a career serving homebrewers, but Denny and Drew know more about brewing than I probably ever will. I've had the privilege of trying some of their wilder concoctions, such as the infamous Clam Chowder Saison for which Drew conceived the recipe, and Denny's Wee Shroomy mushroom Scotch ale, of which I've had a couple of variations. While I might not order a pint of it, the Clam Chowder Saison was quite drinkable, actually reminiscent of clam chowder but without any of the gag reflex you might anticipate with such a concept. I don't know any other brewer who could pull that off. When I sampled Denny's Wee Shroomy during Club Night at the 2012 Homebrew Con™ in Seattle, I expected an urge to spit it out (or hurl). Instead, I found it utterly delicious; I wanted more. I don't typically like Scotch ales, but I won't turn down a chance to sip some more Wee Shroomy!

Before we go any further, I should tell you what this book is not. It is not a book that will teach you how to brew beer for the first time. If you've never brewed before, go get John Palmer's *How to Brew* or Charlie Papazian's *Complete Joy of Home Brewing*, read the first few chapters, brew a few batches of beer, then come back to this book.

For a seasoned homebrewer who might be thinking a title like *Simple Homebrewing* "couldn't possibly be for me," think again. This book isn't about dumbing down the brewing process to the lowest common denominator.

Simple Homebrewing helps homebrewers cut through the overgrown jungle of brewing processes, equipment, jargon, and traditions and get down to the business of making really great beer without taking up an exorbitant amount of your free time while doing it. As Denny and Drew put it, the point is to "Brew the Best Beer Possible, With the Least Effort Possible, While Having the Most Fun Possible." I need to frame that mantra and put it on my brew room wall.

In this hobby it is easy to get caught up with both traditional practices and the need to try out the most innovative techniques. Unfortunately, most of the time those practices and techniques tend to add up to make the brewing process longer than it should be. As far as I'm concerned, the only thing that truly matters is the end result. Why not brew a malt extract recipe using a 20-minute boil if the end result is a great tasting beer? Great tasting beer made with less effort sounds pretty awesome to me!

Simple Homebrewing isn't a guide for a particular approach to brewing that will streamline your process. It's not an Atkins™ diet for slimming down your brewing method. *Simple Homebrewing* gives the reader many examples of how various processes can be simplified to make it easier to brew without compromising the quality of your beer. I recently ditched my homebuilt brew system with the goal of simplifying my brewing and hopefully brewing more frequently, and bought an off-the-shelf electric system that now resides in a dedicated brew room in my basement. Yet, as I read through the manuscript of this book, I still found example after example of ways I can further simplify and probably make better beer, while spending less time doing it.

In *Simple Homebrewing*, Denny and Drew take on some complex issues and make them approachable. I was scarred for life by my experience with high school chemistry and have avoided the subject ever since, so water chemistry for brewers is a subject I've been avoiding in my hobby. But no more! The "Simple Water" chapter and had some easy-to-implement suggestions that I have already begun to follow, such as ditching my carbon filter for Campden tablets to remove chlorine from my brewing water.

I couldn't agree more with Denny and Drew's approach to recipe design, which focuses on how to get a particular flavor profile by thoughtful selection of ingredients. Far too many homebrewers take a "kitchen sink" approach to recipe design, thinking that the more different malts and hops used, the more complex and flavorful their beers will be. The end result of that approach is all too often a muddled mess of flavors. So, read "Simple Recipe Design" and follow the authors' advice.

How to approach this book? Start by reading the first chapter, "What is Simplicity?," which will help you understand the authors' approach. From there, you can bounce around to the subjects you are most interested in. Apply the tips that are most relevant to your method of brewing. Eventually, you'll want to read every bit of this book—there are so many unexpected takeaways offered by Denny and Drew that you'd miss out on them if you don't read it all.

Now, start reading and get on with making great beer, with less work, while having more fun.

Gary Glass
Director, American Homebrewers Association

ACKNOWLEDGMENTS

There's no way a book like this doesn't happen without a ton of assistance. So let's do our best to call it out.

First, a hat tip for the yin to my yang, the Abbott to my Costello—Denny. He has learned to be surprisingly calm with the last-minute high-wire act that is working with me. We've been having fun working together for way too many hours over way too many years now. My hope is we keep getting to do so!

Thanks to all the people who've helped in the making of this book, including all our Profiles in Simplicity participants. It's always more interesting when you can grab someone else's knowledge! The same goes for the members of my homebrew club—the Maltose Falcons—for continuing to challenge the things I think I know.

Thanks to my dogs for not caring one whit about beer and demanding attention and walks instead.

Thanks to beer for being beer!

Lastly, thanks to my wife, Amy, for looking at this hobby gone mad and understanding it, mostly.

—Drew Beechum

None of this would have ever happened if my beery other half Drew hadn't asked me to join him in writing a book years ago. Three books and two podcasts later, I've forgiven him! What can you say about a guy who can make my writing readable and even put up with me being Mr. Grumpy? I love him and look forward to us doing more in the future.

Thanks to Gary Glass and Chris Frey for encouraging me to stay involved. Without their kind words I might have long ago retreated into solo homebrewing.

Thanks to John Palmer for his work as technical editor on this book. I hope we didn't make his head explode with our heresy!

Thanks to my lovely wife, Paula, who not only got me started homebrewing and puts up with it, but encourages me to do some of the crazy things I do.

And a huge thanks to all the homebrewers all over the world. It's you people who restore my passion and give me inspiration. You are truly the reason we do this.

—Denny Conn

INTRODUCTION

The first time beer was made, it probably happened by accident. Apocryphal stories put it on the level of events like "mold formed in my petri dishes" or "you put chocolate in my peanut butter"—in other words, moments that define history. We can't say for certain, because not even Denny is old enough to have witnessed that epic happening.

Since the arrival of beer, we've studied it, experimented with its processes, experimented with its ingredients, explored its ins and outs, and generally complicated the hell out of it. It's what humans do, it's how our great cultural advances came to be. Seriously, we can't leave anything alone. But maybe, just maybe, that kind of scrutiny and control isn't the only way to make beer. Maybe it's time we step back a bit, take a firm grasp on the simple basics, and remember why we brew.

We want you to know that *Simple Homebrewing* is not just for beginners. If you are a beginner reading this book, you will get ideas on how to streamline your process, but we're not going to teach you homebrewing from scratch. There are other books to get you started, like *How to Brew* by our dear friend John Palmer. What we are going to teach you is a different way to brew, how to take the principles outlined in other homebrewing sources

> "If you're not having fun, you're doing it wrong."

and adapt them to your own way of doing things and make brewing fit into your life.

In a great many ways, simplicity is the hallmark of complete mastery. If you're an experienced homebrewer and thinking, "Pshaw! I know all I need to know about brewing," maybe you're right. But maybe, perhaps probably, you've never stopped to ponder the exact reasons for the fuss you put into your beer. We're not arguing for simple mindlessness, we're arguing for simple mindfulness, where everything you do has meaning. A master craftsman will make a process look simple because he has no wasted motion.

We want you to relax and make homebrewing work for you. We want you to imbue your brew days with a sense of Denny's mantra, "If you're not having fun, you're doing it wrong." We're going to explain the working details in an easy way, so you can integrate them into your process and then not have to think about them again. We'll show you how to save time and money when you brew without sacrificing beer quality. We'll show you how to avoid the stress that sometimes drives homebrewers out of the hobby. We're fairly egalitarian, so we won't just pass off our brewing methods as the only true way to simplify your life.

Over our collective years of brewing and researching, we've seen brewers make things more difficult in the name of their MacGuffin. Efficiency, the perfect Pilsner, you name it, whatever you can think of—never-ending debates raging around this or that arcane process that may or may not improve your beer. Arguments about better ingredients, process, technique, or yeast whispering abound in this world. While fun, very little of it has anything to do with making great beer or making lifelong converts to homebrew.

We've been through all that and come out the other side. We're not opposed to expensive equipment or arcane processes. We use multiple processes and approaches based on our mood, goals, and obsessions. But we want you to know that you don't have to be "one of those people" to make great beer and have a great time doing it.

If you're a homebrewer that believes if it isn't difficult it isn't worth it, go forth and make the beer you do the way you do, and enjoy it. We love that you've found your way.

For the rest of you—first timers, semi-lost enthusiasts, the questing journeymen, or the cynical, weary experts—how about you join us on this beer-soaked journey to find the fast, the fun, and the fine? ■

1
WHAT IS SIMPLICITY?

THE INHERENT SIMPLICITY OF BEER

A wise man once said, "Malted barley wants to become beer." But, as with all human endeavors, we've complicated that effort to the point of losing sight of the central truth, which is simplicity in all things.

We're here to help you make your brew day simpler, more efficient, more effective, and more fun without sacrificing quality. It doesn't matter if you've never brewed or if you've been brewing since the Sumerians discovered beer's fundamental awesomeness, there's always a new avenue to explore in making great beer.

Stop and look at the process for virtually any other fermented drink. The only drink more complicated to make than beer is *sake*. Go look at the "simple" instructions for making sake and you'll weep fortunate tears for being a brewer (unless you're a special variety of odd). Look at those same simple instructions for mead, wine, and cider and you'll really feel like they get to cheat. In other words, as brewers, we're already starting with a complicated process, so let's not muck it up any further! We should also realize that we can learn a thing or two from meadmakers, vintners, and cidermakers.

> "In all things, the supreme excellence is simplicity."
>
> — Henry Wadsworth Longfellow, *Kavanagh*

DREW: Longfellow may have done a disservice to my ancestor Israel Bissell by choosing to write about Paul Revere's two-block ride instead of Bissell's multi-state ride to warn the colonies that the British regulars were marching, but he served us well in this case—simplicity is key to having fun. (Don't fret about reading *Kavanagh* though, it's a terrible story, even if it is free.)

DENNY: Pay attention to that word Drew used: fun. That's the reason we do this…well, that and the fact that it's beer! But beer should be about fun and friends, and what we want to do is help you get to the fun sooner and more easily.

THE IMPORTANCE OF A PRAGMATIC FOCUS, OR A BOOK'S MANIFESTO IN THREE LINES

Maybe it's a character flaw particular to Denny, but long ago he decided that work wasn't fun. Sure, the payoff from the work could be fun, but he has never liked the work part itself. On the other hand, Denny likes making beer and he likes beer that doesn't suck…kinda like most people! So, Denny has learned that some work is a necessary evil if you want good beer and he has no problem doing the work if he knows the payoff is going to be better beer.

Denny's pragmatism has driven him to explore which parts of the homebrewing process are essential and which are just work. That's the attitude we're going to share with you in this book, along with the specific discoveries we've made where the payoff is better beer and having more fun when you make it. We'll help you assess your own processes so you can decide for yourself what's working and what isn't. By cutting out the stuff that isn't working for you, you can simplify your process and increase your brew day joy. And that leads us into the mantra for this book…

> **Brew the Best Beer Possible,**
> **With the Least Effort Possible,**
> **While Having the Most Fun Possible.**

Figure 1.1. Found here in it's native habitat, a group of beers remain wary of mighty predators, known as brewers.

Who can argue with that? This is a hobby, and part of the reward is the fun you have. Sure, there's beer too, but isn't beer all about fun? And do you know what the absolute best part is? It's that YOU get to decide what counts as work and what doesn't, what is fun and what isn't, and set your own goals. For some people that might mean one-gallon brew-in-a-bag (BIAB) batches in their kitchen. For others it might mean a gleaming, totally automated stainless steel beast out in the garage, which has also been converted to a taproom/sports viewing center. (For the record, if you've created your own taproom brewer's cave with a big-screen TV, feel free to invite us over for a tasty beverage. Denny prefers movies; Drew likes all Boston sports.)

Isn't that a kick? You get to decide how to do things and what you want to do when you brew your beer. We'll be right here to give you ideas and guidance, but ultimately it's up to you to decide how you're going to brew your own beer. If you've never brewed before, we'll show you a variety of options to get you started.

So, here's a story to contemplate. We've already gotten into mantras, so why not a little Zen to round things out?

> A Japanese master named Nan-in received a visitor. The visitor was a university professor who had come to learn about Zen. Nan-in served the visitor tea, but when the cup was full Nan-in kept pouring. The visitor protested, "The cup is full! No more will go in!" Nan-in replied "Like this cup, you are full of your own opinions and speculations. How can I show you Zen unless you first empty your cup?"

Like the professor, if you approach simplicity with an attitude of already knowing what things are and how to do them you will get nothing out of this book. If, on the other hand, you are an empty cup and open to new ideas, then this book can be your tea.

Maybe not all of the ideas presented here are things that fit your brewing style, but by being open you may come away with a tidbit of knowledge, an inkling of an idea that may set you on a new course for your homebrewing; a sip of tea, if you will. And if you're a beginner, you're already an empty cup waiting for that first pour of tea. That's why we're here—we're gonna fill your cup!

Also, if tea isn't your thing, just change the tea to a pint of cask ale, or a long-forgotten farmhouse ale. No matter how full you are of certitude, no matter how much knowledge you've consumed (along with pints, naturally), there's something lurking out there. Some technique, some style, something you don't know. Odds are good you probably don't need it, but, hey, how will you know unless you try? What have you got to lose?

A WORD TO EXPERIENCED BREWERS

If you're a seasoned brewer, we hope to show you some ideas that might stimulate your brain and break you out of your usual process and try something new. Something that might give your love of brewing a kick in the butt and show you a new, fun side you hadn't considered before.

"Simplicity" can often imply "beginner" to experienced homebrewers. We know the feeling. We've both been brewing a long time (over 40 years combined experience) and have been through a lot of the stages of homebrewing: starting out with minimal equipment and an even more minimal understanding of what we're doing, progressing through fancy and plentiful equipment, and then settling into a deeper semi-scientific exploration of brewing ideas and processes. We get it, we understand your skepticism when you hear the words "simplicity" and "homebrewing" in the same sentence. But maybe it's time to set your prejudices aside. Maybe, just maybe, simplicity can lead to better beer and more fun. Open your mind to new ideas.

THE EFFICIENCY OF SIMPLICITY

If you've been brewing for a while, you might read "simplicity" and think that's for beginners. Maybe you're one of those homebrewers who aspires to have a home brewery that looks like a scaled down version of what a major brewery would look like. Hey, that's fine with us! That's your decision. But we can guarantee you that commercial breweries don't aspire to do things in the most complicated way they can think of. They simplify for the sake of efficiency. Efficiency is the goal, not the simplicity itself. But those breweries make sure they don't simplify to the point where things become ineffective, which can happen if you cut out processes just to simplify. Which brings us to the other half of our mantra. (We're reformed hippies, we love mantras. "Oooommmmmmmm.")

Do Everything Necessary to Make Great Beer, But Make Sure It Pays Off in Better Beer and More Fun.

See, we're not just trying to do the least amount of work—we're trying to do the least amount of work that it takes to make great beer and have a great time doing it. We're not about cutting corners, because that can lead to bad beer. We're about evaluating what works and what doesn't, and focusing on doing what needs to be done in the most efficient way possible. When you eliminate unnecessary effort, you build in more fun.

Here's an example of what we're talking about. When we started homebrewing many years ago, the accepted technique for sparging was what is called continuous sparging, or fly sparging (if you don't know what sparging involves, don't worry, we talk about the process in chapter 4). Fly sparging is a process of rinsing more sugar from the grain that usually takes over an hour and requires near constant attention if you don't have specialized equipment for it.

Denny heard a mention of something called "batch sparging" (see chapter 4) that was a much faster method of getting the sugar from the grain into solution and draining it out rather than rinsing it. It used inexpensive, commonly available parts to make the equipment. Denny tried out batch sparging and found it worked every bit as well as fly sparging, but also saved him a lot of time and effort. He started talking it up and it is now the most popular way to homebrew all-grain beer. That's a perfect example of a simplified process that saves you time without compromising your beer quality. Saving time on the brewing means you have more time for sampling your beer or brewing another batch!

We'll talk a little later in the book about preventing brewing demotivation, a dishearteningly common occurrence among long-term brewers, but simplification can help here as well. To overcome the massive inertia that can build up prior to a brew day, Drew's taken a page from his engineering training—namely, break the process down into simple, easy to execute, easy to build on tasks:

- Make your yeast starters ahead of time. Having the yeast on hand puts a ticking freshness clock in your head. You'll only need to start a day prior to brewing, but it makes a difference. We'll tell you why and how to make starters in chapter 10. For now, what you need to know is that a starter is like a very small batch of unhopped beer that allows the yeast cells to build up to an amount sufficient to ferment your beer. And yeah, it's easier than it sounds!
- Crush your grain ahead of time and seal it in a bucket. We've done experiments that show pre-crushed grain works just fine when stored in a bucket, even a month later.
- Clean your fermentors, chillers, and other equipment.
- Set up your water the night before.

Completing these tasks the day before will simplify your brew day. You can just get up in the morning, light a burner and get your brew day on.

If Drew decides he's going to brew the next day and needs to get some yeast ready for it, all he has to do is grab a jar of premade starter wort and dump his yeast into it. By the time he's ready to make the wort, the yeast is ready to make beer. Efficiency—don't discount the power of having yeast-ready wort on the shelf! (To find out more about "jars of wort," wait until chapter 10 on yeast.)

Figure 1.2. Look at all these lovely jars of wort, safely canned and stored, ready for use in beer making. Now imagine the same sight, just with jars filled with alcohol and spices; those are your tinctures.

Another example is Drew's process of making flavor tinctures for his beer ahead of time. He has shelves in his garage full of alcohol-based tinctures of various ingredients. If Drew gets a wild idea while he's brewing (and we guarantee you that he does), he simply has to grab one of his tinctures to quickly and easily add the flavor he's thinking of.

Simplicity and efficiency are the keys to some brewing equipment. New systems, such as the PicoBrew Zymatic® or Bevie's The Grainfather, are all-in-one brewing solutions that make your brew day easy and efficient. No need to pull your equipment out of storage and set it up. No need for constant attention during the brewing process. Although each of the systems out there functions a bit differently and requires different amounts of attention, they all have one thing in common—their goal is to simplify homebrewing. Yeah, all-in-one brewing systems do cost more than gathering some pots from your kitchen and using those for brewing, but that trade-off is just the right thing for some homebrewers. We'll take a closer look at some of these systems in chapter 5.

What we're trying to do in this book is look at the various parts of the homebrewing process and break them down into steps, showing you what each part is contributing to your brewing. We'll give you guidance through our opinions and ideas, but the ultimate decisions will be up to you. Once you have a few brews under your belt, you'll start seeing the synergy and flow in the process and how various parts of it relate to each other. Once that lightbulb clicks on for you, you can start defining your own process.

A WORD ON PROCESS

You'll notice in the previous section we didn't say that we are going to dictate a process to you. We intend to help you find your process, and we guarantee it's going to be different than ours. In the course of writing *Homebrew All-Stars*,[1] we had the opportunity to interview 25 of the world's best homebrewers (if you include us). We walked through each homebrewer's brew day and looked at their way of brewing, and we found that they all brewed differently and they all had a sort of muscle memory for their brew day setup. Some of the crazier brewers had a few procedures specific to what they were brewing, but those were almost always just branches off their existing process.

If you've never homebrewed before, we recommend you pick up a book for beginning homebrewers like John Palmer's *How to Brew* (mentioned in the introduction).[2] We want to help you make all the instructions and details work better for the way you brew. But whether or not you've brewed before, it's a good idea to break the process down to the basics. Then you can build it back up to be your own customized process. For example, let's try this with the all-grain brewing process.

---

[1]   Beechum and Conn, *Homebrew All-Stars: Top Homebrewers Share Their Best Techniques and Recipes* (Minneapolis: Voyageur Press, 2016).

[2]   Palmer, *How to Brew: Everything You Need to Know to Brew Great Beer Every Time,* 4th ed. (Boulder: Brewers Publications, 2017).

Simplified All Grain Brewing Process

1. Crush your grain.
2. Treat your water (if necessary).
3. Add your grain to the strike water (strike the mash).
4. Batch sparge.
5. Boil your proto-beer (a.k.a. wort).
6. Add your hops.
7. Cool your wort.
8. Pitch your yeast starter.
9. Ferment your wort/beer.
10. Rack your beer.
    a. If bottling, add priming sugar, then siphon to bottles and cap. Leave at room temperature for 1–2 weeks to carbonate.
    b. If kegging, force carbonate.
11. Chill your packaged beer.
12. Serve. (Don't forget to enjoy it.)

Figure 1.3. Cornelius kegs at the ready for beer transfer and force carbonation.

There are other ways to do this. You could use multiple mash steps. You could partially chill the wort and add hops for more aroma, etc. No matter what though, the rest of the deal stays basically the same. We may change the mash regimen based on what we need, but everything works the same general way. We make wort, we boil wort, we cool wort, we ferment wort, we package beer, we drink beer. Some things don't change, because we're comfortable with what we've developed. We always rack the same way, we always carbonate the same way, we always <blank> the same way. It's what we do.

Notice that we talk about kegging the beer rather than bottling it. Almost all new brewers bottle their beer, and that makes sense when you don't know if you'll stay with the hobby long enough to commit to the expense of a keg system. But once you decide you're a homebrewer, you should look into getting some used soda kegs for your beer. The time and effort you save might just make the difference between giving up brewing or staying with it.

There are pros and cons for every method of doing something. Sometimes a method will be traditional because it is the best way, and other times it will be simply because no one has taken the time or effort to come up with something better.

For example, for the first several years he was homebrewing, Denny bottled by putting the bucket of beer on a counter and siphoning into bottles on the floor while he knelt down to fill them. Why? Because that's the way it's shown in Charlie Papazian's great book, *The Complete Joy of Homebrewing*.[3] The method was effective, but by the time Denny was done he could hardly stand up because his knees were so sore.

---

[3] Charlie Papazian, *The Complete Joy of Home Brewing* (New York: Avon Books, 1984).

UNITS OF MEASURE

There are metric conversions provided where appropriate, but note that throughout this book the processes and recipes are based on US customary units. Most of the time we deal with the standard homebrewer batch size of five US gallons, which is roughly 19 liters (L). OK, five gallons is more precisely 18.92 L, but who's counting? Before you start scaling your recipes up or down, just keep in mind the metric conversions have usually been rounded off.

One day Denny was bottling at his friend Kevin's house. Kevin put the bucket of beer on the counter, then brought out two chairs. He put a sheet pan on one chair and sat down in the other. The bottle to be filled was put on the sheet pan to catch spills. It was a revelation for Denny—he could actually stand up after bottling without grunting in pain!

Denny had managed to get away from his painful "tradition" and discover a new, more efficient way to bottle. By watching someone else do the same process in a different way, he broke through his "I've always done it this way" wall and simplified his process.

But, That's Not How the Pros Do It

In their attempts to perfect their process, a common refrain we hear from homebrewers when we advocate for simplicity or breaking from tradition is, "Hey, that's not how the big breweries do it!"

Let's get real for a moment. For all of our flights of fancy—our dreams of manning the giant kettles to supply supreme suds to society—we aren't pros. (And, for the record, neither of us have any desire to turn pro.) While we strive for a certain level of efficiency like professional brewers do, what we do at home is fundamentally different from what any commercial brewery does. Breweries are often trying to solve problems that we, as homebrewers, don't have. We shouldn't expect our techniques and needs to be the same. You don't cook meals for a restaurant full of customers the same way you make dinner for your family. They are radically different. It's the same with brewing. When it comes to quality, there's less difference between what we make at home and what you get from a professional brewery than what we see between home cooking and a multi-Michelin-starred restaurant. Yes, we have echoes of the same processes and the same basic techniques, but it's far less important for us to emulate the pros to get great results than if you're trying to match, say, James Beard award winner Thomas Keller's food.

If cooking's not your thing, how about these examples: you wouldn't build a car at home in the same way an auto factory does; you wouldn't build a chair the same way a factory producing a hundred thousand units would. We can go on. The truth is that everything changes when you scale and when your goal is to produce the same beer over and over and over again. Drew can make a pretty damn fine Pilsner at home without needing to obsess over a mashing detail like "endosperm mashing" a la Trümer Brauerei in their Austrian and Californian breweries.

Homebrewers can use more malt and sparge less to reduce tannins because we're not trying to shave every penny we can from our costs. We can go brew a massive beer and give it endless amounts of time to ferment and age, because, hey, if we need a new fermentor we can just go get a new bucket, carboy, or whatever. Try doing that with a commercially sized stainless tank. Alternative processes, like BIAB and no-chill brewing (where brewers skip the post-boil chill step in favor of a gradual overnight chill), work because our scale is smaller, weights are less, and the thermodynamics are more forgiving.

Seriously, we have so much freedom, it's not even funny. Every brew can be a new idea, every batch can be an experiment. Try doing that when your batches are your profits. We don't have the moral dilemma that comes from dumping a bad batch down the drain, because it's only a few dollars, not a few thousand. That's another reason why the battle cry, "But that's not what X does," is terrible. Almost all of that beloved research that people love to wave around about various magical reactions that can make or break your brew was done at the behest of massive lager corporations for their specific needs: the lowest cost, highest shelf stability, a longer sales period, and shorter fermentation time.

We're now in a time of science-minded homebrewers and craft brewers who are tackling brewing in their own way to efficiently produce flavorful and quality beers. The technical precision needed to make a great IPA is looser than an industrial lager, but there are new questions not answered by existing lager-powered research. We are finding out that we can be less rigid, less formal, and still produce great beer. That's because once you know what the science is and how it works, you can decide what applies to you in your own home brewery and how you want to implement it. Ain't life grand?

WHAT ISN'T SIMPLICITY?

The real key to simplicity and efficiency is an understanding of the brewing process. It goes back to the saying, "Learn the rules so you know which ones you can break." By understanding the core processes in homebrewing, as well as a bit of the science behind it, you can decide which things matter to you and which don't. We'll show you how to combine some processes to save time and energy as well as eliminate others because they don't have a payoff. We are going to break down some of the complex ideas and processes into core components, and you can decide what works for you. Don't worry, it isn't as intense as it may sound! We promise to make the science in this book as painless as possible.

But, before we get going, let's define what simplicity isn't. (You've got to explore the negation, man.) Spontaneity is not simplicity. Brewing by the seat of your pants is not simplicity. Not being prepared on your brew day is not simplicity. Without thinking through what you're going to be doing, you may end up running around your kitchen or garage looking for that one piece of equipment that you really need *right now*! Meanwhile, your kettle is boiling over or you miss the timing for a hop addition.

It's tempting to say that simplicity is a brewing process that doesn't require a lot of hands-on time, but that's not exactly true. Sometimes, by simplifying the tools and equipment you use, you find yourself actually having to pay more attention to the process itself. But again, that's a tradeoff for you to decide. We're here to share various methods and systems and then you get

A FEW WORDS ABOUT THE RECIPES IN THIS BOOK

In order to help you decide when your beer is done fermenting, each recipe includes a final gravity (FG). This is the specific gravity for the finished beer. It's important to under-stand that, like the Pirate's Code, it's more of a guideline than a rule, a target rather than a specific number you have to hit. If your beer has been fermenting for a few weeks and the specific gravity is a bit higher or lower than what we list, don't worry. You'll be fine and you still made beer! If it's a lot higher or lower, like 10 points, it could indicate a problem. But you know what? You STILL made beer!

to put it together into a process that fits what you want to do and the time you have available to do it. Denny's "Cheap 'n' Easy" system (see chapter 4) requires more hands-on time than an automated system, but the saving in cost is the tradeoff he decided on in exchange for having to spend a bit more hands-on time during brewing.

On the other hand, when Denny uses an automated all-in-one system, he can get it started and then monitor the brewing on his phone while he cleans the house, does the laundry, or writes a chapter of this book! He's trading money for his time and effort.

The recipes at the end of the profile on Doug King demonstrate both sides of simplicity.[4] Doug's equipment was about as basic as you can get and he brewed in his kitchen rather than a fancy outdoor setup. But Doug's process was as old-school as you can get. For Doug, his extensive process was part of the fun he was looking for when he brewed.

We would be extremely unlikely to ever do a complicated mash, but we both use more complicated brewing systems to simplify our brew days. Both ways show that simplicity is a personal evaluation. And both ways can make great beer while you have a great time doing it.

That's what the rest of this book is about: discovering your version of simplicity to make the brew day more enjoyable and worthwhile.

[4] By the way, if you're new to brewing, don't worry, we walk you through the anatomy of a beer recipe in chapter 2 on page 26.

PROFILES IN SIMPLICITY: DOUG KING

DREW: Every homebrew club has "one of those members." You know, the brewer who always gets there early and always stays there late; the one who brews constantly and is always teaching. For the Maltose Falcons that member was the late Doug King. Doug attended everything the club did and was crazy enough that he was a member of two homebrew clubs (the other one being the now defunct Clan de Stein Homebrew Club). Doug led special club project brews and taught our all-grain brewing lessons.

Doug's primary obsession when it came to homebrew was the oft-maligned American lager. Yup, good ol' Budweiser. Fortunately for Doug, our club is located in the backyard of Budweiser's second-largest brewing facility. He became close friends with the brewers and learned their secrets.

He got skilled enough at making his Dougweiser ("Beer of the King") that he won the California State Homebrew Competition. Once, on a lark, Doug asked Anheuser Busch to analyze a few of his bottles. He nailed their specifications. That's impressive. What's more impressive, he did it by mashing on his stove top and lautering in a classic Zap Pap setup. (What's a Zap Pap? It's Charlie P's old-fashioned, about-as-cheap-as-it-gets setup of two plastic buckets sitting inside each other with a bunch of holes in the bottom of the top one.) So much for needing stupendously expensive computer-controlled systems to make a delicate beer.

There's also the legend of Dougfoot, a simple extension to Dougweiser that was created on the spur of the moment from the first runnings of the Dougweiser recipe. As the story was told years later, Doug loved the idea and hated the execution ... until he gave it time to age and smooth out. Dougfoot became a club staple. (A few folks still know the magic and make it in remembrance.)

But Doug wasn't just a lager guy—he made everything. He wanted to try as much as he could. He also had a homebrewer's appreciation for recycling and using whatever was on hand. Leftover corn tortillas went into the mash and made Cornweiser; potatoes became Spudweiser; chocolate cake went into his Cakeweiser stout; and on and on it went. ∎

Throughout this book we want to highlight brewers who exemplify the concepts of simplicity. For our first one we figured why not start with the guy who taught Drew how to do all-grain brewing?

DREW: One of the last brew sessions that Doug led for the club was the first all-grain beer I ever helped with. It was May 15, 1999. Doug died tragically in an auto accident just a few months later. He never did get to try the first all-grain beer I made on my own, but his legacy lives on. To this day, the Maltose Falcons continue to honor Doug's memory by holding a competition that focuses on lagers and experimental beers.

Dougweiser (Drew's Simple Version)

a.k.a. The hardest simple recipe you'll ever make

In the spirit of simplicity, Drew utilized flaked rice instead of a traditional cereal mash. We're going to give you both ways to make this pair of beers: the complicated full-throated version with an American cereal mash, and the simple version with flaked rice. I'm fairly certain Doug would grumble about the latter, but I think it works pretty well! Doug also simplified his brew life by maintaining a rigorous fermentation schedule that was always the same and allowed him to know just what to do. For Dougfoot, increase the grain bill by 30% and only use the first runnings.

Batch volume: 5.0 US gal. (19 L)
Original gravity: 1.048 (11.9°P)
Final gravity: 1.010 (2.6°P)

Color: 2.3 SRM
Bitterness: 14 IBU

Malt
- 6.0 lb. (2.7 kg) American two-row
- 0.25 lb. (115 g) Carapils®
- 3.0 lb. (1.36 kg) whole rice, coarsely ground (or use flaked rice for an easier time and skip the cereal mash)

Cereal Mash
- Gelatinize: Add 1.75 gal. (6.6 L) of boiling water to the coarsely ground whole rice. Stir and keep heat on rice mash; always stir while it is boiling!
- Saccharification: Add 0.75 gal. (2.8 L) of cold water and 1 lb. (450 g) of the two-row malt to bring the temperature down to 150-155°F. Rest for 3 minutes and begin the main mash.
- Boil: Return the rice and grain mix to boil for 15 minutes, then add to the main mash.

Main Mash
- 5 lb. two-row and 0.25 lb. Carapils. If using flaked rice, use all the malt here.
- Protein rest: 122°F (50°C) for 30 minutes (no rice, unless using flaked rice)
- Saccharification: 148-150°F (64-66°C) for 60 min. If doing the cereal mash, raise the main mash temperature with the rice infusion.

Hops
- 0.33 oz. (10 g) Willamette, Nugget, or Perle

Water
- Use low-mineral water. Our brewers recommend a 50:50 mix of distilled and tap water.

Yeast
- Wyeast 2007 Pilsen Lager Yeast or Wyeast 2035 American Lager Yeast

Fermentation
- Pitch yeast into 48°F (9°C) wort.
- Ferment for 2–4 weeks at 50°F (10°C).
- Rack to secondary and lower the temperature by 1°F (0.5–0.6°C) every day until you reach 33°F (0.5°C). Hold for 1–2 weeks before packaging.

Schutzen Lite Lager

Don't tell Doug, but we'd both simplify this recipe to a single rest! (Note the fermentation schedule is the same as Dougweiser though.) Schutzen Lite Lager was Doug's final brew on our club's then tiny brew system (the current capacity is about five times what it was for this recipe). You'll notice that Doug continued to have his affinity for multi-step mashes, which tells of his lager-headed background, but notice the simple design of the beer. The recipe is mostly Pilsner malt with a few *Reinheitsgebot*-approved additions (and one non-Reinheitsgebot addition, lactic acid), which yields a light-colored, unboring beer.

Batch volume: 5 US gal. (19 L)
Original gravity: 1.064 (15.7°P)
Final gravity: 1.015 (3.8°P)

Color: 4.5 SRM
Bitterness: 29.4 IBU
ABV: 6.5%

Malt
- 10.0 lb. (4.54 kg) Weyermann® Pilsner Malt
- 0.25 lb. (115 g) Weyermann Melanoidin Malt
- 2.0 oz. (56 g) Weyermann Acidulated Malt

Mash
- Strike at 105°F (40.5°C) with 3.1 gal. (11.7 L) water for 30 min.
- Saccharification rest at 155°F (68.5°C) for 75 min.
- Saccharification rest at 158°F (70°C) for 15 min.

Hops
- 1.25 oz. (35 g) Hallertauer Mittelfrüher 4.5% AA @ 60 min.
- 1.33 oz. (38 g) Hallertauer Mittelfrüher 4.5% AA @ 10 min.

Yeast
- WLP800 Pilsner or Wyeast 2565 Kolsch (for the ale brewers)

Extras
- 2 tsp. (10 mL) lactic acid, added to the hot liquor tank for pH adjustment

Fermentation
- Pitch wort at 48°F (9°C).
- Ferment for 2–4 weeks at 50°F (10°C).
- Rack to secondary and lower the temperature by 1°F (0.5–0.6°C) every day until you reach 33°F (0.5°C). Hold for 1–2 weeks before packaging.

2

SIMPLE EXTRACT BREWING

Historically, the traditional trajectory of a homebrewer's craft started with making beer from sticky malt extract powders and syrups. Maybe it was an old can of something sitting on a dusty shelf, with instructions like, "Dissolve one can and *x* pounds of sugar in hot water and bring to a boil. Cool. Pour into a crock. Pitch the included yeast, cover with cheese cloth …"

You know what? How about we show you some genuine instructions from a Prohibition-era can of Blue Ribbon Malt Extract? It's a piece of history and an efficient brewer's dream. Double win!

> "It is a poor workman that blames his tools."
> — Anonymous

MALT is grain which has been germinated (or sprouted). Blue Ribbon is the concentrated extract of pure malt and is used for many commercial purposes besides in the manufacture of beverages.

Malt extract and clean Hops enables anyone to make a delicious and tasty real Brew of the highest quality, in your own home, in the easiest way and at a very small cost. Pure Brew made with the extract has all the flavor, snap and sparkle you want. It is of better quality than any ready made brew you can buy at bars or cafes. It is very difficult to secure genuine malt extracts or brews in this country. In some of the best known brands, such things as rice, potatoes, bran, molasses etc., are used. (True malts are very thick and of rich brown color). By using Blue Ribbon Malt Extract, you will have real malt and hops Brew at far less than the cost of brewery products.

Follow directions carefully. Use enamel, stone or wooden vessels and do not stir up sediment while bottling, and cork tightly.

TO MAKE 5 GALS. PURE, HOME MADE BLUE RIBBON BREW.

Soft water is best for all kinds of drinks. Never add yeast when water is too cold or too warm (between 70 and 80 degrees F. is right) or it will not be good. Always use fresh yeast and add when liquid is cool (not cold) to your hand. It should be kept at about that temperature until through fermenting.

If sour the cause is over-fermentation or improper corking.

If tasteless, lacking strength, or of foul foreign taste, it is caused by coming in contact with old fermentation or dirt. All vessels and bottles must be thoroughly clean of soap, grease and other matter.

If not carefully strained, there may be a little yeast sediment in bottom of bottle. This is really healthful and often recommended by physicians.

No. 1. Take 5 gals. of water, put in clean vessel and bring to a good boil.

No. 2. Take 2½ oz. good clean hops, tie in loose cheese cloth bag with weight attached. Drop this in and boil from 30 to 60 minutes, according to strength of hop taste desired.

No. 3. Take 1½ lbs. cane sugar, (some prefer light brown sugar) pour this in, stirring well.

No. 4. Take 2½ lb. can of Blue Ribbon Malt Extract, pour in slowly, stirring well, boil all together 5 minutes.

No. 5. Take off fire and let cool until liquid feels cool (not cold) to your hand. Then take one cake of compressed yeast, or 1½ cake dry yeast, (in hot climate ½ cake is sufficient) and dissolve it in some of the liquid, stirring until you have a good foam, then pour into main body of liquid.

No. 6. After adding the yeast, pour into a large stone, enamel or wooden receptacle (which must be thoroughly cleaned) and let stand in a warm place from 40 to 60 hours. A scum will gather on the top which you will skim off.

After about 48 hours the liquid will lose its sweet and take on a bitter taste, then it is ready to bottle.

No. 7. Use small hose to syphon or pour out carefully so as not to stir up yeast. Strain through several thicknesses of cheese cloth. After it is bottled put in ½ teaspoonful sugar to each quart bottle, then cork tightly, set away in a warm temperature for 48 hours, then move to a cool place (ice box preferred) and after 3 to 4 days, the beer is ready to drink. Age improves it.

And then we get the best part of the instructions. Well after variants on making "Kentucky Mountain Dew" and "Cider," there's this warning:

> **WARNING.**
> Be sure to comply with your prohibition laws. If your territory is dry, do not add yeast; yeast will create alcohol; without yeast you will have a snappy, healthful non-alcoholic, hop-flavored drink.

Mmmm…healthful non-alcoholic, hop-flavored drink, just like your granddad used to make.

DREW: Incidentally, this is actually how my grandfather brewed. My mom has always complained that he fermented in or near her clothes, so she always went to school smelling like yeasty beer. I think this might be why she's never come around to "good" beer. Too much childhood trauma!

MODERN HOMEBREWING PIONEERS

Over time, extract instructions got better. Cheesecloth, crocks, and Prohibition warnings went by the wayside. Fresh yeast cakes got replaced with dried yeast, for better or worse. Instructions now include steps about chilling, sanitizing, and, hey, how about adding some fresh ingredients like grain and hops to liven things up!

But you know what, those old instructions for Blue Ribbon Malt up above, they were good enough for some of our heroes, like the good doctor himself, Hunter S. Thompson. Beer lovers know the dean of gonzo journalism for the pithy slogan, "Good people drink good beer." But in a retrospective of his photography, there is a shot of a lone carboy perched on a table, lit by a bare bulb with a blowoff hose curling around in a graceful arc to a round flask with settled yeast.[1] Thompson almost certainly made that batch of beer from extract. He also brewed while living in Big Sur, California during the early 1960s, writing a friend that he was surrounded by "vats of homemade beer in the closet," among other things.[2]

One of our other favorite authors, the perpetually cynical and acerbic H.L. Mencken, was a brewer as well. When he wasn't writing columns for the *Baltimore Sun*, Mencken was an astute student of brewing. During the height of Prohibition he taught homebrewing classes and exchanged beers with friends. He took extensive brewing notes, was not above experimenting, and

> "Puritanism: The haunting fear that someone, somewhere, may be happy."
> —H.L. Mencken

---

[1] Hunter S. Thompson, *Gonzo*, ed. Steve Crist and Laila Nabulsi, biog. Ben Corbett (Los Angeles: American Modern Books, 2006), 33.

[2] Hunter S. Thompson, *The Proud Highway: Saga of a Desperate Southern Gentleman, 1955-1967*, vol. 1 of *The Fear and Loathing Letters*, ed. Douglas Brinkley (New York: Ballantine Books, 1998), 280.

acquired yeasts straight from Munich for his *helles* and lagers.[3] Where others followed those instructions about extra sugar, Mencken was a malt-driven man, adding more extract to his brews while claiming it was the only way to get a respectable beer. Seriously, this man would fit right alongside any of us. Well, except Drew, because he apparently hates people adding strange things to the brew kettle.

Extract was good enough for these towering maestros of American letters. So, we need to figure out why extract has never quite received the respect we think it deserves. Too many look at extract as if it's training-wheels brewing, not worthy of the title "brewing" or capable of making a worthy product.

THE BASICS ABOUT BREWING AND EXTRACT

Ok, let's talk a little about extract. What is it? How is it made? And why should we all respect the technical magnificence of the stuff? To start with, you have to understand brewing, because without brewing you don't have extract.

To make beer or wine, you ferment sugars from fruit (wine) or grain (beer). With fruit, the sugars are easily accessible, just crush the fruit and you're good to go. With grain, though, it's a little more difficult. You need to go through a process of converting the starch in the grain into sugars that you can ferment. As well as barley, grains commonly used in brewing beer include wheat, rice, corn, oats, rye, and even more exotic grains like quinoa and triticale. However, barley became the brewer's grain of choice for a number of reasons:

- The barley's husk material makes it possible to filter the sugar-filled liquor.
- Barley already contains enzymes that can convert complex carbohydrates and starches into fermentable sugars.
- Barley is utterly useless as bread fodder. What's so bad about barley bread? Barley bread, thanks to its composition of starches and proteins, makes for a dense, gritty, heavy loaf without the lightness of wheat bread. Because it doesn't hold CO_2 in the same way a glutenous wheat dough will, barley bread tends to be tough to chew; barley is better suited for making barley cakes or—even better—beer.

So how do we get from grain to extract? Well, the first step is *malting*. A malt-ster converts barley (or other grain) into malt by wetting it and letting it sprout in a very controlled process, which activates the grain's enzymes. Brewers use those enzymes to convert the grain's starches to fermentable sugars.

To stop the sprouting process, the maltster *kilns* (dries) the malt. Kilning at different temperatures, moisture levels, and times produces different colors and flavors of malt. Very lightly kilned malts make beers like pale ale or Pilsner. Heavily kilned or roasted malts provide the deep black appearance and coffee

DREW: I often suspect that part of the distaste among "real" brewers about extract comes back to the purity argument. You know the one where people get their chests all puffed up talking about the greatness of German Beer and how it's due to the *Reinheitsgebot*, which restricts beer to malt, water, yeast, and hops. OK, except the 1516 Reinheitsgebot didn't include yeast and the modern equivalent has so many loopholes that you could use it to strain the mash. Here's the other dirty secret: the 1516 law wasn't really about preserving beer purity. It was about, among other reasons, reserving wheat for bakers to keep bread affordable to the people and army. After all, the elites still granted licenses for brewing wheat beer—for themselves.

---

[3]   Kihm Winship, "H.L. Mencken, Homebrewer," *Faithful Readers* (blog), May 1, 2012, https://faithfulreaders.com/2012/05/01/h-l-mencken-homebrewer/.

flavors in porters and stouts. By using various colors and types of grain, you can produce all the colors and flavors of beer.

Brewers take the finished malt and *mash* it. Mashing is nothing more than soaking the crushed grain in hot water. This reactivates those malt enzymes that convert the grain's starches into sugars. Keep in mind that the darker the malt, the fewer enzymes will be left after the malting process. You need some lighter grains in there to convert the starches in the darker malts (see chapter 4). But don't fret too much—almost all beer recipes start with a base of enzymatically strong pale malts. You won't need to worry too much until you decide to do something outrageous.

To make malt extract, the mashing is done at the processing facility for you. The liquid from the mash, called *wort*, (pronounced "wert") is separated from the now used-up grain. That liquid is boiled for a while, then concentrated under a vacuum at below boiling temperatures to make liquid malt extract (LME), a sweet, sticky, thick syrup. In order to make dry malt extract (DME), the LME is sent to a spray dryer. Nozzles at the top of the dryer create small LME particulates as it is sprayed into the dryer, where the hot air inside dries them out.

It's tempting from our vantage point as homebrewers to think of extract as an inferior product marketed to people who just want to make something cold and wet. The reality is that beer production, whether commercial or homebrewing, is far from the most common use of malt extract. Later on in this chapter we'll talk about the real reason maltsters make their extract products. We're just lucky they're available to us!

RESCUING EXTRACT FROM ITS REPUTATION

Here's a common misperception: we all think—no, we all know—that extract beer sucks. Or is it that extract brewers suck?

Let's take a step back to our childhoods for a moment. At some point, by virtue of being new to the world, we tried something we never tried before. Did we excel at it? Both of us will admit that no, we sucked.

Drew's first solo culinary creations, well, they were interesting. It took years of practice to get to the point of effortlessly whipping out some damn fine dinners. In the meantime, Drew also left innumerable attempts strewn behind him to get better at the drums or guitar, or talking like a regular human being. Maybe one of these days he'll even finish his murder mystery or his children's story, *Toby and the Secret Squirrel Army*.

Denny's first attempts at both cooking and beer went better. His first culinary attempt was a chocolate soufflé that he'd seen Julia Child make on TV when he was 12 years old. Denny found a recipe in one of his mother's cookbooks and produced it one evening when his grandparents came over for dinner. His recollection is that it came out perfectly, but there's a lot of memory fog in the days between then and now.

DREW: Speaking from my own experience, I did six extract batches before I switched to all-grain brewing. I was precocious and obsessed (shocker, I know.) But here's the thing—my beer didn't just magically improve when I made the all-grain transition. It still took time, and for a while my beer actually regressed as I tried to figure out this whole mashing thing!

DENNY: Same for me and I think it's a common experience for all brewers. Practice makes perfect, and the more you brew, the more you learn what works and what doesn't. Because new brewers usually start with extract, it often gets the blame for poor quality beers. The reason is actually lack of brewing experience.

Denny lucked out with his first batch of beer too. It was an American pale ale, with crystal malt as a steeping grain, Cascade hop pellets, and liquid malt extract. It would be interesting to taste that beer today and see if it was as good as Denny remembers, or if the memory fog just makes it seem like it. In between that beer and today, there were some failed beers as he learned what mattered and what didn't.

The point is that we both likely sucked at brewing when we first started. Don't get us wrong, we enjoyed the hell out of what we made (except Drew's second attempt, which was a chlorophenolic batch that was an offense to the brewing gods.) But we're fairly certain those around us nodded politely, sipped their beer, and waited patiently hoping that we'd get better. We'd like to think we have. There's nothing like gleaning experience from mistakes when it comes to learning!

Why Extract Is Awesome

- Using extract allows you to focus on the most important parts of brewing, such as sanitation and fermentation. (This, incidentally, is why Drew always, even in the world of small-batch and easy BIAB mashing, recommends starting with extract. Learn the fundamentals, dangit!)
- Using extract means your brew day goes faster, which means more brewing.
- Extract brewing uses less equipment and takes up less space.
- Extract beers can taste every bit as good as a beer made with only grain. In fact, Denny has judged competition "Best of Show" rounds where an extract beer beat out beers made with all grain. It's about flavor, not ingredients!

Why Extract Is Terrible

- Extract is expensive. How am I supposed to make my beer for pennies per pint when the extract itself is going to cost twenty to thirty dollars per batch? That's more expensive than the grain for a similar batch would be.
- Liquid extract can go stale with exposure to air, meaning you'll make a stale beer before you even get started brewing. (Make sure you buy fresh extract from your homebrew store!)
- It's "cheating" and "you're not a real brewer." (It's not just the internet where judgmental bad attitudes reign supreme!)
- Extract is so delicious that you may end eating it all plain or using it up in cooking. Wait, what? (Malted milkshake, anyone?)

THE SIMPLEST BREW DAY EVER

The malthouse took care of the hard, sweaty mash for you. Your job as a brewer is to finish their work! On brew day, you'll be responsible for dissolving the extract, adding fresh grain character, boiling the results, cooling it, and starting the fermentation. In other words, you've got plenty of work to do, so we're going to set you up with our simple guide!

If you buy a kit of ingredients there will also be instructions that come with it. And there are a ton of really great books out there with instructions about how to get started brewing. We highly recommend *The Everything Homebrewing Book* by Drew, *Experimental Homebrewing* and *Homebrew All-Stars* by the two of us, or *How to Brew* (hey, the title says it all!) by our good friend, John Palmer.[4]

The Oversimplified Explanation of Extract Brewing

Brewing an extract beer will take about four to five hours, but you'll only be actively busy for a couple of those. Spend the downtime cleaning your house or reading one of our other books!

For your first brew, you'll probably want to purchase a complete kit of ingredients, either online or from a local homebrew supply shop. If you don't already have a five-gallon pot and a fermenting bucket, the homebrew supply shop can help you with those parts too! (Also, you'll want a few cases of beer bottles and fresh caps to use.) Other equipment you'll need is a long spoon, a thermometer, and, likely, a strainer. We're trying to keep it simple, so for now just buy the ingredients for a style of beer you like. Once you get a handle on the flavors and interactions between ingredients, you can try one of the recipes we've included in this book or create your own. (By the way, we assume in these instructions, and for a good portion of the book, that we're dealing with the standard homebrewer 5 gal. [~19 L] batch, but these processes all work whether you're making one gallon or 300. OK, maybe not 300, but really, almost.)

The Bare Minimum Equipment

- 5 gal. (19 L) pot
- fermenting bucket
- big spoon
- thermometer
- hydrometer
- food-grade vinyl or silicone hose, ⅜ inch (10 mm) inside diameter, 5 ft. (1.5 m) in length
- 50 12 fl. oz. bottles*
- 50 bottle caps
- 1 bottle capper

- No rinse sanitizer—you'll often see bleach recommended, but not by us! The low cost of bleach is offset by the high cost of having a terrible tasting batch of beer because you didn't rinse the bleach off thoroughly. Even a small amount of bleach left in equipment can make your beer taste like plastic. We recommend iodophor or Star San.

* The equivalent bottles outside the US are typically 330 mL, which is 11.2 fl. oz.

---

[4]   Beechum, *The Everything Homebrewing Book* (Avon, MA: Adams Media, 2009); Beechum and Conn, *Experimental Homebrewing: Mad Science in the Pursuit of Great Beer* (Minneapolis: Voyageur Press, 2014); Beechum and Conn, *Homebrew All-Stars: Top Homebrewers Share Their Best Techniques and Recipes* (Minneapolis: Voyageur Press, 2016); Palmer, *How to Brew: Everything You Need to Know to Brew Great Beer Every Time*, 4th ed. (Boulder: Brewers Publications, 2017).

Give yourself a break and don't go for an extra strong style of beer or a lager—they take extra time and effort to make. Keep it simple and learn the basics. A pale ale, bitter, *saison*, or porter are good styles to start with because they don't require extra steps and can be brewed and fermented in a couple of weeks.

Make sure to read through the whole process and recipe before you start! Treat it like you're cooking a new recipe or assembling a piece of furniture that came with little wrenches. It'll get frustrating if you don't.

READING A RECIPE

If you've never seen a beer recipe, it works a little differently than a cooking or baking recipe. Let's take a look at a simple recipe and help you understand it.

Lazy Day Blond Ale

Batch volume: 5 gal. (19 L)
Original gravity: 1.038 (9.5°P)
Final gravity: 1.010
Alcohol: 3.7% by volume
Color: 4 SRM
Bitterness: 20 IBU
Boil: 60 minutes

Malt
- 6.0 lb. (2.7 kg) Briess Pale LME
- 0.5 lb. (225 g) Carapils
- 0.5 lb. (225 g) aromatic malt

Steep/Mash
- Steep grain with 3 qt. (2.8 L) of 170°F (77°C) water for 30 min. Rinse grain with 3 qt. (2.8 L) of 170°F (77°C) water.

Hops
- 0.33 oz. (10 g) Magnum (pellets) 14% AA @ 60 min.
- 0.50 oz. (14 g) Willamette (pellets) 5.5% AA @ 5 min.

Yeast
- Wyeast 1056 Chico, White Labs WLP001 California Ale, or Safale US-05

What does the recipe tell us about Lazy Day Blond Ale? Let's work our way down the recipe.

Beer recipe stats. The stats for the beer recipe are usually given at the start. The *batch volume* tells you this recipe makes 5.0 gal. of beer in the fermentor after the boil (you'll lose some volume in various parts of the process.) The *original gravity* (OG)—the amount of potential yeast food (mostly) available in your wort—is 1.038 (typically given as "ten thirty-eight" in brewer's speak). A *color* reading of 4 SRM means the beer will be a light gold (the Standard Reference Method scale runs from 1 on the light side to 40+ for the darkest black beers). The beer's *bitterness* is measured in international bittering units (IBU); 20 IBU is rather low for craft-style beers, although mass-produced lagers are usually lower at 8–12 IBU. IPAs and other "hoppy" ales are anywhere from 50 to 100+ IBU. The beer finishes in a normal ferment with 3.7% alcohol by volume (ABV). The wort is to be boiled for 60 minutes.

Malt. The malt list specifies 6.0 lb. of Briess (a malt manufacturer) Pale LME, plus smaller amounts of two grains (not extract) that will get steeped. Extract is always added to the boil kettle.

Steep/mash. The steep and/or mash section gives the time, temperatures, and water amounts you need to steep your specialty grains (in an extract recipe) or to perform your mash (in an all-grain recipe).

Hops. The hops list gives an amount, a variety, a form (pellet or whole), the alpha acid (AA) percentage (higher numbers yield more potential bitterness), and then how long the hops need to be boiled. The first hop addition is boiled for 60 minutes, while the second only needs to be boiled for 5 minutes. What that means is, you add the first addition when the boil starts and set your timer for 60 minutes; when there are 5 minutes remaining, you add the second addition.

Yeast. The yeast lists several choices for strains. In this case, all three are different strains from different manufacturers, but they are the same type of yeast (i.e., all three strains are some type of American ale yeast).

MAKE THE WORT.

The first step is making your wort. Heat up about two gallons of water to just below boiling. You're looking for the stage when bubbles are starting to form or if you have a reliable thermometer, 170°F. If your kit came with "steeping grains," put those in the pot before starting the steeping. Make sure the grain is crushed! To make your life easier, put the grain in a muslin or nylon grain bag, which you can get from a homebrew store. You can even use a paint strainer bag from the hardware store. When the water temperature is about 170°F, remove the steeping grains, take the pot off the heat, and stir in your malt extract. When you add the extract to the water, you make wort. You're fancy now!

BOIL THE WORT.

The second step is to boil the wort you just made. You bring the wort to a boil to kill any nasty bacteria that could spoil your beer. Add the hops according the recipe directions that you are following. A bit of an oddity about hop timing is how it's recorded in a recipe. When you see a recipe say, "1.0 oz. Cascade at 15 minutes," it means you want to boil the Cascade hops for 15 minutes. If your total boil is 60 minutes, then you boil for 45 minutes and then add that dose of Cascade with 15 minutes left to go (also see the Reading a Recipe box). Then move on to finish the beer.

The boil also helps extract bittering and aromatic components from the hops you add. How much of these hop components that go into your beer is the degree of hop *utilization*. Without hops, beer is just sugar water! Killing off the bacteria in the wort is a good thing, but if you don't cool it down before you put your yeast in, the same heat that killed the bacteria can kill your yeast.

CHILL THE WORT.

Chilling the wort has two goals: (1) to quickly cool the wort below the bacterial contamination zone of 90–140°F (32–60°C), and (2) to get the wort into the preferred ale yeast fermentation range of 60–70°F (15.5–21°C). Chill the wort in the kettle to the fermentation temperature range before transferring it to your fermentor and adding your yeast. Don't forget to top up the fermentor to 5 gal. (19 L) with an additional 3–3.5 gal. (11.4–13.3 L) of cold, filtered water. (Boiled and chilled in the fridge is best; chilled means it can help pull your wort down into proper fermentation range quickly.)

FERMENT THE WORT, A.K.A MAKE BEER!

Fermenting the wort is where the magic happens! Put your yeast in (that's called *pitching*) and stand back and wait. OK, you don't need to stand back, it's not going to explode. After pitching your yeast it will take a few days for the magic to happen, so go find a comfy place to sit (although we do recommend watching what happens—it's kinda fascinating). Close up the fermentor once the yeast is in there. Use an airlock to keep dust and foulness out of the beer. Put the fermentor somewhere cool at 60–70°F (15.5–21°C)—a closet, a water bath, your bath tub, etc.—and go to sleep. You deserve a nap!

What to Expect When You're Expecting Beer

The full conversion from wort to beer can take from a few days to a few weeks, depending on the style of beer you make. In general, a week or two is enough. The old saying goes, "Brewers make wort, yeast makes beer." Fermentation is where the little critters do their job! The yeast cells start reproducing, eating that sugar, and giving off alcohol as a by-product of fermentation. Yeast party!

KNOWING WHEN FERMENTATION IS OVER.

How do you know when the yeast is done fermenting? There are two ways. The simple way is to observe the beer. Is it still bubbling? Is there a head of foam (*kräusen* in the brewing world) on top of it? If the answer to both of those is no, then it's a good bet that the yeast is done.

But the simple way won't tell you for certain. That's what the hydrometer in your brewing gear is for. A hydrometer is used to measure the specific gravity of the beer. Specific gravity is the ratio of the wort's density to the density of pure water (pure water is set at 1.000). Sugar dissolved into water makes that water denser. Measuring the specific gravity tells you how much sugar has made it into your wort. Your recipe or recipe kit will tell you what the specific gravity of your wort should be before you start fermenting it. This is called *original gravity*, abbreviated as OG. After fermentation, there will be less sugar and you'll get a lower reading. This is your beer's *final gravity*, or FG. Your kit might list what the FG should be. Hit that number and you know the beer is done. If the recipe doesn't tell you what the FG should be, a good guess is that it should end up at about 20%–25% of what the OG was. For example, if your OG was 1.050, then a good FG would be around 1.010.

By the way, don't panic if you didn't hit your numbers precisely. Let the beer tell you when it's done. If the beer is at 1.015 and is still at 1.015 a few days later, then your yeast is finished working. Proceed to packaging!

PACKAGE THE BEER, A.K.A. BOTTLE OR AND KEG IT.

For most new homebrewers, packaging means putting the beer in a bottle, adding a bit of sugar that will ferment and produce carbonation (this is called *priming* the beer), and sealing with a bottle cap. Sealing allows carbon dioxide (CO_2) to build up in the bottles and go into solution in the beer, carbonating it. Alternatively, a lot of brewers put their beer into a 5 gal. soda keg and inject CO_2 from a tank, but that might a bit beyond where you're at now.

DRINK THE BEER!

Drinking the beer is what you've been waiting for! After a week or two of letting your bottles sit at room temperature to carbonate, it's time to chill some down in the fridge and pour yourself a glass of your own handmade, homemade beer. Please, no frosted glasses right from the freezer! The colder your beer is, the less you can taste. You spent your time and effort on this beer, so you deserve to enjoy it at its finest. (Do we have to tell you that the glasses should be clean too? Dirty glasses make for sad, flat, lifeless beer and sad, flat, lifeless beer drinkers!)

A FEW WORDS ABOUT FERMENTATION

Managing Fermentation
Whether you brew with extract or with all grain, remember that "brewers make wort, yeast makes beer." Meaning that, if you don't take some care with the fermentation of your wort, all the money and effort you've put in at that point can be lost. Yeah, we've said it before but it's so important that it bears repeating: the two most important things you need to think about for fermentation are sanitation and temperature.

As long as your wort is boiling, it's sanitary and anything that comes into contact with it doesn't require sanitation. But as soon as the boil is done, beer-spoiling microorganisms are just waiting to munch on those sugars and turn your potentially delicious beer into malt vinegar. So, once you're done boiling, make sure anything that touches your wort has been sanitized. That means your fermentor, spoon, tubing, and airlock…seriously, anything!

Your other concern is the temperature at which the beer ferments. If it's too cold, the yeast will go dormant and ferment poorly, if at all. For best results, almost all ales should ferment in the range 62–68°F (17–20°C). Note we are talking about the temperature of the beer itself, not the ambient room temperature. You can get thermometers made to stick to the side of your fermentor and they're amazingly accurate.

A simple way to control the temperature is to put your fermentor into a large tub of water. If the temperature is too warm, you can add a few ice packs to the tub to cool it down. If it's too cool, you can put an aquarium heater in the water to warm it up. If you want more info right now, you can skip to chapter 9 where we discuss simple fermentation techniques.

For a really easy fermentation, you can ferment right in the pot you brew in! It's already sanitized from the boiling so all you have to do is cool it down to the correct temperature for your yeast.

Yeast: Dry or Liquid?

Yeast comes in two forms, dry or liquid. Dry yeast looks similar to the yeast you use for baking and comes in a small foil packet (but don't use baking yeast). Liquid yeast comes in a pouch or vial.

A package of liquid yeast usually does not contain as many yeast cells as package of dry yeast. For this reason, you may need to make a yeast *starter* in order to build up the cell count in liquid yeast before you pitch it into your wort. The main advantage to liquid yeast is that there are more strains available and that means you can get a wider range of flavors. There are some brands of liquid yeast that contain more cells than others and can often be pitched without a starter.

There are lots of dry yeast strains available, too, and you can find one that suits just about any style of beer you want to make. Dry yeast is easy to use and less expensive than liquid yeast, so you may want to start your brewing using dry. After you learn the other steps involved in brewing you can give liquid yeast a try and see what you think.

DREW: Why the preference for fresh LME over DME? For me the LME is less processed and has more interesting flavors (and more varieties as well). DME is bulletproof and will withstand the zombie apocalypse, but fresh LME makes better beer. Stale LME? Leave that for the undead.

DENNY: I disagree with Drew on this. I find DME makes a far better beer than LME, and I also find it easier to work with. So, what do you do? Try both and decide for yourself.

TRICKS FOR THE BEST EXTRACT BEER

Respect extract both in its abilities and limitations. You'll be able to turn out pale ales, IPAs, and stouts from extract that are indistinguishable from all-grain versions once you understand the ingredient. A light beer like a Pilsner or a dry beer like a saison is probably not going to be the best choice for extract; but, with the newer pale extracts that have come on the market, you can get a lot closer than ever before.

Liquid extract can go stale faster than dry extract, so use the freshest liquid extract you can get. Dry extract is more shelf-stable, so we recommend that you use dry extract for your brewing if freshness is in question. Because water has been removed from it, dry extract is more concentrated and contains more fermentable sugars than liquid. So, if you're brewing a recipe that calls for liquid extract but you replace it with dry extract, use 80% as much dry extract for every 1.0 lb. of liquid extract in the original recipe. Having said that, if your local homebrew store properly stores fresh bulk LME and rolls through it's inventory regularly, then by all means use liquid. Drew's local store gets big syrup drums and flushes them with nitrogen as the syrup is dispensed. The LME is fresh as it can be and really does shine in making a tasty extract brew.

There are a ton of specialty extracts out there: light, pale, amber, brown, dark, stout, and many more. We find that unless you have a specific need, like wheat or rye, stick with the palest extracts and get your color and characters from fresh grains.

Why use fresh grains? Extract is great, but you'll notice that almost every extract recipe contains grains for steeping, which is essentially a simplified version of mashing. We're not really mashing when we steep, but we're still extracting "fresh" grain character to put our stamp on the base malt provided by the extract. The general rule of thumb is specialty grains (almost any malt called some variation of caramel, crystal, Cara-, roast, or black) can be steeped. Adjunct grains, such as corn, rice, oats, and wheat, need to be mashed properly, which means mashing them with a *base* malt, like pale or Pilsner malt. The base malt provides the starch-converting enzymes that the specialty and adjunct grains don't have on their own.

ADVANCED EXTRACT BREWING

Extract is a great way to get started brewing, but that doesn't mean that you have to leave it behind when you become more experienced. Both of us have quaffed and judged some great extract beers. Denny has judged Best of Show rounds in competitions where extract beers beat out all-grain beers to win the medal. The point is that, if you know your ingredients and take advantage of your experience, you can make killer extract beer that you can be proud of.

When you brew from a recipe kit it's probably best to follow the instructions that come with it. After all, that's the way the person who wrote the recipe intended it to be. But as you learn more about your ingredients and how the brewing process works, you may want to start putting your own recipes together and taking advantage of some tricks that will improve your beer and save you time and effort. Here are a few ideas.

Late Extract

If there's any complaint about extract that is absolutely valid, it's that making a light-colored beer is difficult. Think about the amount of time the sugars have been boiled by the time they've reached the fermentor. Not only did those sugars boil in your kettle for 60 minutes, they also boiled for who knows how long when the extract was being manufactured. In other words, there's been a ton of time under ideal conditions for creating darker colors.

So, skip helping make the sugars darker by not adding all of your extract at the start of the boil. We like to recommend that you only add a quarter of your extract at the start, which is enough to help adjust the pH to a better range for hop utilization. Boil according to your recipe, adding hops as you go, and then add the remainder of the extract to the pot with 10 minutes left, which gives enough time to heat-sanitize the whole volume. Remember to take the pot off the heat when adding the remaining extract to avoid the heavy sugars falling straight to the bottom and scorching against the bare metal.

Full-Volume Boil

Until now we've been talking about concentrated wort boils—a full boil is the other main trick we know that really gets rid of the "extract beer" feeling. If you can use a burner and a big enough pot (i.e., 7+ gal. for a 5 gal. batch), simply add all the remaining water needed for a full volume boil after the steep. Adding all the water at this stage reduces the color change and allows the hops to add more bitterness and flavor. Speaking of which, if your recipe is designed for a partial boil, you'll want to back off the hops by some amount when you convert to full boil to keep your brew from being overly bitter. How much? That's like saying "how long is a piece of string?" Experience will help, but brewing software can be used to determine what the correct amount is. The amount will vary depending on how much volume you boil and what the specific gravity of the boil is.

Use a Chiller

Hand in hand with the full boil, we also recommend getting a chiller of some variety to chill the wort. Copper immersion chillers are far and away the easiest to use, clean, and store. Using one is pretty straightforward, just hook it up to a garden hose (or other cold water source, the colder the better) and drop the coil into your boil with 15 minutes remaining. When done boiling, turn off the burner and turn on the water. Rock the chiller carefully back and forth until you reach pitching temperature or you're chilling water is too warm to push the wort temperature down further. At that point, you should be ready to chill overnight in a fridge if you're still above 70°F, or just pitch your yeast if you're down in the 62–68°F range.

Using a copper immersion chiller is great because it takes minutes instead of hours. Of course, we're going to try and simplify this step too in a little while, so hang on!

Speed Brewing: Beer in 20 Minutes

The traditional method of brewing beer calls for boiling your wort for 60 minutes or more, with hop additions at various points throughout. But who's got time for that? One of the beauties of using extract is that so much has been done for you before you even start brewing! You can leverage that advantage to shorten your brew day. Instead of starting your hop additions early on in the boil and leaving them in there for the entire 60 minutes, you can boil for only 20 minutes by simply increasing the amount of hops you use! Later in this chapter we'll show you some recipes that have been adjusted for the Speed Brewing method.

First, a little background. Hops contain a variety of compounds for bittering your beer and adding flavor and aroma. The longer you boil the hops, the more you extract the bittering compounds and the more you degrade the oils that give you flavor and aroma. Hops are usually boiled for 60 minutes to get bitterness from them, around 15–20 minutes to get flavor from them, and for three minutes or less to get aroma. In order to boil for only 20 minutes rather than 60, you need to increase the amount of hops you use to compensate for the lower alpha acid utilization. Those are fancy terms that describe the actual chemical process, but you can just remember that more boil equals more bitter. Of course, there's a limit to this, but you get the idea.

So, here's the trick: in order to boil for 20 minutes rather than 60, look at the amount of hops the recipe uses for the 60 minute boil and increase that amount by 50%. By only boiling the hops for 20 minutes you'll also increase the amount of flavor you get from them.

In order to speed up and simplify your brew day even more, get an induction burner and a pot made for it. We both use 1800-watt induction plates. They work really well and only cost around sixty dollars in the US; a pot will set you back another thirty or forty dollars.

HOW TO CONVERT TO/FROM EXTRACT

A big challenge for extract brewers is that almost all recipes you'll find out there are going to be all-grain. It's probably because almost all the goofs who've been bitten by the beer-writing bug went all-grain somewhere along the way. Here are a few tricks and tips for adjusting a recipe from all-grain to extract:

- Do not try and go all-extract. Just substitute the extract for a portion of the base malt and leave 1–3 lbs. of grain for your basic 5-gallon batch. We recommend converting all but a pound of your base malt to extract and backing off your crystals and caramels just a bit (25% or so). Your taste buds will thank you for the fresh grain taste you obtain from steeping. Your best grains for steeping are crystal and roasted malts.

- Our general rule of thumb is to treat pale extract as a substitute for the pale malt (i.e., two-row, six-row, Pilsner) and approximately 33% of the crystal malts. In other words, drop a third of your crystal when converting to extract with steeping grains.

- Substitute wheat LME or wheat "solids" for the typical Bavarian profile of a 50:50 or 60:40 split for Pilsner and wheat malt.

- Depending on how you steep your grains (i.e., does the temperature drop to somewhere between 150°F and 160°F), you may want to keep a pound of base malt in the mix. What you're doing here is really a very small mash to activate the enzymes in the base malt to help convert the starches in the other grains into fermentable sugars.

- The most difficult grains to convert from all grain to extract are flaked oats and flaked wheat. (These are fine to steep if you're steeping between 150°F and 160°F and have a little pale malt in the mix).

- As a general rule, LME gives 36 gravity points per pound per gallon, or 36 PPG. DME gives 45 PPG. Pale malt when mashed with a typical efficiency of 75% gives you about 25 PPG.

GRAVITY POINTS PER POUND PER GALLON AND EFFICIENCY

Gravity points are the basic measure of how much fermentable sugar is in grain or extract. The amount of fermentable sugar that extract or grain yields is usually expressed as gravity points per pound per gallon, abbreviated as PPG. If you dissolve one pound of DME into enough water to make one gallon of wort, that wort will have a specific gravity of 1.045. In other words, the typical yield for DME is 45 PPG. Therefore, if you add five pounds of DME to five gallons of water, you have five gallons of wort with a specific gravity of 1.045.

With extract, you don't have to worry about efficiency because you always get the same number of gravity points out as you put in; all of the sugars in the extract dissolve into the wort. Hence, that's how you know DME always yields 45 PPG.

With grain working out the yield in PPG gets a bit trickier, because you can never get 100% of the starch in the grain converted to fermentable sugars and dissolved into the wort. Your efficiency is a measure of what percentage of the total sugar you actually remove from the grain and dissolve into your wort. An efficiency of 75% is the average number for homebrewers. When you start brewing you'll be able to figure out what your own system's efficiency is, but 75% is a good guess whenever you're calculating things.

OTHER EXTRACT USES

Yeast Starters

This should be a no-brainer—use malt extract to make your yeast starter. We'll get more into this in Chapter 10. Frugal minded all-grain brewers like to use the final runnings from their mash tuns to provide wort for their starters, but we appreciate the consistency of extract and knowing what we're growing our critters in. Plus, it's way easier to store extract than it is wort.

Simplifying Your Brew Day

If your brew life is anything like ours, there just aren't enough hours in the day to do all the daily chores and attend to life's needs while also brewing as much as we'd like. There are tons of ways to gain time during the brew day, but most brewers skip over an easy solution to making more beer in less time, and that's using extract as part of your brew day. We're not talking as a starter or booster, but as a way to kick-start an entirely new batch from your leftover sparge water.

Some brewers are precise about their water measurements, using only the exact right amount in the mash tun and the hot liquor tank (HLT, i.e., your kettle full of hot water for sparging and more). But you can take a cue from Drew: he pretty much always refills his HLT throughout the day to have a constant source of hot water, which is handy for cleaning and other purposes. At the end of the day, there is always leftover HLT water that ends up being cooled and recycled for laundry or gardening.

But what about not letting the leftover cool down? If you're like most brewers, you hold onto a certain amount of your original homebrewing gear. What Drew has started doing to help fill out his beer roster (you know, for beer festivals, research, etc.) is to make sure the HLT is kept full while he is making an all-grain recipe. He can take the already heated water from the HLT into a separate boil kettle and start an extract batch. Using a second burner and kettle, you can easily time it so that your extract batch is done within 15 to 30 minutes of your main all-grain batch. (If you're horrifically fanatic about brewing, keep repeating that and you can pull off multiple batches in one go. At some point though, you'll need to knock it off and go to sleep!)

Here follows an extract recipe that's a perfect example of making your brew day fast and simple. In the past few years sour beers have become extraordinarily popular, with brewers developing new ways to shortcut the traditionally long souring times they require. After all, beer sitting in a tank or barrel is beer not being sold and money not being earned! Kettle souring will be covered in depth in chapter 11, but if you've wondered why you see so many Gose and Berliner *weisse* beers on the market these days it's because of the simple sour flavor you can obtain quickly with little fuss. You can whip up this beer at the end of your brew day and not have to worry about boiling until later!

Berliner RoggenWhat Extract Kettle Sour

Batch volume: 5 gal. (19 L)
Original gravity: 1.044 (11°P)
Final gravity: 1.004 (1°P)

Color: 5.4 SRM
Bitterness: 1.8 IBU
ABV: 5.2%

Malt
- 3.3 lb. (1.5 kg) Briess Pilsen Light LME
- 3.3 lb. (1.5 kg) Briess Rye LME

Hops
- 0.125 oz. (4 g) Magnum (pellets) 12% AA @ 15 min.

Yeast/Bacteria
- *Lactobacillus*, use a few ounces (50–60 g) of an active yogurt/probiotic culture or a pack of pure culture from a yeast company
- 1 packet Safale US-05 American ale yeast

Procedure
- Mix LME completely into 4.5 gal. (17 L) of 130–140°F (54–60°C) water and top up to 5 gal. (19 L) total volume.
- Cool to ~110°F (43°C) and pitch your souring culture (*Lactobacillus* and other critters).
- Fill the headspace with CO_2, cover the kettle top with plastic wrap, and add the lid with extra weights.
- After 24–72 hours, depending on culture freshness and desired sourness, bring to a boil and add hops. Quickly chill to fermentation temperature and pitch the yeast. Ferment and package as usual.

Notes
How do you determine if the sourness is where you want it? Some brewers use pH meters and push the sour ferment until the pH hits ~3.5. Winemakers will scoff because pH is a poor indicator of taste impact. They have a test for acidity, but that's way too complicated for us now. Instead, let your tastebuds be your guide. It may sound fun to push the envelope and go EXTREME with your sourness level, but it's not a great tasting experience.

Boosters

Just like you should always keep extract on hand for growing up your yeast, so should you keep it on hand for boosting your wort. There are a few ways extract can come in handy for your brew day:

- Miss your gravity from your runoff? Add some extract to reclaim your ground!
- Want multiple beers? Say you want both a pale ale and an IPA: make a pale ale grist, split the wort into two kettles, and add extract to one kettle to increase your gravity and create a bigger beer. We do this sometimes with our experiments just to help us test things out without requiring more brews.
- Don't want to make a kettle sour with your extract, but still love sour beers? In order to provide a little extra "oomph," Drew likes to keep starter wort on hand. He adds starter wort when pitching *Brettanomyces* to the fermentor and other critters. It gives them a little "go juice" so they make more interesting characters.

BAKING: THE FINAL FRONTIER

Remember earlier in the chapter when we said, "Hey, you know, we're lucky to have malt extract for brewing because that's not why they make the stuff"? Well, here you go—the real reason big maltsters invest time, energy, and money into making extracts is baking. It turns out that malt extract is incredibly hygroscopic, that is, it has a fondness for sucking up and holding onto water. This keeps commercial baked goods moister for longer. The sugars and proteins in malt extract also help in creating beautiful brown crusts with a deep earthy sweetness.

Seriously, go look at the bread in your kitchen. Odds are high that it contains malted barley flour, malt extract, or diastatic malt extract. The diastatic version still contains active enzymes that can attack starches and help make dough more elastic and creates a "fermented" flavor.

How would you go about using your DME? You can replace some or all of a recipe's sugar content with DME or LME (LME requires adjusting liquid amounts). Start with replacing only a small amount of the sugar with extract before you go all homebrewer crazy with it!

Pretzel Magic

As an example, here is Drew's modified version of Jeff Renner's Bavarian Pretzel recipe, which Drew goosed with a little DME and beer to give it some extra "beeriness." Jeff's original recipe calls for a small addition of sugar and water.

To make a pretzel a pretzel and not an odd-shaped bun, you must briefly cook the dough in an alkaline water bath. The alkaline environment causes a breakdown of surface proteins found in the dough and encourages Maillard reactions to create that distinctive brown chewy crust. (Jeff's addition of milk powder boosts this effect as well, so use it!)

Oh, and regardless of lye or soda, do not use aluminum for the water bath. Also, put the pretzels on parchment paper or a silicone mat, not directly on the tray!

LEGAL DANGER SAFETY WARNING:

Most modern recipes call for a baking soda bath, but the proper technique is to make a hot water lye bath. Lawyers and the safety minded get worried around caustic soda because it's supremely easy to chemically burn yourself if you are being inattentive. You can substitute 8 oz. by weight of baking soda for the lye, but it won't work as well. Exercise a well-worn brewer's caution to the lye solution—add your lye to a full pot of water, don't splash water onto straight lye or you're asking for chemical burns!

Malty Bavarian Pretzels

Yields 12 pretzels

Dough
- 1/4 cup (60 mL) warm water between 105°F and 155°F (41–68°C)
- pinch sugar
- 2 packets active dry yeast
- 19 oz. (540 g) all-purpose flour, sifted or whisked
- 3 oz. (85 g) shortening
- 1/4 cup (60 mL) DME
- 1 oz. (28 g) dry milk powder
- 1 tsp salt
- 1 cup (240 mL) beer, a good malty helles or bock (use water if you want less intensity)

Lye Bath
- 1 gal. (3.8 L) water
- 1/4 cup (60 mL) lye/sodium hydroxide/caustic soda

Garnish
- Pretzel salt!

Instructions
1. Preheat oven to 400°F/200°C.
2. Sprinkle the yeast into the water with a pinch of sugar to proof for 10 minutes.
3. Whisk together all the dry ingredients in the bowl of a stand mixer with the dough hook attached.
4. Add the yeast slurry to the bowl and turn the mixer onto low speed. Slowly add the beer and let the mixer knead the dough until soft and elastic.
5. Cover the bowl and let rise until the dough has doubled in size (~30–60 minutes).
6. Prepare the lye bath by adding lye to cold water and bringing to a simmer in a non-reactive stainless steel pot. (Not aluminum—Drew destroyed one beefy aluminum pot with a lye bath.) DO NOT ADD LYE (OR SODA) TO ALREADY HOT WATER—THAT'S HOW YOU GET CHEMICAL BURNS!
7. Divide the dough into 12 portions and roll each into an 18-inch rope. Bend into a U-shape, take the two ends and twist them around each other once or twice. Press the ends into the top of the U to form the classic pretzel "praying hands" shape. Rest on a floured surface with the seams down to help encourage a seal.
8. When fully shaped, carefully lower a pretzel into the simmering lye water with a slotted spoon or spider. Allow to simmer for 30 seconds, gently flip and simmer for an additional 30 seconds. The pretzels will expand and change color. Remove and pat dry with a paper towel. Place onto a parchment-lined cookie sheet and sprinkle with salt.
9. Bake the pretzels for 8–10 minutes or until shiny brown. Rest on racks for at least 30 minutes before devouring.

Malted Chocolate Decadence

Serves 12 to 16.

DENNY: Why should all-grain brewers have all the fun? If you don't have any spent grain, you can still have some malty, tasty treats. Personally, I keep dry malt extract around to make yeast starters. Imagine my glee when I ran across a recipe that uses dry malt extract to combine two of my favorite food groups, chocolate and malt! I made this recipe for my wife for our anniversary a few years back. We both absolutely loved it and I scored a lot of beer points with my wife by using brewing supplies to make a chocolate cake! Give this recipe a try for a special occasion...like say, when it's Tuesday!

Ingredients
- 1/2 cup or 1/4 lb. (115 g) butter or margarine
- 1/4 cup (60 mL) water
- 6 oz. (170 g) semisweet chocolate, chopped
- 2 oz. (57 g) unsweetened chocolate, chopped
- 4 large eggs
- 3/4 cup light DME
- 2 tbsp sugar

Materials
- 9-inch (23 cm) springform cake pan
- Aluminum foil
- Baking pan (for water bath)

Instructions
- Preheat your oven to 350°F/180°C.
- In a two to three-quart (2–3 L) pan over low heat, stir the butter, water, and semisweet and unsweetened chocolate just until smooth.
- Meanwhile, in a mixer bowl, whip eggs at high speed until they double in volume. Beat in the DME at a lower speed, then add the heated chocolate mixture and the 2 tbsp sugar.
- Bring 2–3 cups (0.5–0.75 L) of water to a boil.
- Butter a 9-inch (23 cm) cake pan with removable rim (springform pan). Set the pan on 2 sheets of heavy foil, each about 12 inches (30 cm) square. Press the foil firmly against the sides of pan (take care not to tear foil), letting the ends extend above the top—this is to keep the water out of the cake. Set the pan with foil into a larger baking pan; pour batter into cake pan.
- Place the pans into the oven, on a rack that can extend out a bit from the oven. Carefully fill the outer pan with about 1 inch (2.5 cm) of boiling water. Bake about 45 minutes, or until the center of the cake feels set when gently touched.
- Lift the foil sides to remove the cake from the water. Let it cool on a rack for at least 2 hours or until the next day. Remove the pan rim, serve and enjoy!

EXTRACT BEER RECIPES FROM DENNY

To brew these recipes, use the directions from the "Oversimplified Explanation of Extract Brewing" earlier in this chapter. All of these recipes are made for the Speed Brewing 20-minute boil.

Red Dog Pale Ale

Drew and I are both pet lovers and we each have multiple dogs and cats. So it stands to reason that we'd name the beverages we love after the pets we love. This one was named for my red border collie, Hannah.

Batch volume: 5 gal. (19 L)
Original Gravity: 1.051 (12.6°P)
Final Gravity: 1.012 (3.1°P)

Malt
- 5.5 lb. (2.5 kg) light DME
- 1 lb. (450 g) 60°L Crystal malt
- 2 oz. (56 g) roast barley

Hops
- 1 oz. (28 g) Chinook 14% AA @ 20 min.
- 1 oz. (28 g) Cascade 5% AA @ 10 min.
- 1 oz. (28 g) Cascade 5% AA @ 1 min.

Color: 15 SRM
Bitterness: 38 IBU
ABV: 5.2%

Water
- 1 tsp $CaSO_4$ (gypsum)

Yeast
- Safale US-05 dry yeast

Notes
After boiling, cool wort to 65°F (18°C), transfer it to your fermentor, and add the yeast. Ferment at 65–68°F (18–20°C) for 2 weeks, then package.

Happy Dog Stout

This delicious brew was named for Hannah's buddy, Mabel, a black and white border collie. We said Mabel was "the dog who was always singing a song" because she was such a happy, loving friend.

Batch volume: 5 gal. (19 L)
Original Gravity: 1.055
Final Gravity: 1.015 (3.8°P)

Malt
- 5.5 lb. (2.5 kg) dark DME
- 0.75 lb. (340 g) 60°L Crystal malt
- 0.25 lb. (115 g) black "patent" malt
- 0.5 lb. (225 g) roast barley

Hops
- 2.5 oz. (70 g) Cascade 5% AA @ 20 min.
- 1 oz. (28 g) Cascade 5% AA @ 5 min.

Color: 41 SRM
Bitterness: 59 IBU
ABV: 5.2%

Yeast
- Lallemand BRY-97 dry yeast, Safale US-05 dry yeast, or Saflager 34/70 (choose one)

Notes
After boiling, cool wort to 65°F (18°C), transfer it to your fermentor, and add the yeast. Ferment at 65–68°F (18–20°C) for 2 weeks, then package.

Old Stoner Barleywine

Two of my best friends started brewing about the same time I did in the spring of 1998. By January of 1999, we decided that we needed to get together to brew a batch of barleywine for New Year's Eve of 1999. If you recall, there was a lot of talk at that time about if the world would survive the transition to 2000, and we wanted to be prepared! (You may also recall how that fear turned out!). Fortunately, the world didn't end that night, although by the next day we kind of wished it had after drinking all that barleywine! The best part of the story is that nearly 18 years later on Thanksgiving of 2016, my friend Kevin found a bottle that he'd kept all of those years. We opened it up and truthfully it was one of the best beers I've ever had the pleasure of putting down my throat. Yeah, you can make some fantastic beers with extract!

Batch volume: 5 gal. (19 L)
Original Gravity: 1.114 (26.8°P)
Final Gravity: 1.028 (7.1°P)

Color: 12 SRM
Bitterness: 132 IBU
ABV: 11.5%

Malt
- 11 lb. (5 kg) light DME
- 3 lb. (1.36 kg) American pale malt (Rahr, Great Western, Briess)
- 1 lb. (450 g) 10°L Munich malt
- 1 lb. (450 g) 20°L Crystal malt

Hops
- 6 oz. (170 g) Magnum 13.9% AA @ 20 min.
- 1 oz. (28 g) Chinook 12.6% AA @ 15 min.
- 1 oz. (28 g) Chinook 12.6% AA @ 5 min.

Yeast
- Lallemand BRY-97 dry yeast, Safale US-05 dry yeast, or Saflager 34/70 (choose one)
*Use 2 yeast packets since it's a strong beer.

Notes
After boiling, cool wort to 65°F (18°C), transfer it to your fermentor and add the yeast. Ferment at 65–68°F (18–20°C) for 4 weeks, then package.

AN INSPIRATIONAL MESSAGE TO ALL THE DOUBTERS

Here's the other thing, no one—really, we mean no one whose opinion matters—is going to take away your "brewer badge of badassness" because you make any or all of your beer with extract. If they do, feel free to tell them that Denny and Drew told you it's all good. You can also rest assured they probably feel terribly inadequate about themselves. Let's save the "judging" for things that really matter, like everyone else's terrible taste in music!

Seriously, there is nothing wrong with using extract if what you enjoy about beer is putting together an idea and getting it to the glass in the quickest way possible. In fact, we'd argue that not brewing due to time constraints and other complications is the greater sin!

PROFILES IN SIMPLICITY: JAY ANKENEY

If you've been brewing for a long enough time, odds are you've read a piece by Redondo Beach's master brewer, Jay Ankeney. Jay is a prolific writer covering the tech and broadcast fields. Back before he decided he needed to "make money at the writing thing," Jay wrote the *Zymurgy For Beginners* column for years. He even wrote his own homebrewing book, *Easy Beer*,[5] back when most homebrewing books assumed you knew something about beer right off the bat. (To quote Jay, "I picked up a British brewing book and the first sentence was 'You must rouse the wort'.")

So why profile Jay here in the extract chapter? See, here's what's different about Jay. Jay's been brewing for years, longer than either of us. He started in the early 1980s, you know, back when Ronald Reagan was president of the United States. Jay is also somewhat unique because he never switched to all-grain brewing. Throughout the years of enjoying great beer with both of his clubs, Strand Brewers and Maltose Falcons, Jay has amassed an amazing amount of knowledge about beer and mead, all the while making any number of outstanding beverages without needing to cramp his beachside domicile with a mash tun.

There are easy assumptions to make about brewers who keep brewing extract long after the rest of us have moved onto the magic of mashing. "They're lazy." "They just want 'cheap' beer." "They're not real brewers." "They can't make all the beers."

Jay puts to rest those assumptions. When asked why he keeps brewing with extract, Jay offers a few reasons. The first is the issue of space: his place just doesn't have the space to store a kegerator, a mash tun, and all the other gear you need. But the main reason is the scarcity of that most precious commodity—time. Jay has a busy calendar and would rather be able to brew and get back out in the world doing other things. Start to finish, Jay puts a beer together and the kettles to rest in three hours. Then he's off to find other adventures.

DREW: Seriously, the Beatles are overrated, and so's your favorite band. But Jimmy Buffett is aces!

DENNY: I'd drink a clam chowder saison before I'd listen to Jimmy Buffett! As for beer, keep in mind that it's results that we drink, not the ingredient list. No one's gonna care what you used to make it if it's delicious!

DREW: Whatever. We may not all get to tour with hip new wave/art-rock bands, but I think we can both agree that extract makes some damn fine beer if you follow all of the good brewing practices that you've learned over the years. Let's face it, our job as brewers is to create the perfect party environment for our yeasty friends. Do that and you're 98% of the way to great pints.

---

5   Jay Ankeney and Dan Dennis, *Easy Beer: A Beginners Guide to Home Beer Brewing* (Manhattan Beach, CA: Anthem Enterprises, 1987).

Also, Jay's a strange man in other ways. He's the mythical brewer who loves to bottle. He'll happily sit for a few hours meditating his way through a round of priming, filling, and capping. Not only does it relax him, but he believes it offers him the chance to have more variety since he isn't limited by keg capacity. More variety means more brewing!

Jay's Tips for Extract Brewing

- Find the extract varieties that work for you! Jay is a big fan of Coopers' extract because it literally comes from the same brewhouse as Coopers' beer. Plus, the newer, paler varieties that Briess is producing really allow extract brewers to expand their possibilities to more styles and colors.
- Don't be afraid of the dark extracts. Many folks will tell you to focus your extract choices on the paler varieties and get your color from your grains, but Jay says he loves using a dark extract when he's making porters and stouts (he has medaled before with his porter.)
- Say yes to the grain: a mini-mash is essential to getting the best possible beer flavor from your extract batch.
- Go hands-free when chilling. Jay doesn't have a chiller, but he still rapidly cools the beer with a combination water bath and big sanitary ice cube. The night before he brews, Jay boils water, covers and cools it, then uses it to fill a sanitized Ziploc® container. He freezes the container overnight and uses the ice cube in the kettle as combination chiller and top-up water.
- Jay eschews glass in favor of five-gallon plastic water bottles, but since he doesn't trust cleaning and sanitizing them, he uses 18" × 36" 2-mil-thick low-density polyethylene bags that are sanitary and food safe. (Note that 2 mil is 0.002 inches, or 0.05 mm.) Jay stuffs a bag into the water bottle and then transfers his wort into the bag. After fermentation, he racks out of the bag and pulls the bag from the water bottle. Cleanup is done!
- Jay was also ahead of the curve on the no secondary fermentor front. He even wrote about skipping the secondary as early as 1985!

The next time someone tells you "extract can't make good beer," well, now you have Jay to point to. ■

3

SIMPLE SMALL BATCH

There are two ways to think about "small" in the context of brewing. The first we thought of is brewing "small beer"—or session ales—a thing which we both have an incredible passion for. But maybe small can mean something different. See, we don't know about you, but when we first started with this whole brewing thing, it never occurred to us to think of small as "small batch."

It just feels like, since time immemorial, five gallons has been the size of the batch and the size of the batch has been five gallons. When the first small-batch kits began to appear on the market, we both scoffed. Why, oh why would anyone want to spend just about the same amount of time brewing and only end up with a fifth of the output? (Those first kits were all centered on a one-gallon volume.) Seriously, stop and think about it: you can take six hours and produce roughly 50 bottles of beer or you can take five hours and produce ten.

In our world, that's a no brainer...

But now, we're here to argue in favor of small-batch brewing. There are indeed reasons to get small!

"They have this little test they give you—they give you a balloon... and if you can get inside of it, they know you're small."

— Steve Martin,
Saturday Night Live,
February 26, 1977

IN DEFENSE OF SMALL-BATCH BREWING

As if small-batch brewing needed defending! But, when new brewers ask other brewers about batch size, the common thing to hear is that you can brew twice as much beer in the same amount of time, so go big. But that only takes into account the point of view of the person answering the question, who probably has everything set up for five gallons or more.

You can go small with extract, partial mash, or all grain. Whichever way you prefer to make beer, you can scale it to make small batches. Here are our top five reasons to brew small:

1. Less physical strength needed
2. Smaller gear and less gear needed
3. Less room needed
4. More variety and experimentation
5. Less risk (less money on the line!)
6. And a bonus sixth reason…Less time spent brewing and packaging the beer! If you brew less volume, you can boil and chill more quickly. If you brew smaller batches, you need smaller equipment, which makes clean up faster. How can you pass this up?

Less Physical Strength Needed

Many homebrewers employ small-batch brewing due to physical limitations. They can't lift a pot containing the water or wort in a standard five-gallon batch, so a one to three-gallon batch allows them to brew when they wouldn't be able to otherwise. Small-batch brewing has been a great boon in this regard, making brewing accessible to many more people and extended the careers of many older brewers or people with physical restrictions (say, a bad back) that make five gallons unsafe to manage.

Think of it this way: a gallon of water weighs 8.34 lb. and the sugars you add to the wort (courtesy of sugar, malt, or extract) also adds weight. The easiest way to estimate the weight of your wort is to multiply 8.34 lb. by your gravity and you'll know roughly your wort weight; for example, 1 gal. of 1.050 gravity wort weighs 8.76 lb. (since one liter of water weighs one kilogram, 1 L of 1.050 wort weighs 1.05 kg). That means your five gallons of beer weighs 43.8 lb. (19.9 kg) before you include the weight of the container it's in. Add in the 18 lb. (8 kg) from a glass carboy and you're talking nearly 62 lb. (28 kg). Even a bucket adds another three to four pounds, or around one and a half kilograms, of weight. That's a lot of weight in an ungainly vessel with a dynamically shifting load. Considering that federal and state labor departments get antsy about workers lifting weights over 20 lb. (9 kg) from the floor, even the most strapping and sturdy of us should be a little wary of those big loads.

You can mitigate some of the load with tools like pumps and using CO_2 pressure to move liquid around, but at the end of the day you're still looking at moving heavy amounts of liquid when brewing five or more gallons of beer. Sometimes even the stoutest of us might not look forward to that duty.

Now step back and look at a two-gallon batch: that's roughly 17.5 lb. (8 kg), and when you add the 13 lb. (6 kg) for a three-gallon carboy, you're looking at a total of 30.5 lb. (14 kg). Moving that much around is still a daunting proposition for some, but it's more reasonable to the average person.

Smaller Gear and Less Gear Needed

Brewing small batches requires a bit less gear than you need for larger batches, with the real advantage being that you may have much of what you need in your kitchen already. Clever reuse of colanders, pots, stoppers, jars, growlers, and the like can reduce the need for dedicated equipment; for instance, you may already have a stockpot that you can use as a boil kettle. On a similar note, when you brew big your kitchen stove is going to have a hell of a time raising all that wort to a hearty boil. When you brew small your stovetop works like a charm! Also, a wort chiller probably isn't needed since you can put your pot into a sink full of ice water to cool it down to pitching temperature. All this equates to less storage space since you'll need less dedicated brewing gear. That brings us on to the next point, which is you need less room.

Less Room Needed

Times have changed. Current trends point to more and more smaller living spaces. In other words, less room to store your beer and all the assorted equipment and geegaws you'll accumulate. When you combine that with the increased number of hobbies and activities families are involved in, we're getting cramped in here.

What if you have space limitations in your kitchen? What if you don't have an outdoor area to brew large batches? You can run multiple small batches in a spare closet. Your smaller batches require less fixed space, for example, a set of one-gallon growlers can fit on a narrow shelf! Hey, it even has the advantage that your interior closets are very temperature stable. As you'll see later, small batches allow people in even the craziest cramped New York apartments to create an incredible breadth of fermentation experiments.

More Variety and Experimentation

An immutable fact of nature is that, no matter how much gusto we have for our fermentations, our livers literally cannot handle endless gallons of beer. At least most of the time. If you're not downing gallons daily, then brewing "normal" batch sizes means you're usually faced with the challenge of getting the beer out of the kegs and bottles fast enough to bring new batches online. OK, maybe you need more friends, but, hey, maybe you just need less beer!

Smaller batches give you more opportunities to practice, refine, and decide on new ideas and ingredients. They are the perfect way to test ingredients and learn about their flavors. You can make a number of small batches with only a single ingredient change in each, then assess and compare them. Try different base malts or hops in each one to find your favorites.

DREW: Don't scoff. I had a period of time when I was dealing with terrible shoulder pain. I had to take time off from my brewing schedule to heal and it was miserable. I stopped brewing for months. If I'd had access to small-batch equipment, or even just the knowledge that one could brew small (never even occurred to me, that's how enmeshed I was in my five-gallon worldview), I could have taken advantage of the time to play around with some highly creative and risky ideas or other experiments.
Oh, you want another reason to brew small? It's the way of the brewing scientist. When trying to understand a new ingredient or analyze a new crop or lot, a brewer isn't brewing big to begin with. A good number of exploratory learning batches start in beakers on burners.

DENNY: As I've aged over the course of my brewing hobby, I've found I can't do things that were once doable or that at least they presented a major challenge to me. Lifting is the biggest of those. There are days when I just can't lift a kettle of wort onto the burner. Those are the days that I turn to small-batch brewing. I only have to lift a fraction of the weight that I do when I brew a five-gallon batch.

DREW: Hear us out about this. It all depends on what your favorite aspect of brewing is. For some folks, it's the beer and pouring a pint. For me, I love the act of brewing and I really love the act of designing beer recipes. Less beer in kegs means I have more opportunity to design more interesting pints. When I started brewing 10 gallons I found myself getting bored with the beer, so I started figuring out how to brew more variety. Now, when I brew smaller batches, I can focus on the single recipe, the single experience I'm making, and not feel guilty that I'm not maximizing my output.

DENNY: Another side effect of getting older is that I don't have the tolerance for beer that I used to. I drink a lot less than I did 20 years ago. Small-batch brewing means that I can have fresh beer on hand, rather than a keg that's been sitting there for six months waiting to be finished.

Less Risk

Small batches are also perfect because of the lower risk. Less risk goes hand in hand with testing ingredients and techniques. If you discover you've chosen an ingredient you really don't like, at least you only have a gallon of beer to drink (or dump). It's far less psychologically damaging to pour out that godawful red wine farmhouse *chicha* you decided to make.

Of course, there's the money angle too. When you're talking about 2–3 lb. of grain per batch, along with some hops and yeast, even if you're being wasteful you dropped about ten to fifteen dollars at the most. That's a much easier hit to take than the time Drew dropped close to $100 on a lavender-infused beer that really should never have been born.

Truly, the only risk that you run when brewing small is the risk of wasting your labor. But if you're standing over the kettles, enjoying a beer and playing around with different combinations of ideas and experiences, what have you lost? Hobbies are time sinks by their very nature. There's a reason that only the truly obsessively insane folks tack their labor cost into their bottle cost calculations. (Have you met these people? "I buy grain in bulk on the flip side of harvest season when the moon perfectly balances the price, so I get it for pennies per pound. I've reused the same yeast culture for free since the time of Moses. My hops are thrice-cycled and my labor rate is that of a child working in a Victorian-era mill in New England. So, I make my beer for 3.2 cents per glass. Suck it, big brewers!")

Less Time Needed

Remember Doug King from the "Profile in Simplicity" in chapter 1? Well before the era of small-batch brewing, Doug maintained a separate set of gear dedicated to brewing small so he could repeatedly cycle his recipes until he nailed what he thought was the right combination. Again, this is all pre-1999, so we should all get with the program!

Even if you do the traditional one-hour mash and one-hour boil, you can still brew in less time. Chilling your wort will take less time since there's less volume. Cleaning up will take less time because there's less equipment and it's smaller. When you bottle or keg your beer, it can be over in a (relative) flash because of the smaller volume.

DREW: Here's another point that's really a combination of all the other things. My struggle with brewing is always a matter of dealing with inertia. Between work, writing, podcasting, life, and other projects it's sometimes a battle to get to the kettles. Busting out the brew stand, wheeling equipment around, cleaning and setting and heating all that liquid and grain—it can be exhausting. But walking into my kitchen, dropping a pot on the stove while making dinner and talking with my wife? That's far easier to get moving. Kinda miss those days of coming home at 6 p.m., putting a batch on the stove and finishing at 12 a.m.

So, while some people may take pride in their ability to brew 15 gallons at a time, we can smugly think about how many beers we'll be enjoying while they're still working!

Also, a dirty little secret that we feel y'all should know: you don't have to brew just one size. Keep a few pots around, a grain bag in your kitchen, and your huge kettles in the garage. There are no brewing police who are coming to take away your "official brewer" card just because you switch it up. And if, like Drew, you have odd plans for a nihilistic survivalist future, being able to brew with a tin can and some leftover shoe laces is far handier than needing a particularly persnickety electrical coil for your results.

Small Batch Shortcomings

Let's stop and take a minute and recognize that there are some big downsides to brewing small. As one would assume, the volume being less is an issue for some people. If you're a dedicated small-batch brewer, you'll be hard pressed to supply the summer time barbecue for all your friends. (It's a fun and exhausting challenge and a chance to do a ton of brewing, but make sure your friends do the bottling. Freeloaders!)

There's also the additional challenge of replication. How do you dial in your brewing skills so tightly that batch #354 of your Pale Ale tastes just as good (or better) than batch #353? The answer is the same as getting to Carnegie Hall: practice. Truthfully, brewing is a mechanical skill that requires repetition to perfect.

Now we get down to the brass tacks—the things we think no one else thinks about when they start wondering if there are downsides.

You don't take it seriously.

Don't tell anyone, but the first couple of times we tried small-batch brewing, it felt silly. "Oh, look at me making a wee little batch of beer. Tee hee!" Again, it goes back to that chauvinistic concern over size: "I was taught to make five gallons and anything less is wrong!"

The danger isn't so much the attitude—after all, just get over yourself—the danger lies in not taking your process seriously. What we mean by this is, if you've been inculcated with the notion that anything less than five gallons is a lark and a throwaway, you'll forget your fundamentals, like proper sanitation or fermentation temperature control.

Things just work differently.

We're fond of noting that you can't take everything from a professional brewery's experience and apply it straight to homebrewing. Size and scale really do matter. It's no different here with our small batches. Things like hitting your mash temperatures will likely take some adjustments because the thermal mass of one gallon doesn't shield you from temperature swings the way a larger mass of mash will.

DENNY: OK, maybe the survivalistic fantasy thing is a bit overstated, but I do like to brew in multiple ways and small batch is definitely one of them. Combine this with mead making or extract brewing and, boy, do you have a perfect solution to those nights when you just can't sleep!

The gear is all wrong.

This has been changing in the last few years, but the result of 40-plus years of multi-gallon homebrewing is that most of the gear out there is sized for large batches. As we said above, "Five gallons has been the size of the batch and the size of the batch has been five gallons." All the prefab mash rigs, fermentors, and racking canes, not to mention all the parts for creating your own rigs, target the 5-gallon mark by default. Brewing small batches with gear sized for bigger batches requires careful consideration. Will there be enough liquid to reach your valves? Is your kettle so big that a vigorous boil will boil off more than the usual 10%–20% of volume per hour? Is there too much head space in your fermentor? Most of these concerns can be mitigated by preparation. Verify your pickup volume and slow your boil; don't do a secondary in a large-volume vessel, since fermentation won't fill the headspace with CO_2 (or use a CO_2 tank to flood the vessel).

We are fans of small-batch brewing, mostly for the reasons given above. But don't just take our word for it. If you're on the fence about whether to try it, read through these responses we got when we asked brewers on the American Homebrewers Association discussion forum[1] why they brew small batches:

- Use less water and brew more often with more variety
- Fresher beer, so many recipes and so little time
- I'm the primary drinker of my beer and 5 gallons is too much
- The only way I could make it work space wise and quantity wise
- Faster brew day
- Brew all-grain, indoors
- Smaller equipment is faster to clean
- Brewing more often means more practice at brewing

Convinced now? So were we! OK, let's work through what brewing a small batch entails.

BREWING SMALL: THE TOTAL PICTURE

A Small-Batch Brew Day

The only thing that differentiates a small-batch brew from a normal-sized batch brew is that it's smaller…duh! You use a lot of the same equipment and processes that you'd use for larger brew sessions. But there are a few differences and most of them are actually advantages. So, here's a quick walk through of a small-batch brew.

While there's no reason you can't brew small extract batches, the technique really makes a lot of sense if you brew partial mash or all-grain. Brewing a five-gallon all-grain batch can mean a lot of equipment and space. Not only does small-batch brewing take less of both of those, but because it's easy to do indoors it's a great solution in cold winter or hot summer climates.

1   denny, "Small Batch Brewers - Let's Talk!" AHA Forum, January 18, 2017, https://www.home-brewersassociation.org/forum/index.php?topic=28528.

HEAT THE WATER.

We're going to assume that this is a 1 gal. (3.8 L), all-grain batch. The first step is to heat up about 1.5 gal. (5.7 L) of water. Start with cold water, because many water heaters, especially older ones, can have mineral buildup in them. To speed up heating the water, look around your kitchen for inspiration. Put half the water in the pot you're going to be using for brewing and put that on your stove or induction burner. Put the other half in a microwave-safe container and start heating it in the microwave.

After about 5 minutes on high, check the temperature of the water in the microwave. It will heat much faster than the water in the pot, so the idea is to add the microwaved water to your pot as a "booster" to increase the temperature in the pot. (If you are using extract, you want to get the water as close to boiling as possible.) For your mash, average the temperatures of the two containers of water to help you hit your mash temperature. For example, let's say you want to hit a 153°F (67.3°C) mash temperature. The water heating slowly in the pot is 85°F (29.5°C) and the microwave water heating quickly is 185°F (85°C). The average temperature if you add an equal volume of each together is 135°F (57.3°C). You need to keep heating both. Yes, you do have to do math on the fly, but it's not too painful. And the advantage is that you'll get to your temperature much more quickly than you would if you just heated the whole gallon and a half in the pot.

MASH.

Once you get to your desired temperature, add your grain and check the temperature again. If you're below your mash temperature, keep heating until you just barely get there. If you're over temperature, head to the freezer, grab a few ice cubes and drop them in. Don't worry if your temperature is a few degrees under or over for a few minutes. It won't really make much, if any, difference to your beer. Just get the temperature adjusted within 5 minutes or so and you'll be good. Once you get to temperature, turn your burner off (or down to low), put the lid on the pot, and sit back and wait for the mash to finish. Alternately, you can use your oven to maintain mash temperature. Since most ovens don't allow you to set the temperature low enough for a mash temperature, you can heat up your oven, then turn it off and place the pot with your grain in it.

SPARGE AND/OR PULL THE GRAIN.

Once you've mashed for the amount of time specified in your recipe, strain the grain from the pot. Use a sieve and carefully pour the wort through it or use another strainer device to pull the grain out of the wort. If you're going to sparge (an optional step of using hot water to rinse the grains after being removed from the pot), put your grain in a large strainer or colander and pour

180°F (82°C) water over it. If you're not sparging (which reduces the amount of sugar you get from the grain, but it's way easier), just go ahead to the boil step. (We'll cover other ways you can sparge in "What's in Your Kitchen?" below; the section following that looks at brew-in-a-bag, which makes for an easy way to remove the grain from the pot.)

BOIL THE WORT.

Boil the wort for the amount of time specified in your recipe, adding hops as called for. If you want to save some time, you can add 50% more bittering hops than your recipe calls for and do a 20-minute boil (see "Speed Brewing" on page 32). Keep all other hop amounts as your recipe says.

CHILL THE WORT.

Once you've added the hops and your wort has boiled, you need some way to cool it down before you add the yeast. This is another area in which small-batch brewing shines. Rather than use a dedicated wort chiller, you can simply plop the loosely covered pot into your sink, fill the sink with cold water, and let the wort cool. (We're assuming a metal sink here. If you're using a plastic utility sink, safeguard the bottom!) You'll probably need to change the water once or twice as it absorbs heat. When you replace the water the second or third time, add some ice to the water. You can add ice earlier, of course, but it won't do as much good. The key to cooling is to keep the temperature difference between the water and wort as high as possible. When you first begin to cool, the wort will be very hot and the water very cold. As the wort cools down, that difference becomes less. Adding ice to lower the water temperature at that point will help keep your "delta" (the temperature difference between wort and water) as high as possible.

FERMENT THE WORT.

Cool your wort until the temperature reaches about 65°F (18°C). You can check the temperature with a sanitized kitchen thermometer, just be sure it's really clean! Once you reach the right temperature, you can use a sanitized strainer (and funnel if you ferment in carboys) to help you transfer the wort to your fermentor. Or you can use the really easy method—simply pitch your yeast right into the wort in your pot! The pot is already sanitized from the boil. The upside of this method is that it's easy; the downside is that you can't use the pot again until the beer is finished fermenting. But, back in the plus column, small batches take less time to ferment than larger batches. So many choices, and they're all yours! FYI - smaller batches require less yeast too!

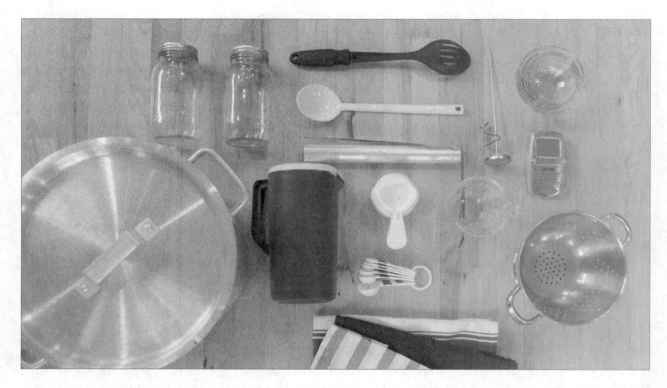

Figure 3.1. Look at all the brewing tools you never knew you already had!

What's in Your Kitchen?

Most people, including us, like to keep separate gear for brewing and cooking. But you can certainly use the same equipment if that fits your style. Just make sure what you use for brewing is clean and clear of cooking residue! There are many things you can commandeer from the kitchen:

- stockpot
- plastic spoons*
- thermometer (make sure it's accurate)
- strainer
- bowls
- pitchers
- measuring cups and spoons
- towels (if you're like Denny, LOTS of towels!)
- milk and/or juice jugs for fermentors*
- jars or resealable plastic containers to store yeast for reuse*
- aluminum foil (a.k.a. homebrewer's duct tape)
- timer

Okay, that's the small stuff. Now let's think bigger. We've already talked about using your microwave to speed up heating. Let's look at some other stuff you might have around your kitchen.

---

*   Be aware that plastic implements and containers can sometimes retain flavors or aromas from their original use, especially from contact with strong-flavored foods like pickles, chili, and curry. Make sure yours don't!

A NOTE ABOUT ELECTRIC HEATING

If you're in America, a standard US household 120 V household circuit will be installed with a 15 A or 20 A circuit breaker. That means at most you'll be able to put 1800 W of load on a 15 A circuit or 2400 W on a 20 A circuit. For safety's sake, it is recommended you do not load your circuits to the maximum load. We also recommend that you stick with commercially made electric heating products instead of homemade systems (unless you're experienced with electrical work).

Induction burner

An induction burner is one of the coolest kitchen toys to use when brewing. It heats really quickly, is easily controllable, and stays cool when you use it. Better yet, it's inexpensive. We both use 1800-watt models that sell for less than sixty dollars. (Here's where we get to be jealous of people in countries with high-voltage systems—looking at you Australia and Europe with your sweet 220/230 volts.) Be aware that you need special cookware designed to be used with an induction plate. But, both the cookware and the burner can be a big plus in the kitchen for when you're cooking too, so the moderate cost is amortized even more.

Sous vide circulator

Sous vide has become such a popular way of cooking that sous vide circulators are showing up in more and more kitchens. If you haven't seen one, it's a heating element and pump in one unit. For cooking, you seal your food in a plastic bag and put it in a pot of water with the circulator running. The food gets cooked to exactly the temperature you have the circulator set to. For our purposes, these circulators act like a perfect temperature control heating element. Some brewers have reported good results doing small batch mashes with the grain and circulator separated by a grain bag. The key is not to gum up the works of the circulator with grain. (For the record, many manufacturers recommend that you only use their circulators with water and that other uses will shorten unit life.) Even if you don't mash with a circulator, you can use the circulator as a water heater and get your strike water ready without needing to keep an eye on the pot.

French press

You can use your French press (*cafetière* or coffee plunger) with hops instead of coffee to make a hop tea to add to your beer post-fermentation. Using a hop tea to add hop aroma to your beer is a process that has gained in popularity, with many people finding it preferable to dry hopping. The hop tea process gives you a lot of hop aroma without all those beer-absorbing hops!

Drip coffee machine

Speaking of coffee, we know it seems that everyone uses single-cup brew systems, but you can use your old drip coffee maker as a hot plate and mash vessel. Throw a coffee filter in the top, put your mashed grains into the basket, and let the drip system sparge into the pot. This works for any typical instant 5–14 cup brew system. (If you're really ambitious, you can convert a full size "church" coffee pot into a system as well. Some of the commercial all-in-one brewing systems seem directly inspired by that form.) Just be sure to clean that coffee maker first, unless you're making an espresso stout.

Metal cocktail shaker

At various times during your brew you'll need to take specific gravity readings of your wort in order to see how your mash or boil is going. Hydrometers are made of glass and don't like super-hot stuff, so an easy way to quickly cool the wort for a reading is to put 6-8 fl. oz. (2 L) in a metal cocktail shaker and swirl it around in a bowl of ice water. In 60 seconds or less you'll be at a safe temperature to get an accurate reading.

Whisk/handheld electric mixer

Yeast needs oxygen to ensure a healthy and complete fermentation; a great way to oxygenate your wort is to sanitize a wire whisk or the beaters of a handheld electric mixer and use it to whip air into your wort. That will help make sure your yeast party rocks out. Even earlier in the process, you can skip a fancy mash paddle and use a whisk to thoroughly mix the mash and avoid the dough balls.

Figure 3.2. Using a whipping siphon might sound complicated, but these are the only parts you need. In this picture, we're about to create 4 fl. oz. of intensely coffee-flavored vodka using a stainless steel whipping siphon (for safety's sake, we only recommend the all-metal models).

Whipping siphon

Kind of like using a French press to make a hop tea, you can use a whipping siphon to make tinctures quickly, whether with hops or some exotic flavoring that only a mind like Drew's can fully comprehend. Don't know what a whipping siphon is? Think your visits to the ice cream store or coffee shop—that fancy gadget they spray whipped cream out of, that's a whipping siphon. Put a bit of vodka (4 fl. oz. or 120 mL) along with your hops or flavoring into the siphon body, then screw on the cap and a nitrous oxide cartridge; release the gas from the cartridge into the siphon, remove the cartridge, and repeat with another cartridge. Open the siphon to release the gas and add the now flavored vodka to your beer.

Spray bottle/mister

No matter how much Denny plans ahead, he always seems to forget to sanitize something until the moment he needs it. By having a spray bottle or (new, clean) mister full of sanitizer, you can give the stuff you forgot a quick spritz and it'll be ready to go. You can also keep another spray bottle of water to knock down the foam that rises as your wort starts to boil.

Figure 3.3. Brew-In-A-Bag, known to most brewers as BIAB, allows for a simpler process.

Brew-in-a-Bag

Another way to make your small-batch brewing simpler is to use the brew-in-a-bag method (hereafter called BIAB, because brevity is the soul of wit). This is a brewing process where the grain is put into a mesh bag and then immersed in the heated water for the mash. You can use an inexpensive muslin bag from your homebrew shop, a paint strainer bag from the hardware store, or a bag made specifically for BIAB brewing, available from one of several suppliers. The advantage of BIAB is that it makes the grain easy to remove once the mash is done. With the proper equipment BIAB can be used for five-gallon or larger batches, but it's really ideal for small-batch kitchen brewers. It just makes your life easier and who doesn't want that? We'll talk about BIAB more in chapter 4.

Itty Bitty Pale Ale

A BIAB, No-Sparge Brew

Batch volume: 2 gal. (7.6 L)
Original gravity: 1.053 (13.1°P)
Final gravity: 1.012 (3.1°P)
Color: 7 SRM

Bitterness: 25 IBU
ABV: 5.4%
Boil: 60 minutes

Malt
- 4.5 lb. (2 kg) pale malt
- 0.5 lb. (225 g) 60°L crystal malt

Steep/Mash
- Put bag in pot. Add 2.75 gal. (10.4 L) water and heat to 165°F (74°C). Add grains and the temperature should settle around 153°F (67°C).
- Steep grains for 20 minutes; stir occasionally, if you feel you need to.
- Remove grain bag and let drain.

Hops
- 0.75 oz. (21 g) CTZ* 11.4% AA @ 20 min.
- 0.5 oz. (14 g) Citra 13.4% AA @ 0 min.
- 0.5 oz. (14 g) Bravo 13.6% AA @ 0 min.
- 1.0 oz. (28 g) CTZ 11.4% AA @ dry hop

*A blend of Columbus, Tomahawk®, and Zeus.

Water
- Use reverse osmosis water for mashing.
- Acidify sparge water to pH of 6.

Yeast
- WY1450 Denny's Favorite 50 Ale™ (use activator pack, no starter)

Notes
- Boil 60 minutes, with boil hop additions as per schedule.
- Cool pot in sink to reach fermentation temperature (65°F /18°C) and pitch yeast.
- Ferment at 65°F (18°C) until done and keg with the dry hops.

SMALL PROCESSES

While we're getting small, let's look at some small processes to complement small-batch brewing. As we and others have noted (see Mary Izett's profile at the end of this chapter), small batches make all the processes associated with brewing easier. But some brewers have taken that even further by devising clever ways to do things.

We picked up the following tip from a listener of our Experimental Brewing website podcast.[2] Nelson Crowle runs the website ReggieBeer.com, which is the home of his beer competition software, Reggie. Nelson likes to make *eisbock*, a style of beer where you freeze the beer and remove the frozen water; you're left with a thick, rich, delicious (and high alcohol!) beer. Most of the time people freeze the entire five-gallon batch, but that requires either a very large freezer or a cold climate. Nelson came up with a smaller, faster, easier method.

---

[2] "The Podcast," Experimental Brewing, https://www.experimentalbrew.com/podcast.

I just wanted to share my Eisbock (or Eis-ing in general) process that has yielded two competition Best of Show awards (in 700-entry competitions).

I use 2 L Mountain Dew bottles to Eis. Filled just above the top of the label (50-ish ounces), then squeezed to remove some of the air, then on their side in the freezer to give good surface area (and a thinner layer of liquid to freeze). They freeze fast, and you can eyeball the progress, and squeeze the bottle for firmness. When a good slush forms all the way through the bottle, I pour out the liquid yummy stuff.

For Eisbock I usually start with a hefty Doppelbock (10–12%), then Eis gives me around 18%.

Two notes on brewing Eisbock:

1) Consider lowering the hop bittering in the base beer (I shoot for the low end of BJCP guidelines for Doppelbock), because the bittering is concentrated too, and a higher-bitter base beer may become too bitter when Eis'd.

2) That leftover ice? Melt it and drink it! It's still a 5–6% beer, and I've entered the Eisbock Eis-only beer in competitions as a Dunkel.

DREW: Sigh. That line is clearly Denny's.

Very cool!

OK, that was bad…but since we've started looking at 2 L PET bottles, here's another idea. Bottling has got to be one of the most onerous tasks in homebrewing, at least for us. Washing and sanitizing bottles, filling them, capping them…even for a small batch it feels like a large hassle! Kegging makes things a little simpler, but still requires a fair bit of effort. But using 2 L PET bottles and a carbonator cap makes bottling and carbonating a breeze.

If you haven't seen one before, a carbonator cap is a plastic cap that's threaded to fit a standard PET bottle. The other end of it has a CO_2 fitting. You simply fill a PET bottle to about the top of the label (this allows head space for CO_2 and it's recommended by the manufacturer), squeeze out the air above the beer, and screw on your carbonator cap. Hit the beer with 30 psi (207 kPa) of CO_2 and put it in your freezer for 45 minutes. When the time is up, you'll have cold, carbonated beer in a fraction of the time that traditional bottling or kegging takes. This makes getting a bead on where your beer is a lot quicker and simpler.

Bonus points for those seeking to make something non-alcoholic either for yourself, a non-imbiber, or as a project to work on with the young. The 2 L PET bottle with carbonator cap is a great technique for making soda as well. Just dilute a flavorful soda syrup, chill the soda, and hit with the CO_2 to make fast, fizzy fun. You can either use a commercial soda syrup like you find in a coffee shop or make your own. Make your own syrup by boiling a 1:1 water and sugar solution with spices and/or herbs of your choosing. Strain, cool, and add to the water in your desired amount.

So, there you go, bigger is not always better. Sometimes smaller is the way to go and it can be simpler. We really think there's value in learning how to move between batch sizes so you can always be brewing. Even if you want or have all the big toys, make yourself a small-batch system for playing around with before you go big. By the way, if you go to larger brewery operations you'll see they have "pilot" systems that follow exactly this idea, offering smaller systems to go explore ideas on. Why shouldn't you?

PROFILES IN SIMPLICITY: MARY IZETT AND CHRIS CUZME

Mary and Chris are the powerhouse fermentation New York duo behind Cuzett Libations. Mary is a homebrewer and the author of *Speed Brewing*.[3] Mary got her start in the brewing world because her degrees are in biology and horticulture: it's a very easy leap from there to "fermentation rocks." As we write this, Chris is the cofounder of Fifth Hammer Brewing in Long Island City, New York and a serious saxophone player—you'll find him at Homebrew Con serenading the crowd with his musical talents. Between the two of them they've got the world of fermentation cornered.

Mary's the specialist in all things small at home and her book not only dives into very simple rules for brewing beer, cider, mead, kombucha, and many other things, but it's almost exclusively all about the small batch. This is driven in part by the size of her New York City residence—NYC apartments are expensive and sized so small!—but also by safety concerns. It's much easier to handle 1–3 gal. than it is 5+ gal., which is a boon when you're moving things up and down stairs, as you tend to do in a packed city. Even though Mary and Chris live in a tiny apartment and brew small batches, they have four (four!) chest freezers that they use for fermentation. Some things are priorities!

We sat down with Mary and asked a few questions about the importance and execution of small batch brewing.

D&D: Why did you get into small-batch brewing and what is your average batch size?

Mary: I started with five-gallon batches, and then started experimenting with one-gallon batches for my more "exotic" beverages. I was brewing five-gallon batches in my backyard and fermenting them in a shared basement. I had to carry the carboys downstairs to ferment them and back upstairs to bottle. When the three-gallon BetterBottle (plastic carboy fermentors) came out I got into doing split batches. And then from there I moved to smaller batches because I enjoyed using the smaller fermentors. Also, because I go out so much I found five gallons of beer at a time was more than I needed.

---

3   Mary Izett, *Speed Brewing: Techniques and Recipes for Fast-Fermenting Beers, Ciders, Meads, and More* (Minneapolis: Voyageur Press, 2015).

D&D: What are your favorite processes and equipment for small batches?

Mary: Brew in a bag! I sew my own bags. Small BIAB batches worked because I couldn't physically lift a 12-gallon brewpot with six gallons of wort. I've made bags for every single one of my different-sized brew kettles.

D&D: When you do BIAB, do you sparge or do no sparge?

Mary: I basically do a "dunk sparge." After the mash I let the bag drain, then dunk the bag in a bowl of warm water. I'm not too concerned about getting a 170°F temperature. Then I'll go ahead and add that dunk liquid to the wort from my mash. I haven't actually done any comparisons, but I think I get better and more consistent efficiency by doing that.

D&D: Do people wonder why you only brew small batches?

Mary: My husband, Chris, started as a homebrewer and now is a professional brewer. He always says, "Why would you only want to make one gallon when you can make five gallons in the same amount of time?" But I've found that the small batches are worth it because BIAB is so fast that it actually takes less time. Also cleaning goes faster and it takes less equipment, so you have less to store. [Denny: Remember, Mary lives in a very small apartment.] Also, since there's less liquid to heat, you can get to your mash temperature or a boil a lot quicker. I mash in the oven, so I get my strike temperature, add the grain and put it in the oven. I can make dinner, clean, or get some work done or read while I'm waiting for the mash. The BIAB method is pretty hands-off. It's really easy and it's really convenient to fit into your lifestyle. I have several 1.75 and two-gallon kegs and it's really fast and easy to keg those small batches. I can put the kegs in a backpack and take it on the subway with me.

D&D: If you're using liquid yeast, do you make a starter?

Mary: No, no need for a starter for a small batch. But I never use liquid yeast any more. I tend to brew pretty simple these days. Most of the time dry American or British ale yeast or dry saison yeast.

D&D: You brew on your stovetop?

Mary: Yes, we live in an old-school industrial loft and have no outdoor space. I have a gas stove that works pretty well. I have a squat, wide kettle that fits over two burners. You kinda have to match the stove and kettle you use.

DREW: Who doesn't love portable beer? Is the "subway beer" the big city "shower beer"? Make sure to follow all applicable local laws regarding the public transportation, serving, and consumption of beer.

D&D: If someone wants to get into small batch brewing, what's the minimal equipment they'd need and what tips would you have for them?

Mary: Obviously you're going to need some sort of kettle. For small batches you may already have a stockpot around that would work great. You should get a bag. Either sew one yourself or buy one of the commercial ones. I think the trickiest thing with small-scale brewing is how you're going to package it. Obviously bottles work great, but so do small kegs. A small auto-siphon is great, too. If you're doing small batches, you'll lose too much beer with one of the normal sized auto-siphons. Plus, the "normal" sized ones may be too big for your fermentor. One other tip is that when you're ready to boil and you remove your bag, a slotted pizza pan or cooling rack is a great way to drain your bag. I put it in the ring from a spring form pan to contain the bag as it drips. You could also use a colander or a sieve. The point is that when you're doing a small batch you probably have a lot of stuff around the kitchen that you can use, so think about repurposing. ■

4

SIMPLE ALL GRAIN

Most homebrewers start out by brewing with extract, viewing it kind of like spring training prior to the big-league experience of all-grain brewing; they can learn the basics of brewing while getting ready to step up their game (see chapter 2 for why we think that's a myopic view). But for a lot of homebrewers, all-grain brewing is as intimidating as a rookie batter facing an all-star pitcher with a 95-mile-per-hour fastball. You hope that you're gonna hit the ball and not vice versa! But some days you're the Louisville Slugger, some days you're the ball. The only thing we can do to help is improve your odds.

"It turns out that all-grain brewing can be just as straightforward and fun as extract brewing."

DENNY: That was me. I really longed for the brewing experience and variety of ingredients I'd get from all-grain brewing, but every time I started to read about it I was overwhelmed by the gear and process. Multiple vessels, pumps, complicated mash schedules, PIDs…I mean, I didn't know what half the stuff was and I certainly didn't know what it was for or why I needed it!

DREW: I was the opposite. I was the precocious kid brewer (twenty-five, oh, to be that young again!) and was into all-grain shortly after brewing. Like Denny, I read everything I could get my hands on, but, and here's where the advantage of having my local club comes in, I was able to filter the myriad approaches through the things I was seeing from my fellow brewers. Today's brewers have it even easier with free podcasts and internet videos providing more feedback. (Shameless plug: listen to Experimental Brewing via your favorite podcast source or download episodes at https://www.experimental brew.com. I've got no shame.)

It turns out that all-grain brewing can be just as straightforward and fun as extract brewing. There are two ways to approach it, understanding a method or understanding the "why."

Understanding a method is the quickest way to get started: "Get these parts, put them together this way, raise water to this, blah, blah, blah…" It's a formula, a recipe, a to-do list—as long as everything goes to plan, you're golden and in beer galore. Naturally, we'll give you several methods because, let's face it, making beer is tons more fun than someone hitting you over the head with elementary quantum mechanics to understand your mash chemistry! (Yup, we've seen this approach—it gives Denny a headache and reminds Drew too much of college.) But if things go pear-shaped, well what then, Sparky?

While understanding the "why" behind what you're doing is arguably harder to achieve, once you get those ideas grokked, the methods behind all-grain brewing will make sense to you. When the pears come falling out of the tree, you'll be ready to adjust and keep the brew day on track. Plus, your understanding of those basics will let you decide what matters and what doesn't. In other words, you'll be defining your take on simple.

We're going to explain the science behind all-grain brewing, but we promise it will be painless! Then we'll pass on some of the tips we've learned that can make your all-grain brew day fun and rewarding. We'll even show you how to build inexpensive all-grain brewing equipment. Your inexpensive system may not be quite as shiny as some of those big, complicated ones, but it will make beer that tastes every bit as good as the beer you make on a fancy system. And we'll pass on some techniques for both shortening and extending your brew day in order to make brewing all-grain beer easier.

So, step into the batter's box, take a couple practice swings, and get ready for us to pitch you the big meatball that is simple all-grain brewing. Of course, if you're already brewing all-grain, we encourage you to stick around because we're offering up some world-class simplification techniques here!

THE STRICT WORLDS OF FERMENTATION

When it comes down to it, the difference between beer and wine is that wine is made from fruit and beer is made from grain. In other words, we are fermenting different sources of sugar into alcohol. With wine it's easy, you just crush or press the fruit to free the sugar-laden juice, pitch some yeast, do a little dance, and you're mostly done. (OK, not really, but this isn't *Simple Winemaking*.) With grain, our initial work is a bit more complicated, but you wanted to earn that beer, right?

It Wasn't Always So

Way back in the far reaches of prehistory, when humanity was first working out the idea of civilization, the rules weren't so fixed about what made a beverage a beverage. The earliest discovered examples of fermentation currently come from China. Dr. Patrick McGovern of the University of Pennsylvania Museum in

Philadelphia did a chemical analysis of jars from China dated to 7000 BCE and discovered trace residues of a beer-wine hybrid made with rice, grapes, hawthorn berries, and honey.[1] It's all the food groups in one beverage! Even the beer made by Babylonians and Sumerians included date wine and honey in the ingredient list for their barley beers.[2] Somewhere, a tradition-obsessed brewmaster just shuddered.

Making Malt

Cereal grains, the grasses that have fueled humanity's growth, contain long complex chains of sugar molecules called starches. Starches can be chopped, sliced, and chemically altered into simpler fermentable sugars by enzymes like alpha-amylase and beta-amylase. Miracle of miracles, those enzymes are built into barley and, to a certain extent, most other grains—but they're really present in barley! This is a big reason why barley is the grain of choice for brewers.

The malting process activates enzymes in the grain that convert starch to sugar. Malting starts by soaking the barley kernels to allow them to germinate, which is where they sprout and begin to grow. The enzymes will allow the new sprout (acrospire) access to the starchy fuel in the endosperm. When the grain has softened, the maltster intervenes and stops nature dead in its tracks by drying the kernels and killing off the sprout. This locks the malt's starches, enzymes, and other proteins in a useful state.

After the grain has been dried, it's kilned to produce different colors of malt, from very pale (like the malt used to make Pilsner) to very dark (like the roast barley that gives stout its deep color and flavor). The catch in all of this is that the darker the malt is kilned, the more enzymes that are killed off, as we mentioned in chapter 2. That's one reason that dark malts are always used in much smaller quantities alongside lighter malts (the other reason being their disgusting taste!).

On to Brewing

When brewers start to formulate a recipe, they begin with a base malt; think "domestic two-row" or "pale malt" or "Pilsner" at the top of the grain bill. Much like when you bake a cake, you begin with flour (fairly bland) and add other flavors to it in smaller portions (chocolate!). In general, most beer begins with a light-colored malt as the base, then brewers use darker malts to add flavor and aroma: crystal or caramel for color and sweetness; toasted malts, such as Munich, Vienna, aromatic, and biscuit, for bready, rich tones; and roasted malts, like chocolate and black "patent" malt, or even unmalted roasted barley, to provide coffee, chocolate, and burnt flavors. The roasted malts can be added in various combinations to it to get the color and unique flavor the brewer is looking for. There are some beers that are made using only one malt (see chapter 7), but the majority of beers use a mixture of malt types to achieve the desired impact.

DREW: The previous few paragraphs are a radical simplification of the complicated art of malting. Suffice it to say that your ability to make beer begins well before you get involved. One of the great advantages brewers have over vintners is the consistency of our starting ingredients thanks to highly skilled folks like maltsters. Malting used to be done as part of the brewing process, and brewers would malt the barley themselves. Now maltsters operate independently, giving all of us access to their best products. Seriously though, praise to the men and women behind converting barley into our foundational ingredient in all of its varieties!

1   Patrick E. McGovern, *Uncorking the Past: The Quest for Wine, Beer, and Other Alcoholic Beverages.* (Berkeley: University of California Press, 2009), 37–39.

2   Ibid., 97.

DENNY: I brewed about half a dozen extract batches and one partial-mash batch before deciding to be brave enough to venture into all-grain brewing. The incentive was that I was dying to make an *altbier*...kind of a German amber ale. All the recipes I could find used Munich malt, and I knew that you had to mash it. It couldn't be steeped like some of the specialty grains you use in extract brewing. Fortunately, by that time I had run across information from two gentleman named George Fix and Ken Schwartz. George had written about a brewing process known as "batch sparging" that simplified and sped up all-grain brewing. Ken had come up with an inexpensive, easy-to-build piece of equipment that was perfect for mashing the grain and using the batch sparge process. I built my first mash tun following Ken's instructions and made a 2.5-gallon batch (I was still boiling on my kitchen stove and that was all it could handle) of altbier that was so good that I was hooked and on my way to bigger all-grain batches.

Figure 4.1.
Denny's original altbier recipe.

Sg. @ 09

ALT 1 - 2.5 gal. - all grain - 2/27/99

3 lb. HFC pale malt
3 lb. Munich malt.
2 oz. Chocolate Malt
2 oz. 80° Crystal malt
1 oz. Spalter Select @ 5.8z - 6.0
1/4 tsp. rehydrated Irish Moss
Wyeast 1338 - repitched 2nd time -
        2x 500 ml. starter
Mash w/9.5 qts @ 155° - 1:10 P.M.
FIRST RUNOFF VOL. = 11 7 qts.
KIRST RUNOFF GRAV. = 1.066
SPARGE WATER VOL = 1.5 GAL @ 170°
SECOND RUNOFF VOL. = 1   -5 to
SECOND RUNOFF GRAV. = 1.025
TOTAL BOIL GRAV = 1.049   147 pts.
TOTAL BOIL VOL. = 3 gal. 67% ex

Bring to boil, add 1 oz. Spalter
Add Irish Moss @ 45 min.
Knockout @ 60 min., cool in ice w
Final Vol. = 2.25 gal.
        top w/ 1 qte water
pitched @ 6 P.M. - 78%
OG = 1.058   = 8.25%
Sec. 3/7/99 = SG = 1.015 = 2%
3/10/99 - outside!
Bottled 3/24/99 FG = 1.014 = 6.25%

After the you determine which malts to use and in what proportion, the malt is crushed to expose the innards (endosperm). The grain is mashed by mixing it with hot water and letting it sit for a while. The heat in the water reactivates the enzymes and finishes the conversion of starch to fermentable sugars. After an hour or so, the liquid (which is now wort) is drained off from the grain. At this point, the grain has given its all for the beer, but the spent grain can be repurposed as feed for farm animals, or as an addition to pizza dough, bread, or even homemade dog cookies. Yep, your best friend can even benefit from homebrewing! At the very least, you can recycle the grain via composting it yourself or through your city's composting scheme.

At this point, all of the work you've done in making the wort is the same as what extract manufacturers do for brewers and bakers, that is, concentrating the wort. From this point on, the brewing process is pretty much the same whether you're brewing with extract or all grain. You boil the wort, add hops, cool it down, pitch the yeast, and ferment.

Nothin' to it!

RECIPE

Denny's Alt #1 Recipe

Note: The process in this recipe has been simplified from my original all-grain batch for two reasons. First, because I've learned a lot since then. Second...well, look at the book title!

Batch volume: 2.5 gal. (5.7 L)
Original Gravity: 1.062 (15.2°P)
Final gravity: 1.012 (3.1°P)

Color: 17 SRM
Bitterness: 41 IBU
ABV: 6.6%

Malt
- 3 lb. (1.36 kg) pale malt
- 3 lb. (1.36 kg) Munich malt 10°L
- 2 oz. (56 g) chocolate malt
- 2 oz. (56 g) crystal malt 80°L

Hops
- 1 oz. (28 g) Spalter Select 5.8% AA @ 60 min.

Extras
- 1/4 tsp Irish moss @ 15 min.

Yeast
Wyeast 1338 German ale yeast (no longer available, substitute WY1007)

Brewing Notes
- Mash: 9.5 qt. (9 L) water to hit a 155°F (68°C) mash temp.
- Sparge: 6 qt. (5.7 L) of water at 170°F (77°C).
- Boil: 60 minutes with hops, add Irish moss with 15 minutes remaining.
- Fermentation: 68°F (20°C) for 2 weeks, then cool to 35°F (2°C) for 2 weeks before bottling or kegging.

DREW: A long time ago in a galaxy far away I used to do catering as a way to add some money to my college's coffers. When I graduated and got an "adult" job, I stopped cooking because I lacked the time. Part of the draw of brewing was getting back to creating. Since I'm the kind of guy who baked his own bread, I wanted to get as real as possible, so I got a pot and carefully built a copper strainer, etc. Looking back...man, I wish I had known about the batch sparging method. It would have saved so much time and money!

For some homebrewers, it's all about the gear and trying to brew like a commercial brewery. Not us—we like to keep it simple! If you're one of those brewers who likes to have a garage full of shiny stuff and another project always in the works, be our guest. We won't be joining you in that quest. We admit that once you get all that stuff put together you might have a simple brew day. But we both prefer brewing to building gear, and we both like to brew pretty much the same way we cook, which is hands on. While having the right equipment is obviously necessary, it's important to note that the brewer makes the beer, not the equipment … well, at least not on its own! We'll also talk later about why, sometimes, the equipment actually gets in the way of you making the beer.

So, with that in mind, we're going to show you how to build and use simple, inexpensive equipment to turn out delicious all-grain beer and have a great time while you do it.

MASHING FROM START TO FINISH

The Super High-Level Process of Mashing

In case you've never brewed an all-grain beer before by batch sparging, here's a quick overview of the process:

1. Crush the grain using a proper grain mill. Your homebrew shop can do it, or you can buy your own grain mill if the mood suits you.
2. Heat up your strike water (~1.2–1.5 qt. water/lb. grain, or 2.5–3.1 L/kg) to about ~10–15°F (~6–8°C) above the target mash temperature.
3. Soak the crushed grain in the hot water for 60–90 minutes. Drain the wort from the mash into the kettle.
4. Stir 170°F (77°C) sparge water into the now-drained grain.
5. Drain the new wort from the tun into the kettle.

And that's pretty much it! From here on, you boil, add hops, and chill just like you would for an extract- or partial-mash brew. There are a few details that we'll get into now, starting with making your own mash tun.

The Cheap 'n' Easy Mash Tun

When building a mash tun, keep the general brewing process in mind. You heat some water, mix it with some grain, and keep it hot. After an hour, you drain the sugar water (wort) from the grain and bring it to a boil. You then chill the wort and ferment it with yeast. The primary difference for you, the all-grain brewer, is the addition of a mash tun, which holds your hot grain and allows you to separate the wort from it.

A mash tun needs to have a few specific properties in order for it to be useful. First, it needs to hold hot water without leaking. We suppose you could use a leaking mash tun, but we prefer our shoes to stay dry. Second, to avoid ending up with really chewy beer, your mash tun needs to have a way to separate the wort from the grain. So, unless you enjoy the tedious job of straining, you'll want an easy way to drain the wort from the tun while leaving the grain behind.

When we first started brewing, the solution everyone sought was a big stainless steel pot with a fancy false bottom or slotted copper pipes. Oh, the copper pipes that we used to diligently hacksaw slots into every quarter inch… the sheer numbing boredom leading to slipped attention, leading to a slipped blade, leading to sudden blood loss via hacksaw. Those were fun times and made all-grain an adventure!

While there are a lot of things that can satisfy the above requirements, the easy, inexpensive solution is a picnic cooler and some stainless steel hose braid. A 48 to 70-quart (45–66 L) cooler is a perfect vessel for a mash tun for 5 to 10-gallon batches (19–38 L). Coolers are made of food-grade HDPE (high-density polyethylene) that is safe up to 248°F (120°C) for short periods and good for extended use up to 230°F (110°C), which is a lot hotter than our mash will ever get!

Why did people futz with pots and slots and whatnot? We think it as a case of, "That's what the big guys use—they have metal pots they can heat!" Lots of folks believed you had to be able to heat the mash through multiple steps in order to brew proper beer. Never mind that countless breweries in beer havens like Belgium have the big equivalent of our cooler: an unheatable, separate lauter tun with just a screen.

To build your Cheap 'n' Easy mash tun, you'll need the following parts:

DREW: I have to admit, if you're big into the concept of multi-temperature, multi-step mashes (for various reasons), decoctions (please, why?), or worried about not hitting your temperatures precisely (stay calm and carry on), I can see the attraction of being able to directly heat your mash. You don't need the direct heating capability for your whole mash. If you must adjust temperature, you can always add a little hot water or pull a small portion of the mash, heat it to a boil while stirring and add it back the main mash. The latter is known as a decoction mash and, yes, I know what I just said. I just don't like decoctions as a necessary thing in your mash.

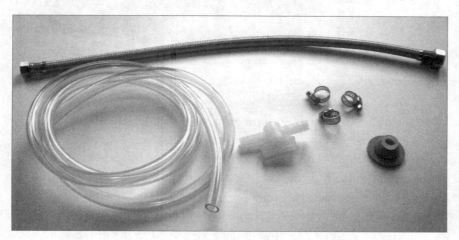

Figure 4.2. The parts for a do-it-yourself mash tun are relatively cheap and simple. Pictured here is a stainless steel hose braid, some vinyl tubing, hose clamps, and a mini-keg bung. You'll also need food-grade silicone sealer and, obviously, a picnic cooler.

DREW: Want to witness the silliest holy war ever? Look online for raging debates over which cooler is better—the blue or red Coleman!

- **48–70 qt. (45–66 L) cooler.** The Coleman Xtreme® is one brand of cooler that works really well, although there are others. You want to look for a drain spigot that can be removed (there will be a nut inside the cooler) and can be replaced with a ball valve. That will ensure you get complete draining.

- **Stainless steel hose braid.** First, a word of warning: there are plastic braids that look like stainless steel. Don't get one of those! Between the weight of the grain and the heat, plastic braid will collapse and not drain properly. Denny uses Lasco brand hoses, part # 10-0121. Drew uses some military-spec braid that's about as big around as most people's wrists. Yeah, he's an overachiever!
- 6–8 feet of ⅜-inch ID (inner diameter) vinyl tubing (1.8–2.4 m, 10 mm ID)
- ⅜-inch (10 mm) plastic ball valve
- 3 hose clamps
- Mini-keg bung
- Silicone sealer/adhesive (food grade)

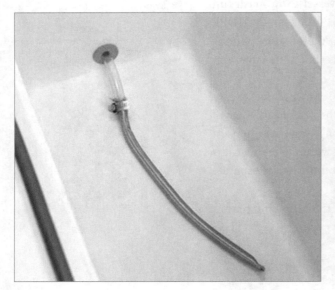

Figure 4.3. Inside view of the mash tun, showing the braid construction.

Figure 4.4. An assembled cooler mash tun showing the ball valve and connected vinyl tubing.

Start by unscrewing the nut inside the cooler for the drain spigot on the cooler and remove it. Put a thin bead of the silicone around the hole inside the cooler. Insert the mini-keg bung into the hole from the inside, with the conical part going in first so that the flange on the bung lays flat against the inside of the cooler. Give it at least 15 minutes or overnight for the silicone to set up.

While the silicone dries, let's take the hose out of the braid. The braid is all we're interested in using. Start by cutting each end (with the threaded fittings) off of the hose. Denny uses the brute force approach and chops the ends off with a hatchet. Feel free to use a more refined method, like a Dremel® tool or hacksaw, if you have one. Once the ends have been removed, gently push each end of the braid towards the middle. That will expand the braid and allow you to pull the hose out of it. Discard the hose or use it for some other important household project. Fold about ½ inch of one end of the braid over on itself three times and either smack it with a hammer or pinch it with pliers to keep it closed.

Next, cut off about 6 inches of your vinyl tubing. Slip the open end of the braid over one end of the tubing and secure it with a hose clamp. You want the clamp tight enough to hold the braid on, but be careful not to crank it down too much or you'll close off the tubing. Push the other end of the tubing through the mini-keg bung from inside the cooler (fig. 4.3). You want about equal amounts of the tubing inside and outside the cooler. On the outside, insert one side of the plastic ball valve into the tubing from the cooler and secure it with a hose clamp. Attach the remaining tubing to the other side of the valve using your last hose clamp (fig. 4.4). The tubing should be tight enough in the mini-keg bung that it doesn't leak, but if yours isn't tight enough just use some silicone sealer.

And that's it! Admittedly, Denny has had practice making a few of these, but excluding the drying time it only takes him about 15 minutes for the entire process.

OK, the tun is dun…er, done! Let's mash something!

Mashing

We need to start by converting the starches in the grain into sugars we can ferment. We activate the enzymes that carry out this conversion by soaking the grain in hot water. Most mashes take place at temperatures between about 148°F (64°C) and 158°F (70°C), but the exact temperature is recipe and style dependent.

Hitting your temperatures

In order to hit your mash temperature, you need to account for heat loss from your cooler and the grain. In most cases, heating the water in your hot liquor tank to about 15°F (~8°C) hotter than the desired mash temperature works well, but it will depend on ambient temperature, grain temperature, and the amount of grain and water you're using. (How much water should you use for your mash? We look at how you can calculate this below.)

Most people use some sort of software to calculate how hot to make their mash water. Beersmith™, Promash, and Brewer's Friend are popular calculators, but if you look around the internet you can find a lot of different ones. Or you can use the old method of trial and error. Start by making your mash water 10–15°F (6–8°C) hotter than your desired mash temperature and see where that gets you. It may not be exactly where you wanted it to be, but you'll still make beer! Take careful notes and adjust things the next time you brew.

Add grain to water

Add your heated mash water to your mash tun and then add your grain.

DREW: This is Denny's classic rig. As alluded to earlier, I use a massive braid that came from a shielded military video communications cable that a fellow brewer dug out of a scrapyard for cheap. (Scrapyards are a handy brewer's best friend. Handy brewers are a DIY-hapless [like me] brewer's best friend.) My braid is hooked up to some copper plumbing fittings and then secured by silicone tubing to a 1/2-inch stainless ball valve. It's hearty and will outlast the cooler. Actually, strike that—it will outlast me. Look upon my mash tun, ye mighty, and despair!

DREW: For me, the difference is usually about 12°F (~7°C), but I live in Southern California, where my garage is barely below mash temperatures some days.

DREW: I measure my water volume before heating and then dump the whole thing into my cooler.

DENNY: I measure my water after heating and use a plastic half-gallon pitcher to scoop water out of the pot and add it to the tun.

Once all the water is in the tun, slowly pour in the grain as you stir. By stirring as you add grain, you minimize the chance of "dough balls." Dough balls are lumps of grain that stick together, meaning that they stay dry inside. If the grain isn't in contact with the water, you can't convert those starches, so make sure to stir thoroughly as you pour in the grain. Some folks use a special "mash paddle" to do this, but in reality almost anything works as long as it's sturdy! Lots of people swear by a massive wire balloon whisk to really work the grain out.

Calculating Your Mash Water Volume

We've been pretty vague about specifics when it comes to water, because that would mean we have to do some math to determine how much to use. There are a lot of theories about how water volume will affect your mash, but in the end that variable has a minimal effect on beer flavor in terms of how it effects conversion. What it can affect is your efficiency—how much sugar you get out of the grain. Obviously, more is better!

A QUICK LOOK AT EFFICIENCY

Efficiency is a measure of how much sugar you get from the grain compared to a theoretical maximum. Each type of grain will vary a bit, but in general you can expect a theoretical maximum of 36 gravity points for each pound of grain in each gallon of water (i.e., 36 PPG). In other words, if your mash and lauter process were an inhumanely perfect 100% efficient, one pound of grain mashed in one gallon of water will yield a specific gravity of 1.036.

For example, if you mash 1 pound of grain in 1 gallon of water and get a specific gravity of 1.027, your efficiency is 75% (i.e., 27/36 = 0.75). Make sense? Many homebrew systems will average between 70% and 80% efficiency without much problem.

Homebrewers usually mash with 1.25 qt. of water for every pound of grain (this equates to 2.6 L per kilogram). But if you mash with more water, you can get a higher efficiency. Now, efficiency is not the be-all and end-all for homebrewing, but more is better. By using 1.5–2 qt. per pound of grain (3.1–4.2 L/kg) you can gain a few extra points of efficiency.

The key to figuring out how much to use is to look at the final volume you want to boil. Ideally, half of that volume will come from the mash and the other half from the sparge. You don't have to be exact. Actually, if they're within a gallon of each other you'll be fine.

But there's a catch ... isn't there always? You are starting with dry grain, which means it will absorb water. Generally, the rate of absorption is about 0.5 qt. for every pound of grain (roughly 1 L/kg), so you'll have to take that into account for your mash.

Let's walk through an example by assuming you want to boil 7 gal. of wort. That means we want to get about 3.5 gal. out of the mash. Let's also assume your recipe calls for 12 lb. of grain. We know that 12 lb. will absorb 6 qt. of water (because $12 \times 0.5 = 6$), which is equal to 1.5 gal. Add that 1.5 gal. to the 3.5 gal. you want to end up with and you'll find that comes out to 5 gal. of water to use in the mash. That didn't hurt too much, did it?

(Exercise left to the reader: How much water do you need to heat up for the sparge? The answer is 3.5 gallons, naturally, because the grain is already wet and won't absorb more.)

So, assuming you want a mash temperature of 153°F, you'd heat 5 gal. of water 15°F higher to 168°F and add to your tun before stirring in your grain. Software may get you a bit closer, but that's a pretty accurate seat-of-your-pants method to get you started.

Batch Sparge

After the mash sits in the hot water in your tun for the recipe-recommended amount of time, it's time to drain it into your boil kettle. But first, we want to clarify it a bit. For this step you'll need an extra container, something like the half-gallon pitcher Denny mentioned earlier. Put the end of the tubing coming from the mash tun into the pitcher and crack the valve slightly open until wort starts to slowly flow. As you're doing this, look through the tube and down into the pitcher. What you're looking for is pieces of grain and husk ... we don't want those! These pieces should start to clear up after a quart or so (~1 L). We're not looking for so clear that you can read a newspaper through it, we're looking for free of chunks and grain pieces. Once it looks clear, transfer the end of the tubing to your boil kettle and slowly pour the wort in your pitcher back over the top of the grain in your mash tun. The grain bed along with your braid acts as a filter, keeping your final beer from being too chunky. If you want to impress people (well, nerds anyway) you can tell them that the term for this process of recirculating the wort until it clears is *vorlauf*, from the German word, *vorläufig*. They probably won't throw things at you.

Once you have returned the wort in your pitcher to the mash tun, you can open up the valve all the way and let 'er rip! You can turn on the heat for your kettle at this point in order to get a jump on boiling, but keep it fairly low. Once you have collected all the wort you can, crank it up and get boiling!

DREW: When I first started brewing, I learned to fly sparge, which we won't cover because it's well documented and annoying, although it has its adherents. When fly sparging, common practice is to not open the valve all the way, and even though I've batch sparged for more than a decade, I still leave the valve halfway open at most. It only really costs me time.

Bloody Head Stout

DREW: Sometimes brewing requires a blood offering to atone for whatever sins against beer we've committed. After my first book was released (*The Everything Homebrewing Book*[1]) I was flush with pride and decided to buy a new kettle (actually still my main kettle, 26 gallons). To christen the pot, I decided I had to tackle a stout. In the middle of the boil my garage door slammed into my skull, dosing the beer with a bit of me. Turns out the beer was great, but ouch.

Batch size: 5.5 gal. (21 L)
Original gravity: 1.067 (16.4°P)
Final gravity: 1.014 (3.6°P)

Color: 40 SRM
Bitterness: 37 IBU
ABV: 7.0%

Malt
- 7.0 lb. (3.2 kg) Maris Otter malt
- 3.0 lb. (1.36 kg) US-grown Pilsner malt
- 1.0 lb. (450 g) British 55°L crystal malt
- 1.0 lb. (450 g) flaked oats
- 0.75 lb. (340 g) roasted barley
- 0.25 lb. (115 g) Weyerman Carafa® III Special malt, debittered

Hops
- 0.6 oz. (17 g) Magnum 12.9% AA @ 60 min.
- 0.75 oz. (21 g) Crystal 3.25% AA @ 20 min.
- 1.0 oz. (28 g) Amarillo 8.5% AA @ knockout

Yeast
- Wyeast 1056, WLP001, or Safale US-05

Brewing notes
- Mash at 153°F (67°C) for 60 minutes.
- Add hops according to schedule.
- Chill and pitch yeast.
- Ferment at 65–68°F (18–20°C) until done.

OTHER MASHING REGIMENS

Short Mash and Boil

Traditionally, a mash lasts for 60–90 minutes and a boil is about an hour. Why? Well, because that's the way it's always been! But in chapter 2 we talked about a recipe that requires only 20 minutes each for mashing and boiling. What's up with that? Well, a couple of things.

First, malt these days is a lot more modified than it was 200 (or even 20) years ago. *Modification* refers to the degree to which the enzymes have released starches from the kernel during malting. The more highly modified

[1]   Beechum, *The Everything Homebrewing Book* (Avon, MA: Adams Media, 2009).

the malt is, the more quickly and easily it releases the starches and breaks them down during the mash. There are ways to determine the degree of modification by looking at the soluble/total protein ratio (called the Kolbach index). However, you can safely assume that any grain not billing itself as "undermodified" can convert during a short mash. (Undermodified malts are used to recreate older styles like classic Pilsners, but the stuff is hard to find and a real complication to your brew day, which is what we're explicitly avoiding!)

An hour boil is likely a holdover from the days when longer boils were needed to deal with inferior malts, efficiencies, and concentrations of wort. Also, boiling hops for an hour is an efficient way to get the most bittering from the least amount of hops, but you can make up for that by simply using more hops for less time. One of the greatest advantages of being a home-brewer is that our ingredient costs are incredibly low. Commercial breweries strive for better efficiency and utilization numbers because the extra costs cut into their very narrow profits. What's another buck or two to us hobbyists? If you're parsimonious, feel free to squeeze every drop of sugar from the malt. For us, we'll take the extra time we save.

It's true that mashing for a longer time will increase the fermentability of the wort, but that makes a minimal difference that really doesn't matter for most homebrewers. If you're mashing for a style that wants a very dry finish, like a Belgian *tripel*, where you want to have maximum fermentability, then mashing for 60–90 minutes might make a bit of a difference. Part of deciding how long to mash is based on how fermentable you want your wort to be. The longer you mash, the more time the enzymes have to break down less-fermentable sugars into more fermentable sugars. So, for something like a Pilsner or tripel, where you want a very light, crisp body, a longer mash can help you get there. But it's a very subtle effect, and the fact is that most malts made these days are so fermentable that you may get very little of that added effect for your investment of time.

So, if you've got a tight schedule, a 30-minute mash and 20-minute boil will suffice for almost any style that we enjoy. A rule of thumb for hopping short boils is to use twice as much hops by weight than you would use for a 60-minute boil. That will get you darn close the same IBU level, or you can use software if you want to get closer.

You'll also want to crush the grain as fine as your lautering system allows. If you're using the same braid that Denny uses (see "The Cheap 'n' Easy Mash Tun" above), you can crush very fine. The same goes if you use a bag in your mash tun as a lauter system. By crushing as fine as possible, you make sure that as much starch as possible is exposed to the mash water. That will help ensure complete conversion during your short mash.

30-Minute Man Tripel

Batch size: 5.5 gal. (21 L)
Original gravity: 1.084 (20.2°P)
Final gravity: 1.015 (3.8°P)
Color: 3.8 SRM

Bitterness: 20 IBU
ABV: 9.4%
Boil: 30 minutes

Malt/Sugar
- 15.5 lb. (7 kg) Pilsner malt
- 1.5 lb. (680 g) table sugar

Hops
- 1 oz. (28 g) Magnum 12% AA @ 30 min.

Yeast
- Wyeast 3787 Trappist High Gravity

Brewing notes
- Single infusion mash at 150°F (66°C) for 30 min.
- Mash quick, run off, and boil for 30 min.
- Chill to 63–65°F (17–18°C) and pitch with a healthy pitch of yeast.
- Ferment until done—usually 2 weeks based on the fall of the krausen and activity of fermentation.

Overnight/Extended Mashing

Denny usually uses the downtime during his mash for household chores… cleaning, laundry, that kind of thing. Not only is it an efficient use of time, but it does wonders for marital harmony. But how about taking that downtime during mashing one step further? In keeping with the line in Denny's chapter 1 mantra about "the least effort possible," how about mashing while you sleep? It just doesn't get easier than that!

Sitting at the other end of the mash spectrum, a long mash, even overnight, can really make your brew day shorter and easier. Imagine if you get a mash going during your lunchtime from work, or before you go to bed at night, and finish the brew after work or the next day. Two short brew days beats one long one!

Just as a short mash doesn't make a huge difference to the fermentability of your wort or the quality of the finished beer, neither does a really long mash. The minimal increase in fermentability can either be ignored or compensated for by adding a bit of less fermentable malt (like crystal or Carapils®) to your grist.

There's one worry about an overnight mash, and that's having the temperature fall so low (i.e., below 140°F, or 60°C) that bacteria, like the intense souring agent *Lactobacillus*, begin to grow on your grain. There are several ways to avoid this:

- Wrapping your mash tun in a blanket or sleeping bag overnight will help hold in the heat. Not to mention, think how much your mash will appreciate being put to bed for the night!
- You might also want to try overshooting your targeted mash temperature by a bit. For example, if you're targeting 153°F (67°C), shoot for 157°F

(69.5°C) when you actually mash in. The extra few degrees won't have a major effect on your beer and they'll give you a bit of a cushion as the temperature falls overnight.

- There's another path you can take…go ahead and do your mash and sparge, and then bring the wort up to boiling for a minute, or at least 170°F (77°C) for 10 minutes. The heat will pasteurize the wort. Then you can use the lid of your kettle, aluminum foil, or some other clever method to seal your kettle overnight. The next day, you bring your wort to a boil and continue as normal.

Whichever of the above methods you choose, you'll shorten your brew day. Or from another point of view, you get to extend the fun for two days!

DREW: Some additional tips from my attempts to split my brew over a few days. *Lactobacillus* is on every grain you use—it's no big deal, but some brewers will attempt to do a "sour mash" and purposely leave the mash for long periods warm (24 hours or so). That can lead to some extraordinary off-flavors. We'll cover a more surefire method of making quick sours later, but be really careful about leaving the mash for too long. This also applies if you're just leaving the spent grain in your mash tun overnight. We've done that before and, oh boy, does it smell like death. (Seriously, don't do this. You'll wish your sense of smell had never been born.)

RECIPE

Overnight Scotch Ale

Batch size: 5.5 gal. (21 L)
Original gravity: 1.072 (17.5°P)
Final gravity: 1.018 (4.6°P)
Color: 22 SRM

Bitterness: 17 IBU
ABV: 7.4%
Boil: 60 minutes

Malt
- 15 lb. (6.8 kg) Maris Otter malt
- 6 oz. (170 g) roasted barley

Mash
- Single infusion at 155°F (68°C) overnight (see Brewing notes).

Hops
- 0.5 oz. (14 g) Target 11% AA @ 60 min.

Yeast
- Wyeast 1728 Scottish Ale

Brewing notes
- Begin your mash at night, say, after work. Stir it up and close up your mash tun. If you're not mashing in an insulated vessel, wrap your mash tun with blankets (make sure any flames are off!). In the morning, lauter as normal and make your beer. Ferment your Scotch ale on the lower side of ale fermentations, say 65°F (18°C).

Brew-In-A-Bag: One-Pot Brewing

The whole mash tun system we've described above, well, it shouldn't surprise you that it's not the only way to brew, just the most common. Walk into a professional brewery today and you'd be able to suss out the same elements: a vessel designed to hold a mass of hot grain and then separate the sugary liquid from the remaining solid mass. There have been other systems, like the historically common "shove a woven basket strainer into the mash and ladle out the liquid that flows into the basket." (Can we admit that if that was still the way we brewed, few of us would?)

Our equally beer-mad and possibly more frugal brewing compatriots in Australia turned the whole lautering notion on its head. What if, instead of creating a vessel that you removed the liquid from, you created a way to remove the grain from the liquid?

That thought resulted in "Brew in a Bag" and no surprise, it's like using a massive tea bag full of grain. The BIAB notion is the pinnacle of simplicity. Take a finely woven bag, something sturdy and heat resistant like nylon or polyester, and fill it with your crushed grain. Fill your boil kettle with all of the water that you'd use for a traditional sparge (remember, mash ratio isn't a super impactful thing in the light of other variables). Heat the water, drop the bag into the water, and work it to fully wet the grain.

Allow the bag and water to rest for the mash, like you would in a cooler-built mash tun. When the mash timer is done, lift the bag and suspend it above the pot. For smaller batches, you can put it in a colander; for larger batches, you'll see brewers rigging up winches to hold the bag above the kettle. Now just let the bag drain. To improve efficiency (a common early complaint lobbed against BIAB), most brewers will don thick gloves and squeeze the bag to work out the liquid. Old brewing practices cautioned against squeezing the bags of grain for fear of tannin extraction, but it's pretty clear that tannin extraction is a chemical process that you don't need to worry about (except in extreme cases). Squeeze away! Your muscles ain't pulling harsh flavors into the beer.

The early homemade bags were made from cheap muslin fabric. The fine weave keeps the grain in while letting the liquid out. These days, if you're so inclined, you can find custom-made bags from tougher materials.

The major advantage of BIAB is massive savings, both in money and space. Even Denny's vaunted "Cheap 'n' Easy" tun is more expensive than the cost of a mesh bag. You also have less gear to store and the path to upgrade from extract brewing to all-grain has never been simpler.

How do you really do BIAB? How about we turn to an expert with our next profile! In the first of two profiles that bring this chapter to a close, we take a look at how Chip Walton tackles BIAB. Our second profile introduces Jeremy Jalabert, who is living proof that you can turn out award-winning all-grain beers while spending less than four hours on your brew day.

PROFILES IN SIMPLICITY: CHIP WALTON TEACHES US ABOUT BREW-IN-A-BAG

Chip is a one-man video crew of homebrew madness. Back in the day, he joined Mike Dawson and Jake Keeler to launch and host a YouTube video show for the homebrew shop they worked for.

After leaving, Chip bounced around the beer industry, but never quite forgot his days of being a homebrew host. He now runs the YouTube channel, *Chop & Brew*, dedicated to brewing and chopping— I mean, cooking.* The Alabama native (now firmly ensconced in the snowy climes of Minneapolis), along with a stalwart crew of fellow homebrewers, brings you a series of misadventures and silliness, including some pretty rad home cooking.

We've both played with the BIAB method of mashing, but Chip is a master at it. So, do you want to learn from some scrubs or from someone who really walks the walk? Also, as a bonus, we include Chip's King Cake Ale recipe that he made with some pointers from Drew. Look, it's a homebrew twofer! Chip is originally from the Gulf Coast where King Cake is a pre-Lent tradition, so he wanted to make a beer in honor of his childhood.

Chip was a stalwart extract brewer, preferring to stay with syrups to keep his knowledge sharp for customers new to brewing. Plus, the level of seriousness he saw in his colleagues made all-grain seem more intimidating. Once Chip discovered BIAB in 2011 he went all-in, making both small and large batches of beer with his bag, kettle, and pristine, never-used-for-grilling grill grate. Over time, he's settled into a happy medium of three gallons, feeling it's the right balance of beer produced versus weight of all the wet grain.

Chip uses a thin mash ratio of 1.75 qt./lb. (3.65 L/kg). He clips his bag to the kettle and slowly streams in the grain, stirring gently to thoroughly wet all of the grain. When Chip wants to raise his mash temperature, he pulls the bag off the bottom before igniting the flame and "bouncing" the bag to keep everything moving. Once done with the main mash, he pulls the bag and sets it on a clean grill grate over the kettle to drain. He does do a fairly light sparge of a few quarts (~2 L) before letting the bag sit for a little longer. This is so he doesn't have to squeeze the hot bag of grains.

But Chip's main advice is to get yourself out there and brew. If he can brew outdoors in a Minnesota winter, what's your excuse?

---

* ChopAndBrew (YouTube user), *Chop & Brew* (webshow), https://www.youtube.com/user/ChopAndBrew/.

King Cake Ale

Batch size: 3 gal. (11.4 L), BIAB
Original gravity: 1.058 (14.3°P)
Final gravity: 1.018 (4.6°P)
Color: 34 SRM

Bitterness: 7 IBU
ABV: 5.2%
Boil: 60 minutes

Malt
- 5.0 lb. (2.3 kg) Weyermann Barke® Pilsner Malt
- 1.0 lb. (450 g) flaked wheat
- 0.5 lb. (225 g) Golden Naked Oats®™
- 0.33 lb. (150 g) aromatic malt

Hops
- 0.75 oz. (21 g) Hallertau 4% AA @ 60 min.
- 1.0 oz. (28 g) Lemondrop 6% AA @ 5 min.

Extras
- 1 tbsp. (15 mL) cinnamon @ 5 min.
- 1 oz. (28 g) dried lemon peel @ 5 min.

Yeast
- Wyeast 1968 London ESB

Brewing notes
- Mash at 153°F (67°C) for 60 minutes and remove the bag to a grill grate over your kettle to drain.
- Boil for 60 minutes, adding hops and extra ingredients as per schedule.
- Chill to the low 60s Fahrenheit (16–17.5°C) and pitch yeast.
- Ferment at 65°F (18°C).

PROFILES IN SIMPLICITY: JEREMY JALABERT—AWARD-WINNING, BUSY DAD BREWER

Jeremy Jalabert is a busy guy. He works as a senior management analyst in the mental health field. I mean, just the title sounds daunting! He and his wife have two kids, ages four and eight, which keeps him even busier. But, somehow, Jeremy had enough time to crank out lots of award-winning batches to become the Oregon State Homebrewer of the Year for 2017. How does he do it?

Jeremy simplifies things. He uses his analyst skills to look at his process and decide what works and what doesn't. He's cut his equipment down to what's essential, practical, and efficient. Consequently, Jeremy has cut his brew time without sacrificing quality. He's living, breathing, award-winning proof that simplicity isn't just for beginners!

Here's Jeremy explaining some of his ideas:

The main things that speed up my brew day is a big kettle (22 gallons) and doing super-duper no-sparge. I abandon water-to-grist ratio and just fill that mash tun to maximum capacity, run off [without a pump] and get to boiling. I sold my fancy plate chiller, pump, bottle filler, etc., and use exclusively my JaDeD* chiller and I've shaved down my brew day from 8+ hours down to <one hour—not bad for ending up with 10–12 gallons of wort to ferment. I also typically only use Imperial Yeast® straight up (note: Imperial yeast is sold with high cell counts, so for most beers it can be pitched directly without making a starter) or a slurry from a local brewery. I like starters, but it's been way faster going my current route.

I've really focused on fast, but still really fun, brew days—and using only the freshest ingredients I can get my hands on (and can afford). I only bottle using the Gordon Strong PET bottle-style filling,† which saved hours of dealing with bottle fillers, etc. [We describe this method in chapter 3 on page 58.] I also follow a lot of your recommendations: don't drink much on brew day, clean all my gear as I go, have fun, experiment, etc. Lately, and this is going to sound soooo Eugene, Oregon, I've been brewing more with "vibes," which is to say, I'm trying to brew a bit more intuitively on brew day. That is, when I see/smell/taste a variable, I call it good and don't worry so much about the timer and exact temps, etc. This is partly due to my interest in brewing history and thinking that brewers way back in the day were probably using some "vibes" and less science to make their beer. My main thing these days is going back to basics, just with bigger-volume tools and more stainless steel.

We're loving his "brewing with vibes" attitude! In 2017, Jeremy took Best of Show at the Sasquatch Homebrew Competition with his recipe for a "Glen Beer." The competition honors the memory of brewer Glen Falconer, and includes a category for beers like he would have made. Denny wrote the style guidelines for it, and it's been a mainstay of the competition for many years. ■

---

* The JaDeD Hydra chiller uses three concentric cooling coils connected to a single inlet and outlet, which, in effect, triples the chilling power.
† Strong, *Brewing Better Beer: Master Lessons for Advanced Home Brewers* (Boulder: Brewers Publications, 2011), 294–95; this method involves filling a clean one- or two-liter soda bottle, attaching a carbonator cap, then squeezing the air out and blanketing with CO_2.

Glen Tribute Beer 2017

All-Grain Red IPA

Batch size: 12 gal. (45.4 L), BIAB
Original gravity: 1.072 (17.5°P)
Final gravity: 1.019 (4.8°P)
Color: 14 SRM

Bitterness: 125.5 IBU (Tinseth formula)
ABV: 7.0% (est.)

Malt
- 16 lb. (7.26 kg) Vienna malt
- 5.0 lb. (2.27 kg) pale malt (Jeremy used Maris Otter)
- 4.0 lb. (1.8 kg) Munich malt
- 3.0 lb. (1.36 kg) flaked rye
- 2.0 lb. (910 g) Carared®
- 1.0 lb. (450 g) acid malt
- 1.0 lb. (450 g) 40°L caramel/crystal malt
- 0.5 lb. (225 g) roasted barley

Hops
- 2.5 oz. (71 g) Magnum 12% AA first wort hop @ 60 min.
- 2.0 oz. (56 g) Simcoe 13% AA @ 60 min.
- 2.0 oz. (56 g) Centennial 10% AA @ 50 min.
- 2.0 oz. (56 g) Centennial 10% AA @ steep/whirlpool
- 2.0 oz. (56 g) Simcoe 13% AA @ steep/whirlpool

Yeast
Wyeast 1056

Brewing notes
- Mash in with 11.5 gal. (1.4 qt./lb.) strike water at 166°F (74°C). Mash at 156°F (69°C) for 45 min.
- Recycle first runnings and verify grain temperatures are 162°F (72°C).
- Batch sparge with, 7.66 gal. of 168°F (76°C) water.
- Boil 60 min.
- 2 Whirlfloc® tablets @ 15 min.
- Pitch yeast at 65°F (18°C). After 3 days, let the temperature start rising to 68°F (20°C) for 3 days, then to 72°F (22°C) for 3–4 days. Fine with gelatin if desired, then bottle or keg.

5
TECHNOLOGY
SERVING SIMPLICITY

W hen this whole brewing thing began it was a remarkably primitive process. A couple of clay pots, a basket, and some less splintery reeds. When brewing left the homes, bakeries, and temples to become an industry, the whole thing was still a flying-by-the-seat-of-your-pants and rule-of-thumb type of operation. Even the famed German immigrant-led brewing practices in 1840s America relied on St. Louis' natural cave systems, with tradition emphasized over technology. It took the rise of science and an increasing aversion to losing industrial capital to bring the tech into place.

So, naturally, when a semi-hippie nuclear engineer took a swing at brewing and started teaching brewing courses, the natural place to go was low-tech—namely, a couple of buckets, an airlock, and the ingredients. You could have stuck a Babylonian brewer next to Charlie Papazian's brewing getup and they would have grokked the whole thing.

"We're geeks, we're gear heads, we like toys, and commercial breweries have all the best toys."

DENNY: Drew and I have always looked at brewing equipment mainly as a means to an end. Yeah, some of it is really cool and gets our geek side all fired up. But in the end, all we really want is a way to make beer that's fun and easy. But for other homebrewers it's all about the gear, and to them building a brewing system is as important as producing beer with it. This chapter is where we look at both sides. We'll talk about some really cool ready-built systems you can buy, and we'll show you how to build your own electric system if that's where your jollies lie. Something for everybody!

DREW: By the way, that's not saying that we don't love some of the new gear out there. We've been fortunate to try a number of the systems we write about below. I think it's fair to say that they all have their pluses, but, ultimately, you can brew beer without them. However, sometimes these things make it a lot simpler! (That is, if you've got the money and patience to learn how they work and what the limitations are.)

Charlie was an atom smasher, Denny's an audio engineer, Drew's a computer guy—let's face it, we are always going to be jealous to some extent of the toys that commercial breweries have. We're geeks, we're gear heads, we like toys, and commercial breweries have all the best toys. Big, gleaming stainless steel monstrosities; computer screens that read like NORAD with constant updates of a brew's vital statistics; motors and gears to crush a man's skull; controls that minimize the need for human attention spans—all of these beckon to our brewing minds like gleaming chrome headers call to the motor head.

DREW: Seriously, one of the most beautiful things I've ever seen in my life is the "new" New Glarus Hilltop Brewery. From the outside it looks like a ginormous Disneyesque rendition of a German or Swiss village. The inside, though, is an epic ode to stainless steel piping in all of its glory. But even that's not the best geeky equipment part. On the other side of the wall from the main brew deck (clad with copper uppers for that traditional feel) is a small homebrew-sized pilot system. "Yawn, Drew, every brewery worth its salt has one of those!" But not like New Glarus they don't—it's a perfectly scaled down rendition of the main brew deck, all the way down to vessel geometries and ratios. I'm still geeking out about it now a decade later!

Even in the early days of homebrewing, we saw guys attempting to cheaply recreate their favorite gadgets and control systems. But it took some real skilled geekery to know how to wire a system and understand tuning a proportional–integral–derivative (PID) controller. The average layman brewer, with a longing gleam in their eye, could only sigh.

But now, with the rise of the everyday cheap computer and microcontroller (like those from Arduino and the Raspberry Pi Foundation, for instance), it's become even easier to get your gear on. There are new companies out there taking advantage of new tech and rolling out affordable, automated, "simplified" brewing experiences for us all. Plus, the internet has given everyone access to a worldwide bazaar of goods, meaning it's easy to obtain the parts to put together your own toys.

So far, we've looked at brewing with equipment you already have around your house, like pots and stoves, or that can be easily and inexpensively assembled, like the "Cheap 'n' Easy" mash tun. Now we're going to take a look at items of equipment for brewing, fermenting, and serving your beer that are more complex and sophisticated. Some of these items are perfect examples of throwing money at something to make it easier! And if you have the money to buy some of these systems, or the time and energy to assemble others yourself, you'll find that a brew day can be as simple as getting your ingredients together and then pushing a few buttons.

One caveat here before we dive in: the systems we mention here are the most well developed, easy to use, and easy to obtain systems at the time of this writing. This aspect of homebrewing is still in its infancy, and a few years down the road there will be new players with new innovations and some of the current crop may be gone. But the examples we'll talk about here will give you a good idea of what's available now and where things may be headed. We've even asked some of the industry leaders to break out their crystal balls and give us their ideas about the future of high-tech brewing systems.

> **NOTE FROM DENNY AND DREW:** What follows is not intended to be a comprehensive review or endorsement of any particular system or piece of equipment. Although we use and love some of this stuff, we want you to weigh up all the information and decide for yourself.

AUTOMATED SYSTEMS

The example systems that we will look at below are representative of the modern, all-in-one, automated brewing systems currently available. Why are these fancy systems in a book about simple homebrewing? Because they allow you to simply add your ingredients and water, start the system, and come back later to find wort ready to chill and ferment. There are some advantages and disadvantages to these automated systems.

Advantages:

- Automated systems can save you set-up time because there's not much to set up.
- All-in-one systems can save space when stored or in use because they all have a small footprint.
- Automated systems can save you time when you use them. They don't necessarily brew more quickly, but, once you have the ingredients loaded and start them up, they don't require further attention until the end of the brew.
- Because all-in-one, automated systems are programmable, you get repeatability—your recipe will turn out the same every time you brew it.

Disadvantages:

- You're not a "real brewer" in the eyes of some when you let the machine do all the work around wort production.
- The fully automated systems tend to be more constrained in terms of recipe execution, ingredient amounts, and deviations from the "standard" brewing process.

PicoBrew

PicoBrew (https://www.picobrew.com) in Seattle, Washington was started by former Microsoft execs and engineers in partnership with a food scientist. That heritage is apparent both in the concept and design of the equipment they make. PicoBrew's lineup covers a range of high-tech brewing equipment.

PicoBrew entered the market with the Zymatic®, a stainless steel beauty slightly larger than a regular microwave. Weighing in at about 50 pounds, the Zymatic produces a small batch size of 2.5 gallons (9.5 L) in about four to five hours. An opening on the front of the unit houses the "step filter," a heat resistant, food-safe polycarbonate box. The step filter is sectioned into a "mash compartment" (i.e., a grain bin) in the front and four "hop cages" in the rear, with a "pass through" in between for when you want water or wort going through the heat exchanger but not the grain or hops. The cages each hold up to an ounce of whole hops, or several ounces of pellet hops. A rotating robotic arm in the top of the unit moves to the proper position for each step and delivers water or wort through a lid on the top of the step filter, which has several holes to allow liquid to flow to either the mash compartment or any of the hop cages.

The Zymatic was in production for several years before being replaced with the Pico Z. While the internal design of the Z Series is different from the Zymatic, the basic operation remains the same. One big plus for the Z Series is expandability. You start with a 2.5-gallon unit that has the "brains" for the whole system. Then you can add on more 2.5-gallon brewing compartments, up to a total system capacity of 10 gallons (37.8 L).

One of the beauties of the PicoBrew systems is programmability. You can even program the unit to do first wort hopping, a favorite of Denny's. The overall process for a brew day with a Zymatic works as follows. Using the online Recipe Crafter software, you can choose a community user recipe or enter grain and hop types and amounts, then a mash schedule. The software tells you how much water to add to a 5-gallon Cornelius (corny) keg that you connect. The keg serves as your hot liquor tank and doubles as the kettle for wort boiling. Because the Zymatic is connected to your PicoBrew account, you can use your computer or phone to monitor your brew throughout the brewing process. It shows you where you are in the process and a graph of the times and temperatures during your brew.

When brewing is done, you're left with 2.5 gallons of wort in your 5-gallon keg. Chill that using any method that works for you, and either ferment in the keg or transfer the wort to another fermentor of your choice. When fermentation is complete, keg or bottle the beer as you normally would.

Besides the ease of use and hands-off nature of the Zymatic, one of the best things about it is the repeatability factor. You know your mash temperatures and times will be consistent from batch to batch, so a beer from a specific recipe will turn out the same every time. This makes experimenting with a specific ingredient a cinch because you can be sure that the ingredient you change will be the only change in the beer.

The other big change in the Pico Z from the Zymatic is that not only can you use your own ingredients, but you can also brew PicoPak™ recipe kits (they come in a 5 L batch size specifically made for PicoBrew's Pico® device) or ZPaks, which have a 2.5-gallon batch size.

And to make sure you get your money's worth, you can even do sous vide cooking with your Zymatic! The even temperature of the water in the Zymatic makes it a perfect sous vide machine.

The Pico® is more of a beer brewing appliance. As automated as the Z Series is, the Pico takes simplicity up a notch. The Pico is a bit larger than a coffee pot and produces about 1.3 gallons (~5 L) and takes two to three hours to brew. The big difference is that the Pico uses prepackaged ingredients called PicoPaks. Like the Z Series, the Pico connects to your PicoBrew account when you turn it on. You then fill your brewing keg with water, hook the keg up to the Pico, and slip a pack into the opening in the front. The Pico reads a radio frequency identification (RFID) chip in each pack to know what the recipe is and what brew schedule to run for that pack. When the brew is finished, the brewing keg has wort in it, which you cool and pitch yeast into.

PicoBrew licenses recipes from breweries and homebrewers. Its devices are aimed more at the beer enthusiast who wants to easily and quickly make great craft beers, rather than the "average" homebrewer who wants full control. For those who want to brew their own recipes, PicoBrew allows you to design a recipe online and will assemble and ship the PicoPak to you.

Figure 5.1. PicoBrew Z1 control unit.

Brewie+

The Brewie+ (https://brewie.org/) is a stainless steel box that measures 29 × 13.3 × 18.4 inches (73.7 × 33.8 × 46.7 cm). It makes 2.6–5.3 gal. (10–20 L) all-grain batches based on the BIAB principle. The touch screen is centered on the front of the unit and it has Wi-Fi capability. When you open the lid you see two compartments separated by a center divider, with four "hop tank" compartments that hold the hop cages. On the back of the Brewie+ are connectors for the water inlet and outlet, as well as a wort outlet.

The overall process for a brew day with the Brewie+ goes as follows. A false bottom is put in the right-hand compartment and a bag of grain on top of it. You can use either premade Brewie Pads recipe kits or a proprietary Brewie Bag that comes with the machine for using your own grain. The recipe can be provided via a tag on the Brewie Pad, a downloadable recipe, or your own recipe entered via the front panel screen. After selecting or entering your recipe on the touch screen display, the left-hand compartment fills with water (you can also add water manually if you don't connect the Brewie+ to a water supply) and begins heating to your mash temperature. When it gets to temperature, the water is pumped to the grain compartment, where it is recirculated while your mash is held for the specified amount of time. When the mash is done, the wort is pumped back to the left-hand compartment for boiling. Wort is circulated through the hop cages per your hop schedule.

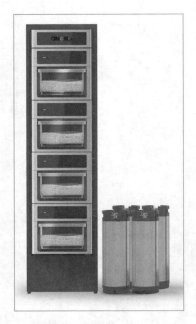

Figure 5.2. PicoBrew Z4 system for 10-gallon batches.

Figure 5.3. Brewie+ system.

Once the boil is complete, the Brewie+ cools the wort to "a temperature of your choosing" (it's limited by the temperature of your water supply) by running water around the outside of the boil compartment by way of the water inlet on the back. When the wort is cool, you connect a sanitized hose to the wort outlet and run the wort into your fermentor. You pitch yeast and ferment as you would any other brew. You can also connect several Brewie+ units together for larger batches.

ALL-IN-ONE MANUAL SYSTEMS

All-in-one manual systems leave some of the work of brewing up to you. They're integrated systems in terms of the hardware, but some of the brewing processes still require hands-on attention from you. In addition to the manufacturers we describe below, note that there are other options in the "all-in-one" space, like RoboBrew; also, some units are less feature-filled and more affordable, like the Brewer's Edge® Mash And Boil. All-in-one manual systems have some advantages and disadvantages.

Advantages:

- The integrated system saves you time during set up.
- The integrated system saves room when you come to store it.
- All-in-one systems save time and effort in cleaning due to the reduced number of pieces.
- Manual systems are more accommodating to variances in your brewing process.
- Using a manual system "feels" more like brewing.

Disadvantages:

- Manual systems lack the full "walk away" automation of automated systems.
- Because all-in-one systems are electrical, low mains voltage in most US households may mean slower temperature rises and boil times.

Figure 5.4. The Grainfather Connect system.

Grainfather

The Grainfather (https://www.grainfather.com), based in New Zealand, offers an all-in-one brewing system based on a traditional fly sparge setup. The Grainfather Connect is a vessel within a vessel. The outer stainless steel container has a heating plate in the bottom and a built-in pump on the outside that you use to recirculate wort. The inner container has screens to hold and filter the mash. During mashing, another tube runs from the pump to recirculate the wort. The attached smart controller can be programmed for multi-step or single infusion mashes, and includes a delayed start option. The smart controller has Bluetooth® connectivity so it can be controlled or monitored remotely. The Grainfather Connect also comes with a counterflow chiller to cool your wort quickly. Other add-ons for the Grainfather system include the Graincoat, a neoprene jacket that slips over the outer vessel to help maintain heat, and a pot still attachment.

When using the Grainfather Connect, you fill the inner container with water and program your mash schedule using the smart controller. Next, you insert the inner container with the bottom screen in place and put a cover on the inner tube to prevent grain from going down it. You stir the grain into your strike water and place another screen on top of the grain.

After removing the stopper you put on the glass lid, which has a hole in the center to allow you to direct the outer tubing back over the grain for recirculation. When you start up the pump, wort is pumped from the bottom of the unit up and over the grain in the basket.

Once your mash is done, you lift the inner container and set it on supports built into the outer container. As the wort drains out you pour water over the top screen to sparge the grain. (Grainfather also sells a separate unit for heating your sparge water.)

When the sparge is finished you boil your wort in the same unit, adding hops as usual. Near the end of the boil you hook the counterflow chiller up to the pump and recirculate wort through it to sanitize it. When the boil is over you turn on the water to the chiller and run your wort into a fermentor. (Grainfather also makes 25 L stainless steel fermentors that have a tap on them to make it easy to bottle your beer.)

Cleanup is a cinch. Dump the grain from the inner container into your compost pile, then spray out and clean the container like every kettle you've ever known and loved.

Figure 5.5. Speidel Braumeister systems.

Speidel Braumeister

Arguably the great granddaddy of the all-in-one electric brewing appliances is the Speidel Braumeister (https://www. speidels-braumeister.de). They are serious works of art and German engineering with a substantial price tag to match.

Speidel is a mid-size company in Germany that has been in the container manufacturing business since 1912. They build brewing and fermenting systems, as well as grinders and presses for cider making. Although Speidel makes their Braumeister system in sizes up to 500 L (132 gal.) for commercial use (or REALLY enthusiastic homebrewers!), their smaller 10, 20, and 50-liter systems are what most homebrewers will be interested in. Like the Grainfather, the Braumeister uses an outer stainless steel jacket as the combination hot liquor tank and mash tun, with an inner perforated basket to hold grain.

The Braumeister can be purchased alone, or in various starter sets that come bundled with items such as fermentors, chillers, mills, and other pieces of brewing equipment. An optional internet-enabled Wi-Fi module allows you to download software updates, synchronize recipes to your Braumeister, and monitor the brewing process.

With a Braumeister, the brewing process begins by adding water to the hot liquor tank. You program your mash and boil schedule using the front panel controls or transfer your schedule to the Braumeister using the My Speidel software. Next, you pour in your mash water and heat it to the desired strike temperature. Once your water is at the right temperature, you insert the grain basket with the "sieve inserts" (perforated screens that go below and above the grain), inserting the lower screen first, stirring in your grain, and then placing the other insert on top. You screw down a "malt pipe" across the top of the container to hold the inserts in place and then switch the pump on to recirculate your wort through the grain container during the mash. Unlike the Grainfather, which has a tube running up the outside of the unit from the pump and recirculates over the top of the grain, the Braumeister recirculates from the bottom of the mash tun.

Once the mash is complete, you remove the grain container and allow it to drain into the outer container. You can sparge if you want by pouring water into the grain container. After lautering and sparging, you switch the unit to boil and manually add the hops per your hop schedule.

Here's what we like about these manual all-in-ones: they straddle the line between the burly all-manual means we're used to and the fully automated computerized brewing systems like those from PicoBrew and Brewie. They help make your brew day easier, but you're still hands-on.

RECIPE INTERLUDE

Here's one of the reasons to love these integrated all-in-one systems. They make doing more complicated mash schedules a matter of adding steps to an app instead of manually stirring and adding heat or decocting or infusing hot water. Sometimes you want to do a multi-step mash just because it's tradition (the actual utilitarian value of more complicated brew schedules is somewhat debatable.) Here's a perfect example of a stronger version of a German altbier that uses an old-school mash schedule. On our automated systems, the only extra work is having to wait a little while longer!

Double Secret Probation Sticke Altbier

Batch size: 6.0 gal. (22.7 L)
Original gravity: 1.082 (19.8°P)
Final gravity: 1.018 (4.6°P)

Color: 15 SRM
Bitterness: 55 IBU
ABV: 8%

Malt
- 17.5 lb. (7.9 kg) Pilsner malt
- 0.5 lb. (225 g) Caramunich® malt
- 0.3 lb. (140 g) Weyermann Carafa II Special, debittered

Hops
- 1.5 oz. (43 g) Magnum 12% AA @ 60 min.
- 2.0 oz. (56 g) Willamette 5.5% AA @ whirlpool for 20 min.

Yeast
- Wyeast 1007 German Ale or White Labs WLP036 Düsseldorf Altbier

Mash
- Protein rest: 122°F (50°C) for 20 min.
- Low rest: 148°F (64°C) for 30 min.
- High rest: 158°F (70°C) for 30 min.
- Mash-out: 168°F (78°C) for 10 min.

Brewing notes
- Pitch yeast and ferment this beer between 55°F and 60°F (13°C and 15.5°C) for 2–3 weeks, then lower the temperature to near freezing for 2–4 weeks to age and clear.

SIMPLE FERMENTATION SYSTEMS

The real challenge for most homebrewers when trying to simplify their brewing process isn't providing the heat, it's providing the cool. The old standbys have been the classic water bath, which Drew still regularly uses, or the "brew fridge/freezer" with an override thermostat to set the temperature. On the high end, as we write this, more and more professional "consumer-sized" glycol chillers are appearing, but for those not made of money they're not practical.

Simple fermentation systems maintain your fermentation temperature for you. They're easier and more compact than the refrigerator or chest freezer typically used by homebrewers for temperature control. In addition, some provide you with a way to serve your beer directly from the fermentor.

BrewJacket Immersion Pro

BrewJacket, Inc. (https://www.brewjacket.com) takes a different approach to cooling or heating wort and it works brilliantly, particularly for those trapped in smaller brewing spaces. The BrewJacket Immersion Pro setup consists of a big insulated bag that goes around your fermentor to help control heat transfers, and a heavy anodized aluminum rod that you submerge into the beer. The rod connects to a lid and controller unit with a fan and a heat sink. Through the magic of the Peltier effect, the BrewJacket absorbs heat through the rod and expels it out the top.

Figure 5.6. A "cool" way to keep your beer at a constant temperature. The BrewJacket Immersion Pro is a fermentor inside of a jacket.

Figure 5.7. BrewJacket Immersion Pro system without jacket.

In a space no bigger than your fermentor, you can successfully hold your vessel at roughly 30°F (16.5°C) below or above room temperature using the BrewJacket system. That means if your wort is in a climate-controlled room you can still do a lager in your house year round!

Vessi Fermentor

The Vessi® Fermentor (https://wlabsinnovations.com/pages/vessi) is an integrated fermenting and serving tank from WLabs, a division of appliance giant Whirlpool. WLabs is Whirlpool's approach to developing innovative consumer products, and the Vessi is definitely innovative.

The Vessi Fermentor consists of a temperature-controlled 8-gallon conical fermentor (designed for 5-gallon batches) mounted below a work surface that's set on an outer shell about the size of an average kegerator. The work surface includes a beer tap that is connected to the fermentor. The idea is that you can ferment and serve from the same device. This saves time when compared with cleaning and sanitizing separate pieces of equipment. The Vessi also includes connections for CO_2 so you can carbonate your beer, and a beer outlet connector so you can choose to keg or bottle your beer separately.

Bob Schneider, a Vessi Fermentor owner and Whirlpool Corporation employee, assesses the Vessi like this:

Figure 5.8. Innovation in the form of fermentation and serving from the same vessel; meet Vessi.

> We see ourselves as the ultimate home-level uni-tank for fermenting, removing sediment, clarifying and conditioning with the added bonus of being able to dispense directly, keg, or bottle! This allows you to significantly cut down your cleaning, transferring, and various pain points of the traditional homebrewing process, all the while reducing risks of contamination and oxidization.

HOME CANNING

One of the biggest changes in the craft beer world has been the influx and rapid proliferation of the beer can. Long derided as the receptacle of bad beer, the can has taken on the sheen of respectability as consumers have realized its value in terms of protection from both light and oxygen. The beer can has been around since the 1930s but the technology has remained firmly in the hands of the big guys, until now.

Aside from the small machines being run out of mobile canning lines and the six pack-sized machines that both Oskar Blues and 21st Amendment used to publicly kick off the craft can revolution, there's never been a reasonable way for a craft beer homebrewer to take advantage of everything the can has to offer. The place where most of us are probably interacting with small-batch canning is the Crowler™, a 32 oz. can substitute for the growler fill. The can seamers that seal crowlers are works of early industrial art, but at around $3500 each they are out of the price range for all but the most ambitious homebrewer.

Wisconsin Aluminum Foundry (WAF), probably best known for making the line of All-American® pressure cookers that your grandmother would have passed down to you if only you had asked, has been making canning rigs out of big hunks of metal since the 1920s. WAF has recently begun exploring the homebrew market with its hand-cranked (or drill-powered) seamers, which cost a much more reasonable 600–700 dollars. Still not cheap, but far better

And then there's the new kid on the block, Oktober Design's MK16. It's more expensive than the WAF seamer, but for $1500 you get a slick, modern-looking, fully motorized unit that makes short work of can seaming.

Figure 5.9. A Wisconsin Aluminum Foundry can sealer.

All of the options above still come with a few problems. First, the expense. Second, they work best with already carbonated beer and you'll definitely need a way to purge the cans prior to filling. Professional systems usually use nitrogen, but we can use our trusty CO_2 from, say, a BeerGun™. Lastly, there's the small matter of the cans themselves—they're recyclable, but still single use from our perspective and you get your best savings when you buy in bulk, such as a pallet of cans in a single go.

As we write this, we're in the early infancy of canning at the homebrew level. Maybe these machines never move below the homebrew store or club level, but they could still provide an awesome service for your store regulars or club brewers. It will be exciting to see where this goes because cans rock and this is just another great option.

As for why we're including canning seamers in a book about simple homebrewing? We strongly feel like this is a place people will want to go. Homebrewers love to emulate the pros and the can has a number of advantages as a packaging format. It's only going to get simpler as we go!

SOME ASSEMBLY REQUIRED

We're going to pull a Carnac the Magnificent here and predict that a fair number of you are saying one of the following things.

"drool"

OK, that's not a saying, but suffice it to say, you're excited by the things we've been showing you and are all ready to plunk down your hard earn ducats. If you're willing to buy everything we just mentioned above, can we interest you in some investment properties that are only suitable to a well-heeled individual as yourself?

For the rest of you, we're guessing you fall into one of two remaining camps:

"That's great and all, but my orchard of money trees hasn't blossomed yet."

Or,

"Man, half the fun of this hobby is having an excuse to be out in the garage/shed/lean-to twiddling with wrenches, screwdrivers, and Teflon tape."

We hear you both, and despite never meeting a piece of gear we didn't at least temporarily fall into limerence with, we know that money can't buy you brewing love.

Bucket Heaters: A Cheap Electrical Assist

Sometimes you really don't need all the fancy PID controllers and automated thingamajigs to make your beer, but you do need an assist. About a decade ago, homebrewers (being the clever sort) began playing with electric immersion heaters, a.k.a. "bucket heaters."

You'll sometimes see the small version of a bucket heater sold as a desktop "coffee warmer." These warmers consist of a few metal loops coiled tightly together to submerge in your cup. They heat by virtue of electrical resistance, causing the metal to heat, rather like friction causing a surface to warm. Plug in your coffee warmer and never have a cold sip again … Burnt and burny tasting, sure, but cold? Never!

But you're not interested in potential office electrocution hazards and absurd desktop murder scenarios; you want the brew applications. Do a search online for bucket heaters. When homebrewers first began using them, they were almost strictly the domain of farms and were used to prevent buckets from icing over in the barn. The early models were fairly primitive and had limited insulation because farmers are used to dangerous implements. Homebrewers began by shielding the exposed wiring and electrical connections using various housings, including PVC pipes and plenty of heat-resistant silicone caulking to keep the wort at bay.

Modern bucket heaters in the 1000–1500 watt range have come a long way in terms of safety. The consumer models won't bring things to a boil, but for a little less than $50 they will help you speed up a stubbornly slow stove top, induction cooktop, and even some of the previously mentioned fancy 110 volt systems. (Most of the plug-and-play bucket heaters have a temperature cutoff of ~180°F, or 82°C.)

A word to the wise: as we noted in chapter 3, on a typical US household with a 15 amp circuit (found in almost every room except the kitchen), you can only put a maximum load of roughly 1800 watts before tripping the circuit. If you have a 20 amp circuit, you can pile on about 2400 watts of load before "click-*wrrr*" and the power goes off. Bear in mind that 1800 or 2400-watt load total includes everything running on that circuit, which means your lights, fans, fridges, and other gadgets in addition to the load brought by your heating elements.

The other use for a bucket heater is preheating brewing water. Some people like to wake up in the morning, turn on the burners, and get their coffee on while waiting for their brewing water to come up to temperature. Others, like Drew, know that every little thing left to be done in the morning is just going to make it that much harder to get the brew going.

You can combine a bucket heater with a standard heating thermostat controller (like the newer models from Inkbird, found online and at your homebrew store) and fire up the heater overnight so you can wake up to water ready to go. If you add a timer switch to the whole assembly, you can even save energy by having the heater flip on at a suitable time before your brew session is scheduled to start. Also, we highly recommend that if you preheat water overnight this way, you use a ground fault circuit interrupter (GFCI) wired outlet for this application to prevent disaster should your heater short out. Much better to have a delayed brew day than your house burn down!

If you're doubly handy (and can trust yourself around electricity), you can buy individual heating elements and install them permanently in a pot or bucket. If you do an internet search you can quickly fall down the rabbit hole of building your own full-on electric brewery (http://www.theelectricbrewery .com/ is one good resource). But please, please, please, for the love of all things beery, you must make sure you know what you're doing. Unlike flame-based systems where you can see the danger, electricity can be sneaky, and any small miswiring can cause serious damage.

Even if you don't embrace the fully automated, fancy-control-panel version of brewing, you'll see some pretty spiffy and simple brewing systems built out of little more than heaters and buckets.

Raspberry Pi and Arduino-Based Systems

Let's say you're not hyped to buy a thing that's all "turn-key," but, like a great many brewers, you're somewhat obsessed with computers because, hey, it's your day job (we bet that applies to at least a third of you reading this right now). One of the coolest developments in the past decade in the computer industry is the return of the microcontroller and microcomputer. The big players are the gadgets from the Raspberry Pi Foundation (https://raspberrypi. org/) and Arduino AG (https://arduino.cc/). Both groups are making it easier than ever for computer-savvy types to bridge the virtual world of computer code with the physical world of motors, switches, and sensors.

The Raspberry Pi series are credit card (and smaller) sized computers that run open-source Linux-based operating systems. Think how powerful your desktop machine was about 10 years ago and now shrink that power into a credit card and pay about $35 for it. Madness! The Arduino series focuses on the microcontroller segment. Basically, they are very simple computers designed for controlling systems as opposed to being a general purpose computer. The Arduino makes for cheap prototyping and is a natural interface for many simple sensors.

NOTE:

We REALLY recommend you use a professionally made bucket heater too. Electricity and water can be a lethal combination. Don't risk your life to save a few bucks!

DREW: Seriously, I suffer from such a bad case of "inertia interrupted brew-dayitis" that I finally had to talk to my doctor about preventive steps. More on that later!

NOTE:

Immersion heating elements should only run while fully submerged. They depend on the heat capacity of the liquid to avoid burning out the elements and wiring. In other words, don't run them without liquid unless you like burning things and wasting money.

DREW: Fun fact, the PicoBrew products started as Arduino-based machines. Once the design was established, PicoBrew could transform the design to custom-printed circuit boards. Go troll through Kickstarter and Indiegogo—most of the interesting electronics projects you'll find are invariably built on a Raspberry Pi or Arduino foundation. So freaking cool to my nerdy, old-school electronics heart.

OK, another fun fact if you want to get cross-compiled terminology stuck in your head. The term "homebrew" originally made the news because of the Homebrew Computer Club that first met in Menlo Park, California in March 1975. They eventually gave birth to the original Apple I computer. Of course, that was a full year after my homebrew club, The Maltose Falcons, first met, so we still claim homebrew supremacy!

Because of their availability, low cost, and embrace of the open-source software (OSS) model, there are scads and scads of projects available to you online that use Raspberry Pi and Arduino platforms. However, the nature of OSS also means that these projects exist in various states of upkeep. Be careful when adopting a pet project, and find out if there's sufficient active support behind things to suit your level of willingness and ability to develop.

One great current example are the folks behind BrewPi (https://brewpi .com/). As of 2018, the BrewPi project is actively evolving around new circuit boards and new ideas moving well beyond the singular scope of just controlling a fermentation fridge.

LOOKING INTO THE CRYSTAL BALL

What do we think the future of homebrew tech will look like? Please remember, we're likely to be as accurate as the folks who predicted people wouldn't need individual home computers or the people who created the Jetsons that made so many of us believe that we'd have personal jet packs, robots, and flying cars.

DENNY: In speaking with the people who are designing and selling these current systems, two words I hear repeatedly are "community" and "connectivity." Homebrewing is, by its very nature, a social activity. Homebrewers like to invite other brewers over when they brew and love to talk about recipes, processes, and equipment. Brewers like to feel that they're part of a larger community. That eases their minds when it comes to support on these new systems. As good as company support may be (and some of them have the most excellent support I've ever run across in any field!), there's nothing like knowing you can call on other brewers using the same equipment when you have a problem. And, of course, things like exchanging recipes and learning about other people's preferences in brewing ingredients and procedures is a huge plus. All of the companies making these brewing systems stress the community aspect as a real benefit when learning to use their equipment and getting continued enjoyment of it.

Connectivity is rearing its head in homebrewing, just like it is in everything from Wi-Fi-enabled refrigerators to toilets that take SD cards and are Bluetooth connected (hey, that's not a joke!). As people get busier and busier, it's great to be able to preprogram your brew and check in via Bluetooth or Wi-Fi to see how things are going and even adjust your system. Kids have a soccer game on the only day you can brew? Set up the brew before you go and use your phone to keep tabs on it. By the time you get home, your wort will be ready to be chilled (or is already chilled!) and go into the fermentor. Yeah, some people will say that's not brewing but, fortunately, YOU get to decide for yourself how you want to brew!

We are seeing a proliferation of systems. The longer they're on the market, the more people will begin to accept them. When this easy-to-use equipment began appearing a few years ago, many homebrewers (including myself) felt that it just wasn't homebrewing, that it was somehow cheating. All it took for me to change my mind was using the equipment. The ease of use and quality of beer you can make convinced me that it was a viable way to brew and did nothing to ruin the fun of homebrewing. Although I still enjoy using my "Cheap 'n' Easy" cooler systems, I also have found that I can brew beer of equal quality with a lot less hands-on activity simply by using one of the high-tech systems now available. That allows me to get done brewing more quickly, not to mention having time during the brewing process to do other things. If you have a family, those can be important considerations.

Another thing I see is that the more people use these systems, the more any shortcomings will make themselves known. The market will come up with ways to address these shortcomings, either through redesigning current systems or introducing new ones. That means that the technology will become easier to use and even more attractive.

I also think we'll see more small systems like the Pico, either with or without prepackaged ingredients. For many brewers a 1–3-gallon batch size is an advantage, not a drawback, and the all-in-one systems are in a perfect position to take advantage of this. At the same time, there is a section of the homebrewing world that would prefer larger batch sizes, and I see the market accommodating this by coming out with systems that will be in the 5–15 gallon range. I think that will be a smaller market segment, but still important.

Finally, I think (and hope!) we'll see more packaging solutions to go along with the brewing systems. The Vessi is a first step toward this kind of thing. But I wonder when we'll see small-scale, affordable bottling and/or canning solutions show up. I think this is the kind of thing that a time-pressed brewer would really appreciate in order to fill the last niche in their simple brewing hobby.

DREW: Much like Denny, my first reaction to a lot of these things was, "Hey, that's kinda neat," which is my geeky side, and, "No sir, I don't like it," which is my culinary hands-on side (also, bonus points if you know the reference). It's real hard arguing between those two sides. I have to agree with Denny, that the time and labor savings, or at least time re-utilization factor, is huge when you're busy and running around. Letting the computers and controllers handle everything else while I tend to the family, the errands, the chores, the writing, etc. really is a boon.

But I'll admit, these systems don't always make me feel completely satisfied. Like a part of the brewing itch hasn't quite gone away. But, hey, what do you know—I still have my original system, I have a BIAB system, I have a garage full of brew parts...so, yeah, stand back and watch me scratch that itch when I need to.

I think another aspect of the rising robot-brewer tide is the expense, but, as with all fields, I think those of us who are early adopters are paying the way for future users. Will an automated system ever be as cheap and flexible as a cooler with a braid? Nope, but it doesn't have to be for most people.

Besides, I really love gadgets in my cold, beeping silicon heart.

PROFILES IN SIMPLICITY: RONALDO DUTRA FERREIRA

Using Technology: From Braumeister Homebrewer to Brewmaster

In 2015, we were invited to Brazil to speak at a homebrewing conference in Florianopolis in the state of Santa Catarina. Our host was Ronaldo Dutra Ferreira, an accomplished homebrewer. His home brewery included an extensive Speidel Braumeister setup, including an electric lift to hoist the grain basket out of the mash tun (this was Drew's favorite part). Soon after we left, Ronaldo opened the brewery Bruxa (which means *witch* in Portuguese) in a sort of co-op brewing facility, sharing the space with other friends running similar breweries. We asked Ronaldo to tell us his story of going from a homebrewer with his Braumeister to a brewmaster with his own brewery.

> During university some friends and I wanted to brew beer, but we all lived with our parents and so the project never took off. We had a deal; when the first of us had some sort of structure, we would brew beer. When I finished building my house, I received a large package full of pots and the works to make beer, an off-the-shelf combo of gear and ingredients, and a note: "It's on your turf! Now learn!" At first, I did not know what was happening until my friend called and explained that he had bought everything. I ordered a whole box of books and began to study. This was February, 2010.
>
> Our first brewing equipment was an all-grain 5-gallon set up. Slowly, we upgraded the equipment with some bells and whistles to make our brewing life easier. All the parts were sourced in hardware stores and imported from the US. At that time, few options were available. I brewed the beer at my house in Brazil along with a friend that had also wanted to brew for a long time.
>
> Afterwards I went to a 250 L three-vessel structure, almost a full-size brewery. Then, I downsized to a 50 L BIAB one-vessel system so I could brew more beers, different styles, and do more experiments.

Brewing with a Speidel 50 L BIAB was very easy and fast. To get some feedback on how good the beers were that I brewed with it, I entered and won a few competitions both at the state level and nationally.

During my homebrew days, we had a club called Armada Cervejeira. We had meetings every two weeks to discuss all things homebrew and to taste each other's and commercial beers. The focus was learning and to increase the learning curve through the sharing of information.

In 2016, that club transformed into a collaborative brewery with 21 taps. We can brew whatever we feel like and enjoy the results with our loyal customers. We have won a number of awards, including a gold medal for a grisette and bronze for a sour fruit beer at the Brazilian Competition for Breweries.

The advice I give for people that want to excel in this hobby is to participate in their local homebrewing clubs, subscribe to magazines, buy books, and study, study, study! Information is never enough, and better beer has a lot of knowledge behind it.

The Recipe

A little about the recipe I'm sharing: I developed this recipe with my friend, Rodrigo Tasca; we won a homebrewing competition sponsored by Cervejaria Bierland in Blumenau, Santa Catarina, and they ended up brewing it for release. It is possible that some changes were made by Bierland, but this recipe is the core starting recipe that won their competition. This is a moderate-strength blonde ale with high drinkability, a sweet, fruity aroma, and dry finish. ∎

Bruxa Belgian Blonde Ale

Batch volume: 5 gal. (19 L)
Original gravity: 1.067 (16.4°P)
Final gravity: 1.012 (3.1°P)

Color: 5 SRM
Bitterness: 28 IBU
ABV: 7%

Malt
- 5.3 lb. (2.4 kg) Castle Malts Pils (1.8°L)
- 5.3 lb. (2.4 kg) Castle Malts Vienna (3°L)
- 0.25 lb. (110 g) Castle acid malt (3°L)
- 3.5 oz. (100 g) Castle Malts Abbey (17°L)

Hops
- 1.75 oz. (50 g) East Kent Goldings 5% AA @ 60 min.

Additions
- 1.1 lb. (500 g) demerara or cane sugar @ 15 min.
- 1/2 tsp. yeast nutrient @ 15 min.

Yeast
- Wyeast 1214 Abbey Ale

Water profile
- Calcium (Ca^{2+}): 90 ppm
- Chloride (Cl^-): 60 ppm
- Sulfate (SO^{2-}_4): 60 ppm

Brewing notes
- Multi-step mash with treated to profile water, 4 gal. (15 L) at 151°F (66°C) for 60 min., raise to 158°F (70°C) for 15 min. Sparge with treated-to-profile water, 4 gal. (15 L) at 172°F (78°C).
- Boil for 60 min., adding hops when boiling starts. Add the demerara/cane sugar for the last 15 min. of the boil. Whirlpool and wait 15–20 min.
- Cool wort to around 70°F (21°C) and pitch yeast.
- Ferment around 65°F (20°C) for three days, then turn off temperature control for 7–10 days. Don't let the temperature go above 79°F (26°C). (I skip the secondary.) Crash cool at 32°F (0°C) for a week.
- Bottle or keg as usual.

6
SIMPLE FLAVOR
IDENTIFICATION

T alk to a bunch of homebrewers and you'll start to notice patterns. We certainly have. You have the gear heads, the rigid traditionalists, or the wacky brewers. There are many funny types, but one that keeps popping up to the point where they nearly define the cliché homebrewer (and some craft brewers too) is the brewer who's happiest creating flavor bombs of various staggering proportions.

A lot of passionate debates rage over the proper way to design a recipe. Heck, plenty of folks are willing to tell you that the recipe doesn't matter at all, the magic all lies within you the brewer. We tend to take a middle view: a good brewer with a bad recipe won't make good beer, just like a bad brewer with a great recipe won't make great beer.

What brewer hasn't spent a slow workday with their mind floating through dreams of malt bills and crazy hop blends? Maybe you're in your favorite chair, eating your favorite food, when a flavor idea pops into your head. You race to the computer to jot down the notes. It's spreadsheets with a purpose and an infinite set of possibilities.

"It's that endless sea of possible choices that is homebrewing's blessing and curse."

It's that endless sea of possible choices that is homebrewing's blessing and curse. With so many combinations of ingredients, homebrewers tend to get giddy and laugh with the panicky laugh of someone verging on madness. Some fall full and hard for the lunacy, indulging in their Bourbon Barrel Blackberry Bhut Jolokia Barleywine (BBBBJBW) or flights of fancy like a Pizza Beer or Clam Chowder Saison. Others laden their recipes with every ingredient in the homebrew shop, to disappointing results.

But how can you avoid the minefield that is the modern homebrew experience where ingredients from every corner of the globe are available? Well, it starts by understanding what flavor is, what it means, and how to think about it. In the next chapter (chapter 7), we'll get into the hard part, developing your recipe discipline and cutting away all the excess to find Michelangelo's malty David hiding in your mash tun.

Oh, speaking of the BBBBJBW, read on to the end of the chapter. (What, you expected us to spoil it now?)

SIMPLIFYING RECIPE DESIGN

There are a couple ways to think about simplifying recipe design. The most obvious way is to design simple recipes, using a minimum of ingredients. While that's a great approach for some beers, it's not true that the simplest recipe in terms of number of ingredients is the best recipe. The best recipe is the one that gets you the beer you want, no matter how many ingredients it does or doesn't have. And that's where other ways of thinking about recipe design come in. You can simplify your recipe design by identifying the flavors you want in your beer, then learning the ingredients that will create those flavors. That's what the first part of this chapter is about. You can also simplify recipe design by looking at other recipes, taking the good parts from them and creating recipe templates, allowing you to adjust or alter one or two ingredients in a template to give you variations on a beer or a different beer in the same general flavor family. For instance, you can turn your American amber recipe into a German altbier recipe with just a couple of ingredient swaps; that's what we'll get into in chapter 7.

UNDERSTANDING FLAVORS AND INGREDIENTS

Flavors in Beer

As your authors, we advise you to drink heavily in order to learn your flavors. All joking aside, seriously, the best way to learn your flavors and ingredients is to keep exposing your palate and evaluating things critically. There's a time and a place for sitting back with a porch beer, mindlessly sipping your beloved barley water, but when you're trying to capture a nuance or figure out the trick choose a commercial sample and pay attention to what you taste!

The first piece is to understand just what is flavor. Put simply, your brain synthesizes a staggering array of inputs from the tongue and the nose to produce a magically woven electrical sensation. That sensation is what we think of as flavor. That's what it really comes down to: chemicals in the food and beverages we consume excite different electrical responses in the receptors of our nose and tongue.

Flavor is even trickier to understand in a universal sense because it is so personal. It's not just that you may or may not like Cluster hops, for instance. Your whole organoleptic system may be supremely sensitive to the compounds found in Cluster hops, giving you a measurably different set of sensations. Look at the burgeoning community of "cilantro haters"—it turns out that for about 10% of humanity cilantro tastes overwhelmingly of soap. To the rest of us, cilantro is a delightfully bright and fresh herb for your chili, tacos, and curries.

DREW: I have a few problems with how a lot of beer judging is done. One is that judges are drilled on finding faults and flaws to make sure they recognize things that have gone pear-shaped. That's fine and a good thing. The assumption is you have more experience recognizing, say, cherry flavors rather than dimethyl sulfide. But it builds a pattern in the judges to always be on the lookout for flaws first. I prefer flavor first and then flaws. The other problem is the use of flowery Robert Parker/Michael Jackson-style language in describing the beer and using certain terms that, while they make sense, don't capture the essence of your subjective experience. If a beer tastes like Hawaiian fruit punch, say so. It's a more accurate and vivid description of what you're experiencing than "fruity and tropical."

DREW: I know this comes dangerously close to those late night, chemically boosted college philosophy discussions like, "What if what I think of as blue is really green to everyone else?" But, this has been shown to be somewhat true. (Stupid brain—where's my beer?)

As BJCP[1] judges and beer nerds, we've run into people over the years who lament that they just don't have the great palates that we do. There are a few things going on here. Everyone's palate is a little different, as we mentioned, but it works on more subtle levels. Drew is highly sensitive to diacetyl (butter/butterscotch), but has a hard time finding the brown-paper-like aspects of oxidation. Denny doesn't have much trouble picking up on diacetyl, although he uses the slick mouthfeel to give him a clue, but he can easily detect oxidation as wet cardboard, sherry, or strange caramel flavors (he does struggle with dimethyl sulfide, though). The real challenge is building the associations and vocabulary needed to express what you do taste.

The point is that our palates aren't perfect, we've just spent a ton of time studying beers and tasting them carefully. We're going to go into a simple process for doing that.

Understanding Ingredients: Build Your Flavor Database

One of the big challenges for homebrewers is that traditionally we've gone about learning our flavors the hard way, batch by batch. If we were commercial brewers, churning out beer day after day, learning the differences in flavor that your ingredients and processes impart is a matter of course. But even the most crazypants brewers we know only hits the mash tun once a week, and most of us are lucky to squeeze in a batch every month!

DENNY: I once received a score sheet that described my beer as having a "dirt aroma." I took that comment as an insult and for many years harbored ill feelings about it. But after doing a lot more judging myself, I realized that it was likely just a descriptor, not an insult. The point is to try to accurately describe what you're seeing, smelling, or tasting in a way that gets the sensations across to the brewer. Use the right words to do that and hope that the brewer knows that you're trying to help them, not insult them!

---

[1]   Beer Judge Certification Program.

There are some folks who can brew single malt and single hops (SMASH) beer one after the other in an effort to isolate and explore their ingredients. May the beer gods favor those hearty souls, but most of us can't. We want to maximize the variety we get out of our brewing. (There will be more on SMASH later.)

For what it's worth, professional breweries need to do this same sort of thing as well. Despite the great efforts put in by maltsters and hop growers to keep our ingredients the same year after year, they are agricultural products. The big brewers have departments dedicated to analyzing new lots of malt and hops using fancy tests and scientific gadgetry. We don't know about you, but that's just not in our realm, even though Drew has been tempted by very expensive instruments. So, are there better, faster, easier ways to help build up your flavor database? We think so!

MALT EVALUATION

Given malt's place as sometimes celebrated, sometimes overlooked foundational base of beer flavor, you shouldn't be surprised that understanding malt flavor is a huge part of understanding and predicting your beer flavor.

Malt Evaluation at Home

The easiest way to evaluate your malt? Eat it. Don't wolf it down though! Grab a very small handful of malt and chew and crush it in your mouth. Don't swallow. Let your saliva hydrate the malt and let its alpha-amylase tackle converting the starch to sugar. As the malt sits in your mouth, you'll begin to detect the change as the sweetness levels rise. Carefully note what you're smelling and tasting. It's imprecise, but it's easy, cheap, and fast to do. As you build your flavor "dictionary," you'll more accurately transform that initial taste sensation to the final product.

So how can you evaluate malt without going through the whole mashing and brewing process? Briess Malt & Ingredients Co. posted a simplified version of the American Society of Brewing Chemists (ASBC) Hot Steep Malt Evaluation Method (an organoleptic focused test mash), which we've adapted here with our own experiences. The heart of the process is simple, make malt flour for your mash—serious malt flour, as in you'll be tempted to make bread out of it. (Don't; barley bread is generally pretty terrible even without the husk.) You may need some base malt in addition to your test malt, depending on the malt being tested. Highly kilned specialty malts often lack enough enzymes to convert themselves in a timely manner, and adjuncts, like flaked corn, lack enzymes altogether. Caramel malts and roast malts don't need base malt to release their flavors.

Hot Steep Malt Evaluation Method

The whole process for malt evaluation at home takes roughly 55 grams of malt, so feel free to splurge. You'll mix the malt powder with clean, mineral-free hot water, steep and keep warm for 15 minutes, then strain the wort and cool it to room temperature before tasting. The real key to the whole process is to hold the temperature fairly precisely. The simple solution is to buy a nice thermos; Drew recommends stainless steel for breakage reasons (he's a klutz). The rest of the process should be familiar to any of us beer drinkers.

Equipment needed:

- mason jar/thermos/other sealable heat-retaining container, roughly 1 quart (~1 L) in size
- water measuring device, with 500 mL capacity or more
- electric coffee blade grinder; clean, unless you want all your evaluations to be "hmm, smells like coffee"
- scale, in grams
- fast-read thermometer
- coffee filter, either cone or paper
- coffee filter holder or a funnel

Ingredients:

- ~52–55 g malt—see instructions for ratio of malts needed based on test malt
- 600 mL reverse osmosis or distilled water, heated to 149°F (65°C)

Extra Parts:

- sous vide circulator (completely optional, but if you aren't using a thermos it's handy for holding the mash temperature)

Process:

1. Grind roughly 52–55 g of malt, husk and all, into a fine powder using the electric blade grinder.
   a. For base malts (e.g., pale ale, Pilsner, Munich—anything you can use as your primary malt) use 100% of the target malt (52–55 g).
   b. For character malts (crystal, toasted malts, adjuncts) mix 50% base malt with 50% target malt (e.g., 26 g two-row with 26 g malted rye).
   c. For roasted malts (very dark crystal, chocolate, or black malts) mix 85% pale or Pilsner malt with 15% target malt (e.g., 44.25 g two-row with 7.75 g Simpsons Double Roasted Crystal).
2. Preheat your "mashing" (holding) vessel with 100 mL (3.4 fl. oz.) of 149°F (65°C) water, then pour out the water.
3. Place 50 g of the malt powder into your holding vessel and mix with 400 mL (13.5 fl. oz.) of 149°F (65°C) water. For ideal mixing, cap the vessel and shake vigorously for 20–30 seconds.

DREW: If you're doing the hot steep evaluation with several malts at once, like I did for the Experimental Brewing channel on YouTube,* it can be expensive to get 5+ stainless steel thermoses. Since the real goal is to hold the mash temp for 15 minutes, I use my sous vide immersion circulator. I use my circulator to heat the mash water and the holding bath to the same temperature. I set the jars in the water bath to heat up as well before proceeding. After that, everything else is just a matter of shake, place the jars back in the bath, and wait patiently. Alternatively, you can use your oven to help hold temperature or a small cooler filled with hot water as well. You really just need to keep the mash hot the whole time because a small mash like this will cool off quickly.

* "Taste Test - Mecca Grade Estate Malts - The Bases," presentation by Drew Beechum, Experimental Brewing channel, video, 18:55, May 30, 2017, https://www.youtube.com/watch?v=fd02QdQNrcc.

4. Set a timer for 15 minutes. If you're not using a thermos or other heat-retaining vessel, keep the vessel warm in a low oven or water bath (a sous vide circulator is useful for this).
5. Wet the paper filter and set in a funnel or cone holder over a receiving vessel.
6. When the timed 15 minutes is up, vigorously mix the solution for another 20 seconds and dump it into the paper filter cone.
7. Allow the solution to drain. Use the first part of the runnings to rinse out the vessel and return that liquid to the filter cone.
8. After it has fully drained (~30 min.), allow the solution to cool to room temperature before tasting. Take good notes!

As you take notes and then brew with your malts, you'll no doubt realize that the mashed grain character will be different than the final beer character. What's a brewer to do? First, realize that while the sweetness levels will change, the high notes of the beer—the toast levels, the malt breadiness or grassiness, roasted tones, etc.—will remain the same, albeit subdued. The real trick is with the sweet malts. What sweetness remains?

If you really want to answer that question, consider throwing the final wort samples into a microwave or saucepan and bring to a brief boil, maybe with a hop pellet for bitterness. Cool, transfer to a fermenting vessel, and pitch with a little bit of dried yeast. Wait two or three days for the wort to finish, crash, and sample. Take a page from Denny and carbonate the beer in a small soda bottle with a carbonator-type cap and some CO_2 (see page 58). Femtobrewing anyone?[2]

An alternate idea: instead of fermenting, mix a little vodka into your boiled and cooled wort. Mix enough vodka to get to around 5% ABV (roughly 15 mL. of 80 proof vodka per 100 mL of wort) and then carbonate that.

Making grain teas

In order to know what various grains are doing to your beer flavor, you can make grain teas and taste them. Of course, fermentation will change the flavor somewhat, but at least you can see where the starting point is. Eventually, you'll be able to extrapolate from the teas to the finished beer flavors. Denny's "Cheap 'n' Easy" grain tea method isn't as sciency as the hot steep method, but it's…well, the clue's in the name.

Cheap 'n' Easy Grain Tea:
- Start by heating 4 fl. oz. (120 mL) of water to about 170°F (77°C) in your microwave.
- Stir in about 1.5 oz. (about 4 tbsp., or 40–50 g) of crushed grain. Let it sit for about 30 minutes. Reheat for about 30 seconds every 10 minutes to maintain the temperature, although you don't have to be exact.

---

2   It's a math joke, micro = 10^{-6}, nano = 10^{-9}, pico = 10^{-12}, femto = 10^{-15}.

- After 30 minutes, put a coffee filter into a strainer and pour your wort through it. Taste the wort and write down your impressions.
- To see what various combinations of grain taste like, simply mix the grains before you do your microwave mash; or make teas from various single grains and blend them.

HOP EVALUATION

Hops are to the modern brewing scene what the development of Technicolor was to film making. Suddenly everything is about the bright colors, so bright they hurt your eyes and drive you mad. But even before this grand period of all things hoppy, hops were still the fundamental spice of beer for a long time (since roughly 800 CE; OK, hops didn't become the primary spice of beer for quite a while after that, but we're not here to talk *gruit* and mystical herb blends, we're here to talk hops).

The Language of Hops

Let's talk the language of hops first before we delve into the evaluation methods. The first thing to understand is that brewers have been trying to define a system to describe their hops for centuries. A favorite means of communicating hop characters (and most flavor characters) has been the use of flavor wheels and spider graphs. The most famous flavor wheel is the UC Davis Wine Aroma Wheel, which allows vintners and tasters to zero in on precise descriptors for their experience. There have been a few attempts to pull the same trick for beer, but it's harder since beer has many different flavor experiences at the same time.

The spider graph (or radar graph) presents a taster with several axes and asks you to evaluate the intensity of sensation along each axis. Get enough tasters together and your graphs can be mathematically manipulated to present a unified theory of organoleptic sensation. In years past, brewers and hop chemists had settled on five primary axes: citrus, floral, fruity, herbal, and hoppy. Spicy and other categories were sometimes included.

With all the new hops that have appeared on the market, all with wildly varying characters, those five descriptors make for a relatively weak communication vehicle. Think about varieties such as the strongly mango/pineapple-infused Citra, Mosaic, and Galaxy, and then compare that to other "fruity" hops like Nelson Sauvin (grapes) and Lemondrop (lemon). Those are some wildly different experiences to capture under the generic term "fruity."

Lots of groups are proposing new language to put a finer point on our hops. The descriptors we've been digging come from a group at the German hop company, Barth-Haas. Georg Drexler and his team worked with a group of aroma-obsessed professionals, a.k.a. perfumers, to flesh out a new vocabulary.[3] The current vocabulary offers the following terms:

---

[3]   Drexler et al., "The Language of Hops: How to Assess Hop Flavor in Hops and Beer," *Master Brewers Association of the Americas Technical Quarterly*, 54, no. 1 (2017), 34–37.

- Floral: elderflower, geranium, jasmine, rose
- Citrus: grapefruit, orange
- Sweet fruits: melon, cherry, peach, mango
- Green fruits: pear, apple, gooseberry, white wine
- Red berries: cassis (blackcurrant), blueberries, raspberries
- Cream caramel: butter, honey, vanilla
- Woody aromatic: tobacco, leather, pine
- Menthol: mint
- Herbal: tarragon, basil, tea,
- Spicy: pepper, anise
- Grassy-hay: green grass, green peppers
- Vegetal: celery, onion, garlic

Evaluating Hops at Home

OK, enough about the language of hops, let's get down to the actual task of tasting them and figuring out just what we want to do. We're still skipping over the SMASH brewing process (we'll get there eventually), so this part is all about the simple things you can do at home to evaluate hops without brewing a whole batch of beer.

Rubbing hops

If you've paid attention to beer commercials over the years, you know brewers love to brag about their trips to hop fields to choose their lots of hops for the year (we're talking regional craft brewers on up to macrobrewers—think Sierra Nevada and Firestone Walker up to AB InBev and MillerCoors). Pictures and videos abound of these trips, with brewers grabbing fistfuls of whole-leaf hops and slapping their hands together and rubbing them gleefully like a mad villain before the hero crashes their scheme. After a brief but vigorous friction party, they open their hands and let the now destroyed hops cascade to the ground. Then, like a huffer turned loose in an aisle of unlocked spray paint cabinets, they take their now sticky paws and cup them around their nose and mouth, breathing deeply to capture the full aroma. By the way, this is an official process—it's the ASBC Hops-2 method. Remember that science is just the documentation of odd behaviors!

What's happening here is fairly straightforward. All of the essential oils and other flavor-impacting chemicals are bound up in the lupulin glands and other structures in the hop cone. When we boil hops, we're depending on the temperature and agitation to extract those compounds and dissolve them into solution. When testers are doing the hop hand jive they're using the friction to smash and volatilize the compounds. It's an imperfect technique, but it does allow you to get a better sense of a hop's character, particularly if there are any potential off-flavors/aromas. Plus, you get to look crazy! (Go wash your hands too, unless you like being a human fly trap.)

Making hop tea

There's a problem with all the rubbing stuff—when's the last time you rubbed the hops in your beer? Rubbing is a fun technique; it gives you a sensory experience that you can translate into beery impact after some experience. Another approach is to make a hop tea. This is exactly what it sounds like: steep your hops in 170–190°F (77–88°C) water for 20 minutes, strain, and sample. We should warn you that drinking hop tea will give you one of the most vile flavor experiences you've ever had, but some people like it! But, if you can get past that, teas can at least give you a way of comparing one hop to another, even if you may not get an absolute idea of what the hop is like. By doing this with several varieties of hops, you can get a bit of an impression on the overall character of the hop—is it sticky, or dank, or clean? How does it compare to another variety? You can also add a bit of the tea to a beer, which will tone it down and place it in context a bit.

We've both had issues with translating the hop tea experience to actual brewing experience. The lack of downward pH adjustment from the malt, the lack of agitation, and other factors come into play. Hop tea doesn't taste the same as using the hops in a beer, but it's an improvement over rubbing, which only gives you an idea of aroma, not flavor. We've used a small amount of malt extract in our hop teas to give a low gravity (~1.010) that provides a more reasonable base for flavor adjustments, but it's still not perfect.

Amanda Benson, who was performing quality control at Deschutes Brewery, wrote a presentation for the World Brewing Congress proposing mixing hot water and hops in a French press and then agitating the mixture for 20 minutes before straining and chilling. The presentation was done in conjunction with others from New Belgium Brewing Company and hop industry notables, Barth-Haas and Hopsteiner. As we write, the process is still undergoing evaluation to verify if the results are repeatable.

Hop teas might be a good use for the stir plate we're about to advocate you tossing. At the very least, hand agitate the wort for a while and you should be good. Do try it with that tiny touch of DME too, we believe it makes a difference. And don't forget those notes!

Dry hopping commercial beer

We'll admit that dry hopping lends characters that are nothing like those you get from rubbing or teas. Makes sense, since the extraction process in dry hopping is all cold side and largely ethanol driven. Since dry hopping really only requires fermented beer, why not just use beer we can buy at the store? We first stumbled on this technique in comments from Anchor Brewing about testing new hop varieties using the cleanest and blandest style of beer out there, the American light lager. You can follow suit or choose your favorite, less-aroma-forward beer to mimic different malt profiles. The process is dead easy and can give you a pretty decent idea of your hop character. Try and find a beer that comes in regular bottles (i.e., crown caps, not screw tops). You'll also need fresh caps and a bottle capper.

DREW: One of my most memorable beer experiences was travelling to Belgium in late 2001. The trip I was on ended up staying for a bit in the town of Poperinge. Pops, as the Brits shorten it, has a long hop history and is home to the Hop Museum (http://www.hopmuseum.be /en) and a big beer and hop festival every three years. I got to witness the big tables full of the year's crop and the strange shuffling, snuffling, judging dance used to pick the winner. Such an incredible experience.

DENNY: The same kind of process happens at Yakima Chief Hops in Yakima, Washington. The 200-pound bales of freshly harvested and dried hops are brought in to YCH for cold storage in their warehouses. When brewers are ready to assess a particular lot of a hop variety, a "cut" is taken from the center of the bale. This is brought into a small wood-paneled room and placed on a table covered with royal blue paper. I'm told that the paper and color are traditional. The brewers then stand around the table rubbing hops and sniffing. The aroma permeates the entire room.

Process:
1. Chill your soon-to-be-altered beer as cold as you can get it without freezing. This will preserve carbonation and protect the beer during the dry hopping process.
2. For each target hop, weigh out roughly 1 gram of pellets. (Or basically sneeze and what falls out of your hand is probably appropriate.)
3. Carefully open the bottle, drop the pellets in, and immediately re-cap. (This may cause a bit of foam to shoot up your nose.)
4. Store in the fridge for 2 weeks or at fermentation temperature for 1 week. When ready, chill, open and decant the beers into a glass, and take your notes.

YEAST EVALUATION

Yeast are our friends that turn the wort we make from grain and hops into the beer that we pour into our glasses. The saying "brewers make wort, yeast makes beer" is literally true. Without yeast all we'd have is a kind of bitter, highly nutritious sugar water. But it seems like a lot of homebrewers don't take the flavor impact of yeast into account when they design a recipe or evaluate beer flavor. As great a thing as yeast does by turning sugar into alcohol, that's only one part of its impact on beer flavor.

The only way you can really evaluate what a yeast will bring to your beer is to brew with it or taste a beer that it has been brewed with. Tasting the yeast itself will tell you even less than you can discern from drinking a hop tea. You may be able to get a bit of a clue by sniffing an open container of liquid yeast, but when you use the yeast there will likely be a lot more going on with it than you can get simply by smelling it. And of course, trying to get an aroma from a packet of dry yeast is more difficult than trying to get Drew to brew a beer without wacky ingredients!

In general, you can think of yeast as having four different flavor profiles. Some yeasts have only one of them, some have more than one. But the flavors you can get from yeast are every bit as important as the flavors from other ingredients. The general yeast flavor profiles are clean, estery and fruity, phenolic and funky/barnyard, and sulfury.

Clean

A "clean" yeast is one that adds little of its own flavor profile to a beer, but lets the other ingredients come through and clearly express themselves. Many brewers have a general disdain for clean yeast, saying that it's boring. But there are times when you want the malt and hops to "speak" and the yeast needs to stay in the background in order to do that. Some examples of the classic clean yeast strains are generally considered to be Wyeast 1056 American Ale yeast, White Labs WLP001 California Ale yeast, and Safale US-05. The Safale US-05 strain is one of those yeasts that can have a dual character, developing some low-level peach esters at lower fermentation temperatures (generally regarded as below 68°F/20°C). Conversely, Wyeast 1007 German Ale yeast is very clean at temperatures as low as 55°F (13°C), but can give a slight fruitiness if fermented at temperatures above 65°F (18°C).

Other yeast strains in the "clean but not quite" category are Safale S-04 English ale yeast (bready phenolics and a very slight fruit character) and Wyeast 1098 British Ale, which can have fruity esters to a greater or lesser extent depending on fermentation temperature and wort composition.

The great thing about using a clean yeast is that you don't have to take its flavor effects into account when designing a recipe. You can concentrate on the malt and hop flavors and know that the yeast will accentuate those without adding flavors of its own. There are even clean yeasts that have no flavor impact but can accentuate mouthfeel, like Wyeast 1450 Denny's Favorite 50 Ale (what, you thought we weren't gonna mention that one?)

Estery and Fruity

If you've ever had one of your beers judged and looked at the resulting score sheet, you'll be familiar with the phrase "fruity esters." It's kind of a redundant phrase because most esters are reminiscent of fruit, although some esters can be solventlike. The general flavors and aromas produced by estery yeast are things like banana, apple, pear, rose, plum, raisin, and honey, although esters are not limited to those. Hefeweizen yeast is a classic example of an estery yeast. Wyeast 3068 Weihenstephan Weizen, White Labs WLP300 Hefeweizen Ale, and Safale WB-06 all produce the classic banana ester that hefeweizen is noted for. These yeasts also produce some clove phenolics, so they fall into a kind of hybrid area.

British and Belgian yeasts are well known for their fruity character, and this can be controlled to some extent by fermentation temperature. These strains can be less fruity if fermented at lower temperature (58–63°F/14.5–17°C) and more fruity if fermented at temperatures higher than the mid-60s Fahrenheit (>18°C). In addition, most Belgian yeasts will also have a phenolic component to them than can be emphasized by elevated temperatures.

Phenolic

When homebrewers think of phenols in their beer, it's all too often in the context of chlorophenols, those nasty plastic and Band-Aid flavors that can occur from using water that hasn't had the chlorine removed. But there are good phenols too—the ones responsible for clove and smoke flavors and aromas, to name a couple. Phenolic yeast strains are also responsible for the spicy flavor in beers like saison, or the "barnyard" flavor in beers made with *Brettanomyces*. Phenols have a chemical makeup that's similar to alcohols, but they are not alcohols. Phenols are more acidic than alcohol and can bring a "sharpness" to a beer's flavor.

Maybe the most classic example of good phenols in beer is German hefeweizen. Hefeweizen yeast converts the ferulic acid in malt into 4-vinylguaiacol, which smells like cloves. Although you may get this in other types of beer if you use a hefeweizen yeast, it's emphasized in wheat beers because wheat contains much more ferulic acid than barley. Many brewers enhance this by doing a mash rest at 110°F (43°C), which will increase ferulic acid production and availability.

Many homebrewers think that a Scotch ale ("wee heavy") should be made with peated malt because they detect a slight smokiness in commercial examples. In truth, that comes from phenols created by the yeast rather than a smoked malt. Please don't use peat malt for your beers, leave it for the whisky makers.

The best examples of yeast strains that are both phenolic and fruity come from Belgian yeasts. The Trappist breweries seem to have a way of combining both characteristics in a beer. Yeast strains from Westmalle and Rochefort exhibit restrained esters and increased phenolics when fermented at lower temperatures, in the range of 60–63°F (15.5–17°C). Above that temperature the profile reverses, with the esters becoming more prominent. The phenols are still there, but the increased esters become the major focus of the flavor.

Sulfury

Sulfury character can come from several yeast strains, but primarily from lager yeast. All beers, no matter what the yeast, produce some amount of hydrogen sulfide during fermentation as a result of processing sulfate. Hydrogen sulfide is the compound responsible for "rotten egg" sulfury aromas. Because ale yeast ferments at a higher temperature and is therefore more active, the hydrogen sulfide gets blown out with the carbon dioxide as the beer ferments. Lager yeasts, on the other hand, not only produce more hydrogen sulfide originally, but because of the less vigorous fermentation less of it gets removed during fermentation.

American and Mexican lager yeast strains generally seem to produce less sulfury flavors than Continental versions. Strains like Wyeast 2124 and 2247, White Labs WLP835 and -838, and Fermentis Saflager W-34/70 will produce detectable sulfur to some extent. A bit of sulfur is usually thought of as the mark of a Continental lager, so if you're making a lager recipe you should take that into account. You may be able to limit hydrogen sulfide production through the use of yeast nutrient. Although barley has pretty much all the nutrients needed for beer fermentation, it can be lacking in zinc or nitrogen. Adding a bit of yeast nutrient can make up for this, which makes for a cleaner fermentation with less hydrogen sulfide.

LEARNING THROUGH DRINKING

Why wasn't school like this? Sounds like not too bad an idea, huh? Actually, one of the best, easiest, and most enjoyable ways to learn about flavors is to sample beer while you read a description of the beer you're drinking. The writer will guide you through the flavors of the beer while you sip and analyze, trying to find those flavors in your glass.

Two of Denny's favorite pieces of writing to use for this are the BJCP's *Beer Style Guidelines* and Michael Jackson's book, *New World Guide to Beer*.[4] Both describe beer flavors using terms that are both approachable and educational (well, Jackson can get a bit flowery, but it's kinda fun). You'll learn about the flavors of a particular beer (Jackson) or style (BJCP) in a way that will help you not only appreciate the flavors but as a way to describe them.

Start by looking through the literature and picking out a couple of beers that sound good to you. Jackson will call out specific beers, while the BJCP guidelines will have a listing of commercial examples of a particular style. Sit down in a quiet room with the beers and books. And please, no smoking! You may enjoy the experience of a cigar with your beer, but that's not the objective here. We want the beer to come through on its own.

Start by doing three short "drive-bys." Move the glass from side to side under your nose while you inhale the aroma. If you have trouble picking up the aroma, try this trick to clear your sense of smell…sniff your shirtsleeve. NOT your armpit! Then go back and do the drive-bys again. You should have a better sense of the aroma at this point. Read the beer description and try to find what the writer says is in the aroma. This method of sticking the beer right under your nose to sense aroma is called *orthonasal olfaction* (directly inhaling aromas through your nose).

Next, take a sip of the beer. Suck in a bit of air along with the beer to aspirate it, which will kind of spray beer all over your palate. You can also swish the beer around in your mouth. At this point, you want to exhale. As we're all well aware, flavor comes mainly from aroma. Exhaling after tasting the beer directs the aroma up and out through your nose, which is called *retronasal olfaction* ("backwards nose") because you're exhaling the aroma rather than inhaling it.

The beer warms while it's in your mouth, releasing more volatile aromas. Coating your mouth with the beer by aspiration or swishing helps disperse those aromas and make them more easily identifiable. Once more, read the beer description while you do this. Do you taste the same flavors? Something different?

Finally, think about how the beer hits different parts of your palate. Think about the flavor on the tip of your tongue, the mid palate, and the finish. Bitter up front, malty mid palate, and a dry finish with lingering notes of tropical fruit? This kind of analysis may make you feel like a pretentious geek, but in truth it's exactly the way you should think about how flavor evolves over the course of a sip of beer. Take another look at your reading material to see what the authors have to say.

And, hey, competition brewers, may we suggest you do the same thing with your returned score sheets? It's tempting to read a judge's comments in the blind and think they're full of it, but sit with your beer and read the comments. Then you can see where you agree and where you disagree, giving you a better insight into what appeared before those poor abused palates.

DREW: This may sound like a joke, but "drink the beer" is seriously one of the best things you can do to learn the nature of beer, and who knows what road it will set you on. I already had a fair love of saisons before studying for the BJCP exam, but one night, sitting quietly with a fellow student, we cracked open a bottle of Fantôme. We poured the incredibly lively and mousse-like beer into our glasses and were amazed at the "pop" the beer had on our tongues. The beer just vanished in an explosion of carbon dioxide, leaving behind these funky, fruity spice sensations. That experience is what inspired my travels to Belgium and my eventual deep dive into the world of saison. But enough about saison—here follows a beer that shows the lessons that I learned by paying attention to my flavors! (And, boy, is this a big 'un).

4   Beer Judge Certification Program, *2015 Beer Style Guidelines*, http://www.bjcp.org/style/2015/beer; Jackson, *The New World Guide to Beer* (Running Press, 1988).

Little Man Barleywine

Batch size: 5.5 gal. (21 L)
Original gravity: 1.112 (26.4°P)
Final gravity: 1.022 (5.6°P)

Color: 19 SRM
Bitterness: 42 IBU
ABV: 13.4%

Malt
- 20 lb. (9 kg) Maris Otter pale ale malt
- 1 lb. (450 g) Simpsons Double Roasted Crystal 100–120°L
- 1 lb. (450 g) dark brown sugar (strong molasses character preferred)

Hops
- 2 oz. (56 g) Target 8.8% AA @ 60 min. (substitute in Magnum or Warrior)
- 1 oz. (28 g) Progress 6.3% AA @ 0 min.

Yeast
- WLP099 San Diego Super Yeast, WLP028 Edinburgh, or Wyeast 1728 Scottish Ale

Brewing notes
- Mash and rest for 60 minutes at 150°F (66°C).
- Boil for 90 minutes.
- Add hops as scheduled.
- Chill and pitch yeast.
- Ferment at 65–68°F (18–20°C) until done.

Bourbon Barrel Blackberry Bhut Jolokia Barleywine

Batch size: 5.5 gal. (21 L)
Original gravity: 1.112 (26.4°P)
Final gravity: 1.022 (5.6°P)

Color: 19 SRM
Bitterness: 42 IBU
ABV: 13.4%

What, now? We did promise.

Notes
- Brew the Little Man Barleywine, and decide to lose your ever-loving mind.
- Soak 2 oz. (56 g) of oak cubes (American oak, medium toast) in a pint of bourbon for 2–4 weeks.
- As primary fermentation slows, add 5 lb. (2.27 kg) of frozen blackberries to the fermentor and allow to ferment out for about one week.
- Transfer the beer to a secondary fermentor (or keg) onto the bourbon-soaked oak cubes. Age for 2–4 weeks. When the beer approaches your desired oakiness, add 1 Bhut jolokia (a.k.a. ghost pepper) to the fermentor. Age one more week and keg it.
- Carbonate and trust in your favorite deity to preserve you as you drink it.

SIMPLE BEER

OK, so the BBBBJBW is way out there, but you still need a beer to get your basic flavors on. We'll talk more about SMASH beers in the next chapter but, for now, here's your most basic beer that will help you learn all you need to know about your malt, hops, and yeast. ■

RECIPE

Simpler Times

Batch size: 5.5 gal. (21 L)
Original gravity: 1.051 (12.6°P)
Final gravity: 1.012 (3.1°P)

Color: 3–5 SRM
Bitterness: 26 IBU
ABV: 5.2%

Malt
- 11 lb. (5 kg) base malt (Pilsner, pale, Munich)

Hops
- 0.5 oz. (14 g) Warrior 15% AA @ 60 min.
- 1.0 oz. (28 g) "exploratory" hop of choice @ 0 min.

Yeast
- Dealer's choice, but a neutral yeast like Wyeast 1056, WLP001, or Safale US-05 will let you explore your ingredients.

Brewing notes
- Single infusion mash @ 152°F (67°C).
- Make a beer, change your ingredients around—slowly—and compare the differences. That's how you learn!

7
SIMPLE RECIPE DESIGN

It seems like once most homebrewers get a handle on the basic brewing process, the next thing they want to tackle is designing their own recipes. Sometimes even before they totally understand how brewing works! There's a feeling of freedom, a sense of "hey, don't tell me what to brew" that appeals to a homebrewer's independent spirit and makes them feel like they *need* to do their own thing. And that's totally understandable. We all have our own tastes, and homebrewers are an adventurous lot. But, all too often, that spirit can get them in trouble unless they start with a basic understanding of the flavors that various ingredients bring to a beer and how the brewing process affects them. They (we!) just start randomly throwing things together to see what will happen. Sometimes it works, sometimes it doesn't. We're going to show you how to improve those odds and make recipe design work in your favor.

> "With careful observation and some experimentation, you can take what you learn at each stage and put it all together to design recipes that really reflect your tastes."

EVOLUTION OF A HOMEBREWER

As a homebrewer, you will probably go through several stages in the hobby. Each stage presents you with different opportunities to learn about ingredients and how they got together. With careful observation and some experimentation, you can take what you learn at each stage and put it all together to design recipes that really reflect your tastes. And even better, you can make damn good beer! So, let's take a look at the typical evolution of a homebrewer. You may have taken some of these steps in a different order, or skipped over a few, or ended up in a different place, but we're sure you'll see some common ground here.

Stage 1: Extract Recipe Kits

Most homebrewers we know start by buying a recipe kit that includes the ingredients you need to make a specific beer. This frees you from having to actually do the recipe design yourself so you can concentrate on the brewing processes and final flavor of your beer. You can make some great beer from extract if your process is good and you start with fresh ingredients.

You can begin getting an idea of what various extracts taste like at this stage of your homebrewing career. In the chapter 6, we talked about understanding how flavors relate to ingredients, and building your own flavor database by separately evaluating malts and hops. Well, you can do something similar with extract kits, but please be aware that anything other than the very lightest extract may very well have more than one grain in it. This makes it difficult to learn the exact flavor of a specific grain, but at least you can compare the flavors you get from various extracts.

For example, an extract labeled "light" may have only Pilsner or pale malt in it, so that's an easy one. But a "gold" extract may have crystal or Munich malt in it. A "dark" extract may have chocolate malt or roasted barley in it to give it a dark color and specific flavor. A rye extract that Denny has used has pale malt, rye malt, and crystal malt in it, practically an entire recipe just in the extract!

As you can see, you may have to extrapolate a bit to determine what the source of each flavor is in an extract beer. Learn the flavors of the extracts available to you; see what differences are imparted by the inclusion of specialty malts, like you might find in the examples above. A big help in this regard is looking up the composition of the extract on the manufacturer's website. By comparing ingredients in different extracts, you can start figuring out what it is that makes one extract taste different from another.

Many extract kits also come with grains that you steep or use in a minimash. Taste a few pieces of the various grains before you steep them and taste the resulting wort after you steep them. That will give you a great way to identify the flavors that those grains will bring to your beer.

Make sure to smell the hops that are included with the kit. Do they smell like tropical fruit? Do they smell like citrus fruit? Do they smell like pine, or flowers, or earth? Do they smell like cheese? (Pro tip: if they smell like cheese, don't use them! That's a classic sign of old hops. These days we have better access to better ingredients, don't waste your brew time with bad ingredients! Although, if you really want to get every cent's worth from your ingredients, you could let them age more and use them for *lambic* or sour beer.) All of those descriptors and more can be applied to hop aromas and flavors. You won't be able to tell much about the exact flavor or quality of bitterness until you actually brew with them, but these first impressions can be really helpful when establishing your flavor database.

And finally, take notes! We're saying that here, but it applies to most of the stuff in this book. Don't trust your memory (especially if you're anywhere near Denny's age). Write down what the grain or wort tastes like to you. Write down your impressions of hop aromas. And when you taste the finished beer, write down your overall impressions about its flavor and what you think each ingredient may have contributed to the overall flavor and aroma of your beer. Next time you drink a commercial beer, pull out those notes and see if you can identify what grain and hops might have been used in the beer. It's educational and it's fun … how many times have you been able to drink beer educationally?

If you intend to stick with extract, a lot of your research is done at this point. But for a lot of homebrewers extract is just the starting point. For them, the next step is all-grain kits.

Stage 2: All-Grain Recipe Kits

Like extract kits, these let you concentrate on the process and learn about ingredients by using a tried and true recipe from someone else. But in an all-grain kit, all the ingredients that might have been together to make an extract are discrete components. This gives the brewer the ability to learn what each of those pieces tastes like and what they each bring to the beer. And while you can make great beer with extracts, there's nothing like the control over beer flavor that you get by choosing an exact ingredient flavor rather than trying to deal with someone else's ideas.

Using the experience you gained from evaluating extract kits, start evaluating each component of an all-grain kit. Taste the various grains. If they're not all mixed together before you get them, you'll have a chance to taste all of the components. Even if all the different grains come in the same bag, try the mixture to see if you can get an idea of where things will go.

Stage 3: Brewing Other People's Recipes

Working from a recipe someone has already designed is kind of like using a kit, in that the recipe is already done for you. Brewing someone else's tried and true recipe allows you to concentrate more on process than the recipe itself. But what you can do is analyze these recipes and try to figure out what the author of the recipe was thinking (or wasn't thinking!) when they included each ingredient.

You will also have access to a much wider range of recipes than you might be able to find with kits alone. But, you will also be on your own when it comes to sourcing ingredients. That can be a real learning experience, since each maltster will have a slightly different take on how a particular malt is produced and how it should taste. You'll soon learn that not all base malts taste the same, and that British and American crystal/caramel malts vary from each other in flavor.

Now, when you start looking at other people's recipes, one of the first things you'll want to do is change something, we can pretty much guarantee it! But please, do yourself a favor and brew the recipe exactly as written the first time you brew it. How do you know what you want to change unless you know where you're starting?

DENNY: I *know* the above is true because I've been guilty of it too many times! Here are some of my examples.

Mash hopping is a technique that's used by some brewers where hops are included in the mash. Yeah, I know, it sounded crazy to me too, but they do it anyway. One time I was getting ready to brew Mike "Tasty" McDole's famous Janet's Brown recipe, which calls for mash hopping. I asked Mike if the mash hops were really necessary, because my previous experience with mash hopping led me to think that it really didn't add anything to the beer. His reply? "I've never done it without, so I don't know." OK, I used the mash hops and then made another batch without them in order to test my theory. I couldn't tell the difference, so I haven't used them in that recipe since.

The second example involves ingredient substitution. Some years back, the AHA chose Scott Abene's "Gennesee My Butt" cream ale recipe as the recipe for the yearly Big Brew day. I didn't have the temperature control to brew lagers at that point, and I didn't have some of the hops that were called for. I emailed Scott and asked him about using an ale yeast and different hops. His reply was very gracious, but reading between the lines it basically came to "sure, but you'll be brewing a different beer." Scott was right—the beer was OK, but it wasn't even in the ballpark of what he'd intended.

Coming from the other side, I often get questions about my much-brewed Rye IPA recipe, asking me about using different hops or changing up the grist bill. My reply, which I try to make as gracious as Scott's, is always, "Do what sounds good to you, but please brew it once as is." Usually I hear back that they've decided not to make any changes at all, which I take as a great compliment. But even if they change it, at least they know where they're starting from and what needs to be changed to suit their own tastes.

DREW: On the other hand, I can't brew or cook a straight recipe without adding my own spin. I recognize that I'm not brewing a perfect clone of this person's beer or that style, but it doesn't bother me—I'm playing. I will say, however, that when you go to make changes, do so with open eyes and a judicious mind. Yeah, I'm not a cloning fanatic, this much is known.

Let's be doubly honest, I tend to goof off because I know my ingredients pretty well. Then again, I taught myself to cook by assembling some of the most godawful creations known to mankind before I eventually learned to follow a recipe. My early efforts were the same random acts of combining ingredients that we see with a lot of new homebrewers. Fortunately, none were as bad as my college roommate's "sandwiches" of white bread, cherry Kool-Aid powder, butter, sugar, and maraschino cherries.

Stage 4: Your Own Recipes

This is what you've been working toward! Whether extract or all-grain, it's time to put all that knowledge to use and create your own recipe—something that's completely yours, something that represents your style and tastes. But is it really all yours?

It's been said that all music has already been written because there are only 12 notes in a scale (at least in Western music). There are a lot of ways you can arrange those notes, but, ultimately, it's a finite limit. Many people say that limit has been reached and all the arrangements possible have already happened. So, any music written now is simply rewriting what's gone before. It's not that farfetched a proposition.

Think of those musical notes as the ingredients you can use to make beer. There are infinite combinations of ingredients that make up a finished beer, but most beers use some variation of the same ingredients. For instance, we know that a hefeweizen will have wheat in it, that a Belgian tripel will have Pilsner malt. So, when we formulate a recipe for beer, we're drawing on a style that's gone before.

Heck, even something as weird as clam chowder saison begins with a saison base. And there's another parallel with music: even if there is a finite number of arrangements for those 12 notes, there are other things you can do to make music seem new and fresh. You can use odd meters, change the tempo, or put in a key change at a crucial moment. The same holds true of beer: you might start with a tried and true set of ingredients (a saison) but throw in some surprises (clam juice, potatoes, herbs) that make it different than what's gone before. Hopefully in a *good* way!

The point of that ramble is to take what's gone before you into account when you make a new recipe. Sure, you may have an idea that you think is going to make a great beer, but the best way to realize that idea usually involves considering what has gone before and drawing on that. Just as there is very little totally unique music, there's also very little totally unique beer. Everything is a variation of what's come before and that's not a bad thing.

In order to help you think through what your original beer recipe will be like, it helps to be aware of the basic approachs to recipe design. Denny and Drew have distinctly different ways to go about it, but both ways are perfectly valid. So, let's take a look.

THE PHILOSOPHY OF RECIPE DESIGN

There are a few basic ways to approach designing a recipe, and a number of thematic variations that fall under those. None of these basic approaches is necessarily better than the other, although some of the variant methods can be kind of dicey. As you read through these, try to find yourself described in one method or another. Then think about if you're happy with the method you're using, or if you think you might be able to incorporate some parts of other methods.

The usual method of recipe design is to think about what you want to make and what you have on hand. You open your recipe software, add a little of this, a little of that, and, hey, the numbers look right! You brew the beer, taste it, and wonder why it isn't what you thought it would be. I mean, five pounds of brown malt gave it just the color I wanted; unfortunately, the flavor... So, you say a prayer, tweak the recipe, and try it again.

The usual pitfall of this method is that you use too much stuff, or you lack understanding of your ingredients (see the beginning of this chapter!), your

DREW: I love how much the clam chowder saison freaks everyone out. Seriously though, without the clams it was really just an herb-infused saison with one alternative adjunct—the potatoes (dried, instant potatoes with no powdered milk or butter).

processes, or even the beer style itself. The biggest pitfall may be that you don't have a clear idea of what you want the beer to be, so you toss stuff in randomly. (But learning through making mistakes can be valuable too!)

When you start to think about a recipe, you can either start with the ingredients you want to use, or you can start by deciding on what the final beer will taste like and how you get there. The first approach is what we call "bottom-up" recipe design and the second is "top-down" design.

Bottom-Up Recipe Design

The bottom-up approach is to look at the ingredients you have or want to use and come up with a recipe using those ingredients. You look through your grain bins or around your kitchen, see some stuff that looks interesting, and start thinking about how those would work in a beer. Sure, you no doubt put some thought into what the beer will taste like, but your motivation comes from the component parts of the beer.

Within the bottom-up approach, there are a few different methods you use as a way to create your recipe. Some of them are more likely to create a great beer than others.

What have I got?

This isn't as much an approach to recipe design as it is housekeeping! You look through your grain supply and decide how much of it you want to toss into a beer. The goal is to use up the stuff you've got (hey, I don't want it to go bad) and creating a great beer is secondary to the pecuniary aspects. It may work or it may not … are you feeling lucky? (Read that with a Clint Eastwood voice.)

More is better

OK, raise your hand if you've done this. And if you didn't raise your hand, you may want to avoid taking lie detector tests! If we're honest, I think we all recognize ourselves here at one time or another. It goes like this … I'll start with pale malt as a base, just because. Then I'll add some Vienna malt for depth, and some melanoidin for richness. I need wheat for head formation and, of course, Carapils for body. Every recipe I see has crystal 60 in it, so I'll add some of that. Maybe some brown malt for color, and, hey, I like Munich malt! I'll use seven different hop varieties for complexity and age it in a Hungarian goulash barrel because I can.

Seriously! We know the rule, "All things in moderation," right? It's a good rule to pay attention to lest you fall prey to the confused and muddy flavors that result from an exuberant hand with the ingredients.

But you don't have to artificially limit yourself either. For example, some brewers say, "I won't use crystal malt," or limit themselves to using only a certain amount of crystal malt, or a certain color of it. Why would you do that? OK, we get that some people may not like the flavors of certain things, but to limit yourself based on an arbitrary "rule" just doesn't make sense. Use whatever it takes to get the results you want to achieve. But you do have to know why every ingredient is there. If you can't imagine or justify the contribution of a certain ingredient, leave it out.

Top-Down Recipe Design

Physics would seem to dictate that if there's a bottom-up way to develop recipes, there's got to be a top-down way too. And what do you know, there is! In the top-down approach you begin with the flavor profile of the beer you're going for and then figure out how to get there. There are two different methods within the top-down approach to recipe design.

Tweaking another recipe.

For the tweaking another recipe method, you start with a recipe and then adjust it to fit your own tastes. Assuming that you know your ingredient flavors (see how we keep coming back to that) and you start with a solid recipe, this can be a great way to develop a beer that fits you while doing some learning at the same time. The key is that you change only one thing at a time and are OK with repeated brewing to get to your destination. This is the method that Denny used to come up with his well-known and often brewed Rye IPA recipe. It began as a "normal" IPA recipe from a magazine. Denny began wondering what would happen if he replaced part of the pale malt in the recipe with some rye malt. He brewed four or five test batches with varying amounts of rye until he came up with what tasted right. Then he began playing with hop combinations, first replacing only one of the two hops varieties that were in the original recipe. After doing that for a batch, Denny decided that he had hit a combination that he really liked. Then he went back to malt, playing with amounts of crystal malt for a few batches. Along the way, he ran across the yeast that eventually became Wyeast 1450 Denny's Favorite 50 Ale and decided he loved the silky mouthfeel it left in the beer. But that mouthfeel also changed the perception of the malt and hops, so he went back to adjusting malt percentages and bittering hop amounts. That took another three to four batches. Finally, Denny thought he had it right. That was confirmed when his wife gave the beer her seal of approval. He then brewed three more test batches to be sure he had it and it was repeatable.

Drew and many other homebrewers would find this anathema. Many homebrewers feel like there are so many beers to brew and so many ingredients to use that they just can't deal with the concept of brewing the same beer many times over. And that's OK, we get it. It's simply one way to approach recipe design and homebrewing in general. But for Denny, it's interesting to assess the tiny changes and see what another tweak will bring. He's weird like that.

DREW: Now this is one thing I will partially disagree on. I think there are sometimes valid reasons to place arbitrary restrictions on your recipe designs and hey what do you know, we have a few of those that exist, both of which are perfect examples of simplicity, but we'll get there in a moment.

DENNY: But that's kind of a different situation. In Drew's examples in "Recipe Templates," you still have an idea of what the ingredients are going to do even if you limit yourself to only one or a few ingredients. Bottom line is that there are many roads to the same destination.

DREW: It's OK to be a bit weird. We wouldn't love Denny if he wasn't and people wouldn't know what to do with me if I wasn't so aggressively nerdy.

The roadmap

The roadmap method takes a different tack to top-down recipe design. As the old saying goes, "If you don't know where you're going, how do you know when you get there?" Tweaking another recipe is a journey of exploration, as you go along you constantly assess where you are and where you need to go next. With the roadmap approach, you start by deciding where you're going and then figure out how to get there, like plotting a route on a map. It still involves repeated brewing after assessing your results, but it's a little more direct.

The roadmap method is the way Denny came up with his Bourbon Vanilla Imperial Porter recipe. He and his wife were discussing what beer he could brew as a Christmas gift for friends. Denny wanted to barrel age something, but there wasn't time before Christmas; and anyway, he didn't have a barrel! He decided on a dark beer like porter or stout, since it seemed to fit the season. He thought about the flavors that might come from a bourbon barrel and decided on bourbon (duh!) and vanilla (oak is often said to give beer a bit of vanilla flavor). Denny set about brewing a test batch of the base imperial porter. It took two or three tries before he nailed what he was going for. After adding the vanilla beans and bourbon, the beer seemed a bit too sweet, so Denny went back for another test batch or two in order to figure out how much to increase the bittering in order to compensate for the perceived sweetness of the vanilla.

You can see that this beer took fewer test batches than the Rye IPA because this time Denny at least had some clue about how he wanted the beer to taste. That's the advantage of the roadmap method, you have a pretty good idea what the destination is so all you have to do is figure out the road to take to get there.

EVERY BEER TELLS A STORY

Once you have some experience under your belt, you can expand on the basic approach to recipe design and incorporate other themes. Making a beer that tells a story is Drew's primary approach, and if you've done your homework learning about ingredients, processes, and styles it can be very effective. Drew likes to design beers around events or parts of his life. That's how the recipe for Saison Guacamole came about. Drew was looking around his backyard near Los Angeles and saw an avocado tree, tomato and cilantro plants, and other guacamole ingredients—he thought of the romantic (a nice way of saying "questionable") story of farmhouse ales being brewed with whatever ingredients were available on the farm and decided he'd take a cue from that.

Another classic "story" beer of Drew's is his Cookie Celebration Ale. The story for that one is that Drew's favorite dog, the aptly named Cookie, was part corgi and unfortunately inherited the breed's tendency to have bad backs. One day Cookie went down paralyzed and was rushed to have spinal surgery. When she finally could walk again Drew immediately put forth a plan to brew a beer to celebrate, and what better way than to make one that tasted like his favorite culinary cookie, oatmeal raisin. The recipe design was pretty straightforward:

toasty notes, brown sugar and cinnamon tones, raisin flavors, and such slick oat characters.

Other stories come to mind, like remembering how Drew got into college. His institute required an essay on any subject you wanted to write about regarding science. Even at 17 (possibly especially at 17), Drew couldn't resist being a smart-ass. He wrote his entrance essay attempting to argue that Marshmallow Fluff was a fundamental element of the universe. It was everything you'd expect from a kid who grew up eating Fluffernutter sandwiches. So, thinking about the classic Massachusetts staple made Drew wonder… what would that look like in beer form? Here we go.

RECIPE

Cosmic Fluff

Batch size: 5.0 gal. (19 L)
Original gravity: 1.064 (15.7°P)
Final gravity: 1.015 (3.8°P)

Color: 10 SRM
Bitterness: 14 IBU
ABV: 7%

Malt
- 6 lb. (2.7 kg) pale ale malt
- 4 lb. (1.8 kg) Munich malt
- 2 lb. (910 g) Golden Naked Oats®
- 0.5 lb. (225 g) biscuit malt
- 0.5 lb. (225 g) crystal 55°L

Mash
- Single infusion mash for 60 minutes at 154°F (68°C).

Hops
- 0.25 oz. (7 g) Magnum 14% AA @ 60 min.

Yeast
- Wyeast 1275 Thames Valley Ale

Extras
- 0.5 lb. (225 g) lactose, added to the boil
- 12 oz. (340 g) PB2® peanut butter powder (defatted), blended with 6 fl. oz. (180 mL) of 150 proof spirit for one week
- 0.5 oz. (14 g) vanilla extract

Brewing notes
- Add PB2 solution and vanilla extract to the keg and let sit for 1–3 weeks before transferring to a new keg (gotta get it off the peanut butter sludge!).

You'll notice that there are a few things going on with the Cosmic Fluff recipe. There's a clear focus on generating baked toast notes (the Munich and biscuit malts) and the oats lend chewiness/nuttiness; the sweet crystal malt provides the sugar of the jam and the yeast gives the fruit. Every ingredient in an otherwise complex recipe has a point and still retains focus.

SINGLE MALT AND SINGLE HOP (SMASH)

We really wouldn't be able to write a book about simplicity without talking SMASH at some point. The term was coined a few years back on HomeBrewTalk. com (https://www.homebrewtalk.com) to describe a simple way of exploring ingredients. The idea is simple: choose one base malt and one hop variety to give you a clean base to focus on what the tested ingredient lends to your beer. Now, in the American way of brewing, that's mostly turned into an excuse for trying different hop varieties in a never-ending parade of single-hopped pales and IPAs; even commercial breweries have gotten in on the action with hop exploration beer series. Both of us think that the whole SMASH pale ale trend is a bit tired and, well, rather weak tea when you stop and try one. Plus, the focus on trying all these different hop types misses out on the wonderful world of yeast and malt. The power of SMASH is its simplicity of execution and ease of understanding. The downside, at least the way it normally gets employed, is the dull and uninteresting beers it produces when all the focus is on hops.

We recommend that, instead of learning your hops via brewing a rather boring pale ale, you try the methods in chapter 6. Also, bear in mind that a great many of the world's classic beer styles are already very simple: take Pilsner, with its focus on a single malt and relatively sparse selection of hop varietals; and the classic English barleywine is really nothing more than filling your mash tun with water and enough pale ale malt that it groans. Just the runoff from a classic barleywine will be rich and decadent enough for a king or a queen.

Applied judiciously, restriction can be a powerful tool. So many beers, both commercial and homemade, suffer from an exuberance of ingredients, a free hand with the malt choices and 29 hop types per beer. With so much competition for your brain's relatively limited sensory processing power, the experience falls flat. Remember back to chapter 2 and Drew's horrific culinary creations? He would have been served far better with a little guidance and a little direction.

SMASH provides very easy direction, but boring results. How about if we open things up, just a bit? Instead of just one malt, how about one base malt, one character malt, one sugar, one bittering hop? You still need to focus, but the beer gets more room to play. This is one of Drew's primary ways of formulating a recipe. Even though he tends to stray from it, the straying is done with a purpose; for instance, blending Maris Otter pale ale malt with US domestic two-row for his IPAs and pale ales gives an extra oomph to his base note.

Choosing Hops

OK, we talked a lot about basic recipe design—top up, sideways forward, use only one thing or the other—but let's take a moment to think about hop varieties. When we first got brewing, there were a few dozen types of hops on the market, more if you got lucky and could find top-notch imported hops. The older hops were mostly meant to maximize bittering potential, often at the expense of finer aromas and flavors. This was mostly to satisfy the needs of the bigger brewers who just wanted a cheap source of alpha acids to dump into their vats, flavor and aroma qualities be damned. In fact, US hops had a global reputation for being pugnacious, even way back in the 1800s. But

DREW: Another good strategy is Munich with two-row. I know some folks love an all-Munich malt IPA, but I find it too much, it's too intense.

DENNY: This is hard for me to grok. Drew likes to bump up the malt background in his beers by using Maris Otter, which I find too much for most American styles. Yet he eschews the use of Munich because it bumps up the malt background! This shows two things...One, Drew is a seriously conflicted individual. Two, learn your ingredients, find out what YOU like, and stick with it!

SUBSTITUTING HOPS

Sometimes you won't be able to find the hops listed in a recipe. Usually, the variety might be available, but the alpha acid content (% AA) will be different. We'll cover substituting one variety of hop for another later, but there's an easy way to adjust the amount of hops you used based on the percentage AA. The concept is called homebrew bittering units, or HBU for short. In a nutshell, you multiply the weight of the hops (in ounces) by the percent AA to come up with how many HBUs they contribute to the beer. By knowing the percent AA of the substitute hops, you can calculate how much to use to achieve the same HBU level.

Here's how it works. Suppose your recipe calls for 2 oz. of 5% AA hops.

$$\text{weight of hop addition in oz.} \times \% \text{ AA} = \text{HBU}$$

$$2 \text{ oz.} \times 5 = 10 \text{ HBU}$$

But the hops of the same variety that you can find are 7% AA. No problem! Since you know 10 HBU is your target, you simply divide 10 by 7 to get the amount to use

$$10 \text{ HBU} = x \text{ oz.} \times 7$$

$$10 \text{ HBU}/7 = x \text{ oz.}$$

$$= 1.42 \text{ oz.}$$

You can round 1.42 up to 1.5 oz. Hey, close enough for homebrew!

with the launch of newer hop varieties like Amarillo and Simcoe, leading to the currently very chic Galaxy and Mosaic, the purpose of hops has shifted away from bestowing a purely bitter punch to now yielding higher and higher quantities of aromatic oils.

That's all well and good, but we both feel these new hops, even at high alpha acid levels, leave a lot to be desired in terms of their bite. This impacts your beers in two different ways. The first impact you'll come across when trying to hit your desired bitterness level is that you end up increasing the hops to the point where the amount of vegetation and the amount of oil becomes detrimental to your beer quality.

The second impact is that we don't think these hops go great in that initial strike of IBUs—they muddy the waters. Over the years, Drew, for instance, has settled on a dependable routine: something high alpha, clean and neutral for bittering, and then use your character hops later. Think Magnum or Warrior, two of the cleanest, most potent hops on the market. Want a little more "oomph"? Try adding a touch of Chinook (say, ¼ oz. per 5 gallons) for just a touch of old-school raspiness. We think your hoppy beers will love you for this, or at least Drew will.

Denny, on the other hand, disagrees (we're sure you're surprised). For instance, Magnum is a great bittering hop when you don't want much character from your bittering, but Denny generally prefers hops like Chinook or Columbus for bittering American styles. He thinks those styles need a punch of bitterness that you just can't get from Magnum. His approach is to consider how you want the bitterness to come across and use the hops that will give you what you're looking for.

DREW: Right now the hot thing to do is throw a metric ton of Galaxy and Mosaic in late additions to the kettle (assuming you can find them). While I enjoy the fruit bomb characters of those hops, I find, when added in mass quantities, that many beers end up smelling and tasting of semi-rotten fruit. Don't do this to me!

Hop Balancing

Here's a problem with hops: it's super easy to throw hops around willy-nilly and get IBU numbers that correctly match your target bitterness level, but there's no good way to calculate actual hop impact in terms of flavor. Ray Daniels in *Designing Great Beers*[1] started down the path of trying to figure this out with his BU:GU ratio (i.e., the IBU level compared to your original gravity). In this system, an IPA would want a BU:GU ratio close to 1:1 (e.g., 65 IBUs for a beer starting at 1.065). This is a good start, but it's still all about bitterness.

RECIPE TEMPLATES

OK, this section is a bit of magic, a bit of pulling back the curtain and showing the wizard for what he is. It's also the simplest way of developing a new recipe.

Almost all of our recipes have a sort of "base" or template recipe attached to them. We may not think of them as such, maybe our rules and preferences are so internalized that we just don't realize we're doing it, but it's true. For both of us, I guarantee if you say "pale ale" we'll both start with a template like Template Pale Ale below. Note the malt combination—pale malt, Munich malt, crystal 60°L—and watch what happens when we need an IPA or a double IPA.

RECIPE

Template Pale Ale

Batch volume: 5.5 gal. (21 L)
Original gravity: 1.054 (13.3°P)
Final gravity: 1.012 (3.1°P)

Color: 7 SRM
Bitterness: 32 IBU
ABV: 5.7%

Malt
- 10 lb. (4.54 kg) pale malt
- 1.0 lb. (450 g) Munich malt
- 0.5 lb. (225 g) crystal 60°L

Mash
- Single infusion at 152°F (67°C) for 60 minutes.

Hops
- 0.6 oz. (17 g) Columbus / Tomahawk/Zeus 12% AA @ 60 min.

- 0.6 oz. (17 g) Centennial 7.8% AA @ 10 min.
- 0.6 oz. (17 g) Cascade 4.4% AA @ steeped/whirlpooled for 20 min.
- 1.0 oz. (28 g) Cascade @ dry hop for 2 weeks

Yeast
- Wyeast 1056, White Labs WLP001, or Safale US-05

---

[1]   Daniels, *Designing Great Beers* (Boulder: Brewers Publications, 1996).

Template IPA

Batch volume: 5.5 gal. (21 L)
Original gravity: 1.069 (16.8°P)
Final gravity: 1.014 (3.6°P)

Color: 7.5 SRM
Bitterness: 57 IBU
ABV: 7.0%

Malt
- 13 lb. (5.9 kg) pale malt
- 1.0 lb. (450 g) Munich malt
- 0.5 lb. (225 g) crystal 60°L

Mash
- Single infusion at 152°F (67°C) for 60 minutes.

Hops
- 1.2 oz. (34 g) Columbus / Tomahawk/Zeus 12% AA @ 60 min.
- 1.2 oz. (34 g) Centennial 7.8% AA @ 10 min.
- 1.2 oz. (34 g) Cascade 4.4% AA @ steeped/whirlpooled for 20 min.
- 1.0 oz. (28 g) Cascade @ dry hop for 2 weeks

Yeast
- Wyeast 1056, White Labs WLP001, or Safale US-05

Template DIPA

Batch volume: 5.5 gal. (21 L)
Original gravity: 1.084 (20.2°P)
Final gravity: 1.016 (4.1°P)

Color: 8 SRM
Bitterness: 76 IBU
ABV: 9.2%

Malt
- 14 lb. (6.35 kg) pale malt
- 1.5 lb. (680 g) Munich malt
- 0.5 lb. (225 g) crystal 60°L
- 1.0 lb. (450 g) table sugar

Mash
- Single infusion at 152°F (67°C) for 60 minutes.

Hops
- 1.75 oz. (50 g) Columbus/ Tomahawk/Zeus 12% AA @ 60 min.
- 1.75 oz. (50 g) Centennial 7.8% AA @ 10 min.
- 1.75 oz. (50 g) Cascade 4.4% AA @ steeped/whirlpool for 20 min.
- 2.0 oz. (57 g) Cascade @ dry hop for 2 weeks

Yeast
- Wyeast 1056, White Labs WLP001, or Safale US-05

Did you pay attention to the malt bill? The numbers change, but the basic approach is still there: pale, Munich, and crystal, and a dose of sugar in the case of the double IPA, and then a handful of American hops. In this case, we focused on the classic "C" hops, but you get the idea that you can put in your favorites and be reasonably certain you'll get a decent beer. Now if you want to play with an odd ingredient, say, Red X or Great Western's Sacchra 50 (two malts designed to give brilliant color with minimal roast or sweetness), you know where to start—in this case, swap out the C60.

Template Pilsner

Batch volume: 5.5 gal. (21 L)
Original gravity: 1.050 (12.4°P)
Final gravity: 1.010 (2.6°P)

Color: 3 SRM
Bitterness: 35 IBU
ABV: 5.2%

Malt
- 11.0 lb. (5 kg) Pilsner malt (use a good flavorful Pilsner malt for this, like the Weyermann Barke Pils)

Yeast
- Wyeast 2124 Bohemian Lager, WLP800 Pilsner Lager, WLP 833 German Bock, or Saflager W34/70

Mash
- Single infusion 152°F (67°C) for 60 minutes.

Notes
- Ferment at 50°F (10°C) for 2 weeks, raise temp. for 2–4 days to 65°F (18.3°C) and then drop to 34°F (1°C) for 2 weeks before packaging.

Hops
- 2.25 oz. (64 g) Saaz 4.5% AA @ 60 min.
- 1.0 oz. (28 g) Saaz 4.5% AA @ 0 min.

We do the same thing over and over again and it makes it a safe bet that you're going to get somewhere in the neighborhood of where you want to be. Here are a few other sample templates.

Template Tripel

Batch volume: 5.5 gal. (21 L)
Original gravity: 1.084 (20.2°P)
Final gravity: 1.013 (3.3°P)

Color: 4 SRM
Bitterness: 25 IBU
ABV: 9.4%

Malt
- 15.5 lb. (7 kg) Pilsner malt
- 1.5 lb. (680 g) table sugar

Hops
- 0.75 oz. (21 g) Magnum 12% AA @ 60 min.

Mash
- Single infusion at 150°F (65.5°C) for 60 minutes.

Yeast
- Wyeast 3787 Trappist High Gravity

Template Saison

DREW: I'm fairly certain there will be a riot if I don't include a saison recipe at some point in my writing, so here you go. This Template Saison and its variants are probably the thing I brew more than anything else.

Batch volume: 5.5 gal. (21 L)
Original gravity: 1.048 (11.9°P)
Final gravity: 1.006 (1.5°P)

Color: 4 SRM
Bitterness: 20 IBU
ABV: 5.5%

Malt
- 8.75 lb. (4 kg) Pilsner malt
- 0.5 lb. (225 g) flaked wheat
- 1.0 lb. (450 g) table sugar

Mash
- Single infusion at 148°F (64°C) for 60 minutes.

Hops
- 0.5 oz. (14 g) Magnum 12.9% AA @ 60 min.

Yeast
- Take your pick from any of the myriad saison strains—it's what Drew does.

Variants
- Endless, but an easy one is steeping an ounce of an interesting hop in the whirlpool for 20 minutes.

Template Stout

Batch volume: 5.5 gal. (21 L)
Original gravity: 1.042 (10.5°P)
Final gravity: 1.010 (2.6°P)

Color: 45 SRM
Bitterness: 26 IBU
ABV: 4.4%

Malt
- 6.5 lb. (3 kg) Maris Otter
- 1.0 lb. (450 g) crystal 120°L
- 0.75 lb. (340 g) roasted barley
- 0.25 lb. (115 g) black "patent" malt
- 0.25 lb. (115 g) chocolate malt

Mash
- Single infusion at 152°F (67°C) for 60 minutes.

Hops
- 0.5 oz. (14 g) Target 11% AA @ 60 min.
- 1.0 oz. (28 g) Fuggle 4.5% AA @ 15 min.

Yeast
- Irish ale yeast (Wyeast 1084, White Labs WLP004)

DREW: On a side note, I'm fairly certain all brewers have blind spots—recipes or styles that for whatever reason just don't gel for them. Mine are porters and stouts. Cannot formulate a winning recipe of my own to save my brewery. Instead I've always leaned on recipes I got from a fellow brewer and have just made slow incremental changes to them over the years. If I try to get too fancy too quickly it all goes pear-shaped in a hurry.

HOW DO YOU KNOW IT WORKED?

So, you've made some changes to a recipe and you're sitting down enjoying a glass of your latest creation. As you sniff and sip, you think to yourself, "Darn, this is so much better than the last batch." But are you sure? How do you know?

When you make a large change to a beer, like adding black "patent" malt to a cream ale, it's pretty easy to tell you've changed the beer. All you have to do is decide if you like the change. But when you make small, subtle changes, like exchanging one hop variety for another, bumping up the IBUs a bit, or using a different but similar yeast strain, it can be really, really hard to discern the difference. And it can be even harder to tell if the change you made had a positive impact on the beer. You may think you can tell, and maybe you can, but it's so easy to fool yourself that we need some way to be certain.

If you're an experienced brewer, right about now you're probably thinking, "These guys are idiots," (OK, well, maybe), "Of course I can tell the difference!" Au contraire, mon brewer friend! Maybe you can, but maybe you can't. There's a phenomenon called confirmation bias. Put simply, it means that you believe what you want to believe even if the evidence points to something else. It's the reason that kids given the same burgers in different bags, one plain paper and one from a fast-food giant, prefer the burger in the fast-food bag. Based on the bag, they expect it to taste different.

One of our favorite examples is a research paper titled "A Study of the Effect of Perceived Beer History on Reported Preferences by Sensory Panels with Different Levels of Training" by John Smythe and Charles Bamforth.[2] They used three tasting panels, one comprised of highly trained Belgian tasters, one of moderately trained Finnish tasters, and one of untrained Irish tasters. The tasters were given two sets of beers, with two beers in each set. In the first set, the tasters were told that one beer was made with a normal length fermentation and the other was made with a new process that sped up fermentation to just a few days. In the second set, the tasters were told that one beer contained all traditional beer ingredients while the other beer used adjuncts.

The more highly trained the tasters were, the more likely they were to express a preference for what they thought were the traditionally brewed beers in both sets. The less trained tasters still showed some preference for the traditional beers, but by a lower margin than the more highly trained tasters. They were more likely to choose one of the nontraditional beers as their preference.

In case you didn't see it coming, all the beers were the same! The tasters were choosing based on their knowledge of the beer, not the flavor of the beer itself. And the less training the tasters had, the less likely they were to be influenced by anything other than the beer itself. There are a lot more studies like this, including ones that show the brain actually undergoes physical changes that lead you to believe you enjoy one thing more than another based on what

---

[2]   J.E. Smythe and C.W. Bamforth, *Journal of the Institute of Brewing*, 108, no. 1 (2002): 34–36.

you've been told. You can probably see where this is going, huh?

When you make a change in a beer, you know what that change was. You know what the intended effect is supposed to be. You know how hard you worked to make that beer. In short, you know too much to be able to make an objective judgment about the beer. Don't yell at us, it's true!

So, what's a homebrewer to do? Fortunately, we have the triangle test and tetra test to help us objectively assess the changes we make. Both tests are done blind so you don't know which of the versions of the beer you're tasting. And both will show you that it's a lot harder than you might think to detect the differences.

So, let's dive in to explaining how to do the tests and evaluate the results.

Triangle Test: The Only Way to Know

You'll hear us and other taste evaluators refer to the "triangle test" constantly. In fact, almost all of the experiments we're creating for our website and this book are based around a triangle test evaluation to determine the truth or falseness of the hypothesis. What follows are the basics of a triangle test.

When you're evaluating beer (or anything else) you have one strike against you before you even start. You have some idea about what you're going for and what you expect the results to be. In order to objectively evaluate the beer, you need to remove those prejudices. And that's where the blind triangle test comes into play.

To do a blind triangle test, you need to have another person pour two samples of one beer and one sample of the other beer without letting you know which is which. You taste all three and pick out the one that's different. If you're unable to correctly identify the different beer, then you can conclude that whatever you're testing for doesn't really make any difference. If you (or your tasters) can identify the different beer, then you can move on to asking them about what differences they detected.

You can also use it to test panelist quality. A better, more trustworthy panelist will spot the difference. You can use this during your panels to select judges for further tastings ("Great! Now tell us about the character differences you perceive and evaluate sample B fully") or to weight their feedback above those who missed the difference.

Now, obviously there are times this isn't going to work. For example, even if you disguise the color, people will be able to tell the difference between a Pilsner and a stout. You need to use the technique on two beers that are basically the same but have a slight difference that you're trying to evaluate; for example, two Pilsners with different hops in each, or a decoted versus a non-decoted beer.

If you want to get all super sciency when you're using a tasting panel, you may want to use weighting to determine how many panelists are likely to choose the odd beer simply by chance. There are resources available

DENNY: Here's an example for you. Many years ago, I wanted to test the difference between first wort hopping (FWH) and a single 60-minute hop addition. I made 10 gallons of pale ale wort and split it into two 5-gallon batches. One batch got an ounce of Cascade FWH as the only hop addition, while the other got an ounce of the same amount of Cascade at 60 minutes as the only hop addition. When the beers were finished and I poured them for myself, it was easy to tell the difference between them... because I knew what the difference was! I had my wife pour two glasses of one of the beers and one glass of the other while I was out of the room; she did this not once, but four or five times. This is the classic blind triangle test scenario. Over and over I tried to pick out the different beer. I got it right less often than I would have if I had flipped a coin. I was flabbergasted. The difference seemed so obvious when I knew which beer was which!

DREW: A word as we get into this whole "tasting" thing: don't get frustrated if you and your tasters can't tell the difference. This is a surprisingly difficult task. When I've done some of these taste tests, I've been fairly certain I'd have zero problem doing it and when I did the evaluation I was dead certain I was right. Only to discover, not so much! The other thing is, don't take the value of a single test to heart. Just like anything subjective, you need multiple passes to know you're right.

online to help you with weighting. However, even though you may learn extra information about the beers, the extra math kind of goes against our "simple" ethos. It just depends on what you want to know and your own idea of simple.

A few years back, Denny had the opportunity to attend Beer Camp at Sierra Nevada Brewing in Chico, California. While he was there, Denny had an opportunity to sit in on a tasting panel led by Cathy Haddock, who is a sensory specialist at Sierra Nevada. Part of Cathy's job is to conduct blind triangle tests of the beers produced by Sierra Nevada. Sometimes a test is to evaluate new recipes being considered for production, and sometimes it's for quality assurance in order to make certain a batch of beer meets Sierra Nevada's high standards and is consistent with previous batches. Cathy has shared a few tips for homebrewers who want to conduct a blind triangle tasting.

Proper protocol needs to be followed in order to trust your results. Proper protocol includes following procedures in which a taster's response is not biased or influenced due to any psychological factors or environmental conditions. The psychological/ environmental factors that can influence a taster's response when doing a triangle test are numerous, but I will sound off on a few that I feel are most important:

1. We do not tell the tasters anything about the samples they are tasting in a triangle test, other than the brand/style, so that they do not have any information to bias their response.

2. We serve the samples in a frosted glass to help eliminate visual cues biasing a taster's response.

3. All samples are poured with the same amount of beer, with careful attention to not have one beer more foamy than the others. If that is not enough, I also ask that they not even look at the samples, just simply grab the glass, noting its three-digit code, and evaluate the sample. This way we can have confidence the tasters are not biased by any visual cues.

We also run the triangle tests in a random balance order to help eliminate First Order effect, which is where the first sample evaluated is perceived stronger—whether negatively or positively—and therefore may be chosen as the odd sample out. This type of presentation format is employed so that the odd sample out is evenly tasted in the first, second, and third position in a three-sample triangle set. I also allow tasters to retaste if necessary.

Other external controls we employ to help offset bias is that other tasters in the tasting area do not verbalize, whether through speech or body language, any opinions on the samples they are tasting in triangle test.

Sample Triangle Test Procedure

Beer 1: A Pilsner made with a decoction mash.

Beer 2: A Pilsner made with a standard infusion mash.

Question: Does decoction mashing have a perceivable impact on the beer flavor/aroma?

Needs: 1 coin, 3 numbered slips of paper, 3 frosted/solid cups per taster labeled preferably with non-biased ordered labels (e.g., red, green, blue, circle, square, triangle, Paul, George, John). Ideally, you have another person pouring the beers and keeping those notes while you observe the tasting.

Process:
1. Flip a coin. Heads means beer 1, tails means beer 2.
2. Put three labelled slips of paper in a hat. Pull the slips. The first two pulled are for the beer selected by the coin flip. The last is for the other beer.
3. Pour the beer selected by the coin flip into the two cups selected by the slip pull.
4. Pour the beer not selected into the remaining glass. You should now have 3 cups of beer with two beers in random pouring order.
5. Serve the beer to the panelists. Give no direction beyond, "Choose the two samples that are the same." If the test isn't about the visual quality of the beer, ask the panelists not to evaluate the beer's appearance. If the panelists choose the correct two samples overwhelmingly, congratulations! You have a determinable difference. Now you need to determine if the difference is actually from your process change or because one sample got infected, was colder, and so on.
6. It's also useful, before revealing the differences being tested, to gather each taster's feedback on the different beers and why they chose the samples they did.

THE IMPORTANCE OF LOCALITY

As all politics are local, so is all beer. The giant ocean of beer styles that face the modern beer drinker and brewer is the result of centuries of adoption and adaption of different ideas. Look at all the variants on Pilsner, for instance: you have the classic original Bohemian Pilsner, followed by others like a north German Pils, international Pilsners, and American light lager. Each of these, and other adaptations like Bavarian helles or Belgian tripel, are unique interpretations based on local desires and supplies.

Before the rise of global trade routes, which now allow us to put our fingers on virtually every ingredient known to man, and before water chemistry was really understood, beer flavor was largely predicated on what was at hand.

What does local mean to you when you can easily click a button and have malt from Germany, the UK, Argentina, or a mom-and-pop farm in the middle of your state delivered to you? Simple, when starting in on a style, start with ingredients local to your beer. Use the right malts and hops. For that first pass at a Bohemian Pilsner, find a good Continental Pilsner malt, like Best Malz or Weyermann from Germany. (We're big fans of Weyermann's heritage malts, such as Barke Pils.) Get your hops straight too and go to the source, or at least find hops that mimic those qualities. As for the water front, well, we'll get there shortly in chapter 8. Water is the chief component of beer, but trying to figure out the "right" profile is exceedingly difficult. Just be sure to get rid of the chlorine and chloramine and learn what beer style your water is best for by brewing beer. Remember, we are trying to help you simplify!

Start with this simple rule of sourcing the "local" or regional ingredients for that style and pay the extra coin for the right ingredients to get your surest start. (And before you know it you'll be like Drew, who keeps enough Maris Otter in his garage to attract English mice.)

Recipe design can be a difficult dancing art. It is a little science, a little feeling, a little…who knows. There's an alchemy in it, true, but nothing so daunting that you can't start making your own recipes. Choose one of our approaches, give it a crack, and next thing you know you'll have your own intuitive recipe design philosophy and think we're completely wrong!

PROFILES IN RECIPE DESIGN: RANDY MOSHER

If you don't know Randy Mosher, well, we don't know what to tell you. Stop now. Go buy *Radical Brewing* (a fundamental book for Drew), *Mastering Homebrew*, *The Brewer's Companion* (Denny's first homebrewing book), or *Tasting Beer*—enjoy.[3] No, seriously, go do that. We can wait.

OK, now that you know Randy, we sat down and talked with him about his history of homebrewing and how he approaches the question of recipe design.

Getting Started

Randy got his start back in college when he was in Cincinnati. At the time there were still a few old regional breweries hanging on in the area, all churning out roughly the same style of beer. But the availability and locality of the beer was a novelty in an increasingly homogenized world. Randy gathered what little information was available and began brewing. Along the way, he hit the books—literally, the books in the library—to combat the paucity of available approachable knowledge. Those efforts led to his first book and started him down the path of becoming a beer guru.

Recipe Design

At first blush, Randy's recipes seem anything but simple. In his work these days with Chicago-based, Latin-inspired 5 Rabbit Cervecería, the beers brim with maddening creativity: mole stouts, beers inspired by bitter liqueurs, or beers that seek to convert the cold street treat, *paletas*, into something more adult. However, when you dig into the recipes you'll notice a pattern. In talking with Randy we came away with a few of his design points:

1. Find a story for your beer, it helps focus your decisions and the experience for the drinker (see the paletas beer, for example).
2. Always taste your malt to keep building your flavor database in your mind. (To paraphrase Randy, the best brewers always have one hand in the malt sack.)
3. Start with your middle-color malts: the crystals and the toasted malts (e.g., Munich, Vienna). They help define the shape of the beer.
4. Use base ingredients with similar characteristics to accentuate your expensive specialty ingredients.
5. Use layered ingredients to build complexity. For instance, one of 5 Rabbits' beers uses three types of cherries, mahleb (a spice made up of ground cherry stones), and cinnamon to produce a full character.
6. Explore the complexity of your specialty ingredients, such as spices. There are many differences between varietals and crop years, but even looking

---

[3]　Mosher, *Radical Brewing: Tales and World-Altering Meditations in a Glass* (Boulder: Brewers Publications, 2004); *Mastering Homebrew: The Complete Guide to Brewing Delicious Beer* (San Francisco: Chronicle Books, 2015); *The Brewer's Companion* (Seattle: Alephenalia Publications, 1991); *Tasting Beer* (North Adams, MA: Storey Publishing, 2009).

at them from a high level is instructive. Randy points to coriander as a prime example—the difference between Mexican and Indian coriander is readily apparent.

Randy is also a big fan of tasting and blending beers on the fly to try and discover what works before stepping up to a big batch. Maybe try a few small batches first; taste and then adjust. Doug King (remember chapter 1?) used to do this as well. Doug was making one-gallon batches back in the 80s as a way to test everything out. For tasting spices, Randy makes tinctures, and blends them into the already finished beer for better control. ∎

8
SIMPLE WATER

Leonardo da Vinci declared that water is the driver of nature. Hungarian biochemist and Nobel Prize winner Albert Szent-Gyorgyi wrote: "Water, the Hub of Life. Water is its mater and matrix, mother and medium. Water is the most extraordinary substance!" Author of *The Little Prince*, Antoine de Saint-Exupéry, proclaimed: "Water, thou hast no taste, no color, no odor; canst not be defined, art relished while ever mysterious. Not necessary to life, but rather life itself, thou fillest us with a gratification that exceeds the delight of the senses." A Slovakian proverb notes that pure water is the world's first and foremost medicine.

You might be more familiar with, "Water, water, everywhere, / Nor any drop to drink," by Samuel Taylor Coleridge. Even Henry David Thoreau gets in on the action, proclaiming, "I believe that water is the only drink for a wise man." OK, maybe we can agree that Thoreau went a little too far there, but it's obvious that water is not only the stuff of life, but also the foundation of our favorite hobby. Water makes up about 95% of our favorite beverage; maybe only 85% if you're a super high-gravity brewer!

For many years, homebrewers were told that if your water tastes good, you can brew with it. That's true to an extent, but without knowledge of your water—what it contains and how to adjust it—you're limited to the few styles for which your

DREW: I prefer Dave Barry who said, "Not all chemicals are bad. Without chemicals such as hydrogen and oxygen, for example, there would be no way to make water, a vital ingredient in beer."

water is ideally suited. Many of the world's great breweries started out by only brewing what the water dictated (we're looking at you, Guinness), but these days few are constrained to one type of beer due to their water.

What we're going to do in this chapter is go over the basic ideas about what your water should be like and how to get there, simply. We promise to go light on the chemistry and heavy on the pragmatism.

You can make really good beer and never worry about adjusting your water if you stick to the styles that your water is suited to. That's what breweries historically did. It's why you get Guinness from Dublin and IPA from Burton-on-Trent. You can even make decent beers in styles your water is not perfect for. But we all know that homebrewers aren't going to be content brewing only a couple of styles of beer. We want it all! And to make great beer in any style, there's no way around getting to know your water and what you need to do with it to nail the style.

DENNY: I have a well that produces great tasting water. I brewed really good beers, some that won awards, for many years without doing anything more to my water than adding a teaspoon of gypsum to the boil for styles like American IPA or pale ale. I learned that I could brew "mid-color" beers without any other water treatment. Sure, I brewed porters, stouts, Pilsners, tripels, and lots of other beers at the ends of the color spectrum and they were pretty good. But not great. My dark beers were a bit insipid, flabby, and the really light stuff had a kind of harsh off-flavor to it. Not bad enough that I didn't brew or drink them, but bad enough that I knew there was something not quite right. I was discovering what those old breweries discovered—just because your water can make one or two styles really well doesn't mean that you can brew ANY style with your water and have it be great. Once I began learning how to adjust my water for dark or light beers, my beers really became something that I could be proud of.

DREW: And for me, I have Los Angeles municipal water, which presents an extra challenge as well—it changes. You may not be aware of this, but we don't have nearly enough water for our population, so we get water from everywhere. Yes, literally. Northern California, Colorado, Arizona, Nevada—if you're nearby, we pay for that H_2O! Politics and dollars aside, the challenge is all these different sources have very different impacts on the brew session. We do need to adjust, but fortunately we're still in pretty good shape to treat our water as a near constant thanks to municipal blending.

So, at the risk of an incredibly bad pun, let's dive in to water! (OK, we're sorry!)

SIMPLE TRUTHS ABOUT WATER

Brewing Water Basics

Before we get serious about water, it's important to understand five basic things. And no, "water is wet" isn't one of them. The following list comes from our good friend John Palmer. We're using it here because we couldn't say it better.

- Bad tasting water generally makes bad tasting beer. If your water smells like a swimming pool, don't brew with it.
- Low mineral water (each mineral less than 50 ppm) is better for extract brewing.
- In general, hardness is good, alkalinity is bad.
- Hardness and alkalinity affect water, mash, and beer pH.
- Sulfate, chloride, and sodium do not affect pH but instead "season" your beer, like salt does for food.

Treat Your Brewing Water

Before we go for our deepwater dive, we want to give you a few simple guidelines you can follow when thinking about what you can do for your brewing water and your beer. You can go a lot deeper, but here's the basic stuff to get you thinking in the right direction.

- Get rid of chlorine and/or chloramine—these will ruin your beer.
- Get your water measured via a third party or a home kit. Everything else starts from here.
- Residual alkalinity is the key to adjusting your water. Use lactic or phosphoric acid to counter alkalinity.
- Water pH doesn't matter, mash pH does; the grains will do a lot of your pH adjustment for you.
- Use sulfates (gypsum and/or Epsom salts) to promote a dry finish in your beer and increase the perception of bitterness.
- Use chloride (calcium chloride or salt) to increase the perception of sweetness and malt.
- When you use a water calculator, add mineral salts first to achieve the flavor profile you're looking for. Then use acid to reduce pH or pickling lime to increase pH if needed.
- The best water treatment is the least water treatment. Do what you need to do and nothing more. More is not better. If you're within 10 ppm of the target in your water program, you're plenty close enough.

WHAT'S IN YOUR WATER?

Before you can figure what to do with your water, you need to know what's in it. How can you decide where you're going if you don't know where you are, right? There are a few key "ingredients" in water that influence your beer. These are what you need to know about:

- calcium
- chloride
- sulfate
- magnesium
- sodium
- chlorine/chloramine

- carbonate
- bicarbonate
- total alkalinity
- pH

Carbonate, bicarbonate, total alkalinity, and pH levels are closely related.

You might also want info on nitrates, nitrites, iron, manganese, and potassium levels, but that's more about overall water quality than suitability for brewing; you just want to make sure all of those are below the taste threshold. Remember, if your water tastes bad you're not spinning gold medal winning beer from it. The list above is what you absolutely must know if you want to get deep into water, but otherwise you really only need to know the levels of calcium, magnesium, total alkalinity, sulfate, chloride, and sodium before you start messing with your water.

OK, so now we know what we need to know, but how do you get this information? All municipalities or water districts can provide you with a water quality report, at least in the US. However, the type of data the your local water utility provides may vary. Sometimes a utility will have all of this info, but many others won't. It just doesn't matter enough to all utilities to track these things. Sure, they have to tell you what is in there that may kill you, but they don't have to report the secondary parameters that brewers need for assessing brewing capability. A water utility may not have the resources to provide you with much more than a yearly average, which is probably sufficient if you're drawing from a steady source of water, but maybe not enough once you get persnickety about brewing and really want to dial in your water.

If a running average isn't good enough for you (and for a number of brewers it isn't), you can find a local company to analyze your water and give you the data you need. Many homebrewers have turned to Ward Laboratories, Inc. (https://www.wardlab.com/), which provides quick, easy, and complete analyses for a reasonable price. Ward has a number of water tests available, but for our purposes test W-6 will tell you all you need to know about your water. All you need to do is take a sample of your water, pay for the test online, mail in the samples, and wait for the analysis. It's easy, as long as you don't mind visiting the post office!

For those wanting more immediate results, there are also home water test kits available. Kits from companies like Lamotte (http://www.lamotte .com/en/food-beverage/brewlab) and Industrial Test Systems' SenSafe® line (https:// sensafe.com/brewing) allow you to do your own complete water analysis at home, at your convenience. There are other products, like the SenSafe iDip® kits, that are bridging the gap between testing and reporting the results via a phone app. All of these kits set you up to understand basic water testing. Shake, mix, and observe or measure a change to dial in your value.

If you don't want to be troubled with frequent testing, you still have a few routes open to you. The cheapest is to become a water sommelier, at least for your water.

Taste your water, observe it, pay attention to it, and you'll notice when it changes. Secondly, and more expensive, go buy your water. Sure, most of the water you buy is just municipal water that's been treated, but the treatment makes it consistent. Lastly, there's distilled and reverse osmosis water. We'll get to those later, but first, let's look at these extra ingredients hanging out in our beer, how they influence it, and finally how to deal with each of them.

DREW: Remember what I said: my water changes, sometimes on a monthly basis, but usually on a seasonal basis. Some of our favorite brewers, like Colin Kaminski, co-author of *Water*,[2] actively pull and test water every brew day just to double check that the water district hasn't made any major changes. If you listen to Colin's stories, he'll tell you of brew days where the water radically changed and affected the flavor of his beer.

2   John Palmer and Colin Kaminski, *Water: A Comprehensive Guide for Brewers* (Boulder: Brewers Publications, 2013).

DREW: Yes, a water sommelier is a thing.

UNDERSTANDING YOUR WATER

We'll start with a sample from Denny's well, since it's a fairly consistent water supply (see fig. 8.1).

Calcium

Calcium is essential for enzymatic activity in the mash and for yeast health and reproduction. In general, barley and wheat, the grains most often used for homebrewing, will provide plenty of calcium for these purposes. Calcium is also essential for yeast flocculation and beer clearing.

In the past, brewers were often told that they needed at least 100 ppm of calcium in their brewing water. More recent studies have found that 50–100 ppm is plenty for ales. Lagers can get by with no additional calcium and in general can be fine with 25 ppm or less. That's because the cold lagering period will help drop the yeast, reducing the need for the calcium to do that.

Calcium also interacts with oxalate, resulting in calcium oxalate precipitating out of solution. Calcium oxalate precipitation leads to the formation of beerstone, a buildup of calcium oxalate and proteins. If beerstone forms on heat exchangers, fermentors, and serving equipment it can make them nearly impossible to sanitize. For that reason, some recommendations are to keep calcium levels at least as high as 40 ppm, which causes calcium oxalate to precipitate in the mash rather than in downstream equipment or the finished beer.

Calcium also reacts with phosphates in the malt, which reduces your mash pH. That's a desirable side-effect, because you want your mash pH to generally be in the 5.2–5.6 range (more on that later). Most water isn't that low, so the calcium in the malt can be one way of reducing your pH to the proper brewing level. In fact most drinking water is mildly alkaline like Denny's. But grain and calcium will go a long way to pull the pH down before you even think about acidifying.[2]

Chloride

Chloride (which is distinctly different from chlorine!) contributes to sweetness and "fullness" in a beer, in that it can enhance the perception of malt. Like everything in life, you want enough but not too much. A range of 10–100 ppm is generally recommended, with the exception of beers that are high in sulfates. Too much chloride in high-sulfate water can create an unpleasant "minerally" taste, which is generally not wanted.

Sulfate

When Denny and Drew started brewing, the rule of thumb was that you added gypsum (which is calcium sulfate) to "hoppy" beers in order to accentuate the hops. Of course, that overlooks exactly what "hoppy" means and

Denny's Ward Labs Water Report
Results For: DENNY CONN
pH 7.4
Total Dissolved Solids (TDS) Est 164
Electrical Conductivity, mmho/cm 0.27
Cations / Anions, me/L 2.8 / 2.7

	ppm
Sodium, Na	11
Potassium, K	2
Calcium, Ca	34
Magnesium, Mg	7
Total Hardness, CaCO3	114
Nitrate, NO3-N	<0.1 (SAFE)
Sulfate, SO4-S	19
Chloride, Cl	3
Carbonate, CO3	<1
Bicarbonate, HCO3	90
Total Alkalinity, CaCO3	74

Figure 8.1. Ward Labs water report for Denny's well water.

DREW: If you do get beerstone in your kettles and fermentors, and we all do, don't try soaking and scrubbing with your regular alkaline cleaners. Most cleaners are alkaline (basic) in nature and don't really do anything to beerstone. Instead, try an acid soak of a nitric acid (or citric or lactic acid) solution. Let soak with warm acidified water for 10–15 minutes and watch the beerstone magically wipe away!

2   "The Oxford Companion to Beer definition of calcium oxalate," *Craft Beer & Brewing Magazine* (online), accessed October 8, 2018, https://beerandbrewing.com/dictionary/ksblED3u4Y/calcium-oxalate/.

what character of hops it supposedly accentuates! More recent thinking says that sulfate helps give the beer a dryness that helps the bitterness stand out. Sulfate is pretty much essential in an American pale ale or IPA to get the hop bitterness character that we expect the beer to have. Sulfate won't really help with hop flavor or aroma other than to dry the beer enough to make those characters stand out a bit more.

In recent years, the flavor impacts of sulfate and chloride have been found to be closely intertwined, but more on that later.

Magnesium

Magnesium is important for yeast health, especially if you intend to harvest and reuse your yeast. You need at least 5 ppm of magnesium for reusing yeast in this way, but wheat or barley should provide you at least that much. You can go a bit higher with the magnesium in order to be certain that your yeast is strong and healthy, but keep it below 40 ppm to avoid adverse effects on flavor. Although magnesium will lower your pH a bit, it's not recommended specifically as a tool to lower pH. We use Epsom salts (magnesium sulfate) to augment gypsum (calcium sulfate) when we want to increase the sulfate level without adding more calcium. This is often good practice for American pale ales and IPAs. A bonus is that we also get the magnesium from it.

Sodium

When used at moderate levels, sodium can boost the malt flavor and sweetness of a beer, especially if present alongside chloride. Any good dessert chef will tell you that even sweets benefit from a pinch of salt to activate your taste buds. In general, you want to keep sodium below 60 ppm; too much can leave a harsh, unpleasant flavor.

It comes dancin' across your water Chlorine Chlorine What a killer.

—(Apologies to Neil Young, *Cortez the Killer*)

Chlorine the Killer

Chlorine is the one you don't want in your beer. As we've brewed for more and more years, one thing we've found is that it's really hard to screw up a batch of beer to the point that it's undrinkable. Poor recipes, out of whack fermentation temperature, no carbonation—all of those are things may not be great, but at least leave you with a beverage that you can usually imbibe. But we've found that there is one flaw that practically guarantees your homebrew will become toilet cleaner, and that's chlorine, along with its close cousin chloramine (a stable chlorine compound that prolongs chlorine's disinfectant properties). The harsh plastic flavors imparted to your lovingly crafted homebrew by chlorine and chloramine will pretty much guarantee a gag-and-spit experience rather than the beery nirvana you were hoping for.

If we had to guess (and we will, since it's our book!), probably 90% of home-brewers are on a city water supply that uses chlorine or chloramine for water treatment. In terms of public health, that's a good thing; you want to know that the water you drink is uncontaminated by disease-causing organisms. But while chlorine-treated water might keep you safe, it's death for your beer.

Every homebrewer is familiar with sodium hypochlorite, a.k.a. bleach. In the early days of homebrewing, bleach was the preferred sanitizing solution, and many people are familiar with the bleach aroma in their water. Chloramine is a little less well known. Chloramine is a reaction product between chlorine and ammonia. Many major water districts have switched to chloramine because it doesn't outgas as readily as chlorine, which means it protects better as the water moves through the long supply runs typical for modern cities.

You can find out if your water contains chlorine or chloramine by contacting your local water board or by looking at their annual water report. If your water contains chlorine or chloramine, you would be well advised to remove it before brewing with the water. Not doing so puts you at risk of chlorophenols in your beer, which produce a harsh, plastic aroma and flavor that is compared to Band-Aids. And let's face it, no one wants their beer to smell or taste like Band-Aids!

Chlorine removal is relatively simple. The easiest way to remove it is to draw your brewing water 24 hours before you brew and let it sit uncovered until you use it. The chlorine will outgas and you will be left with chlorine-free water. Exposure to sunlight speeds this process and can reduce it to a few hours. You can also boil the water to remove the chlorine and be done pretty much when the boil happens. Lastly, you can aerate the water as well to force the offgassing process.

Chloramine is a lot tougher. It won't dissipate if you let the water sit, boil it, or aerate it. That's the whole reason water districts use the stuff! You need to take more active measures. All of these active measures will work for chlorine as well.

Our favorite, easy and cheap method is to use Campden tablets (sodium or potassium metabisulfite) to remove it. As well as Campden tablets, sodium and potassium metabisulfite also come in powder form. Most homebrew shops will carry Campden tablets because it's a popular wine sanitizer. One typical (695 mg) Campden tablet (or a healthy pinch of powder) can remove the chlorine from 20 gallons of water, unless your water has a very high level of chlorine in which case you should use a bit more.

To use, crush the tablet (or part of it, depending on how much water you want to dechlorinate) and mix it into the water. The reaction happens within a few seconds and you're ready to use the water. Some people worry that using Campden tablets might add sulfites to their beer, but that doesn't happen. The end byproduct is chloride (in the case of chlorine), and also hydrogen, sulfate, and ammonium (for chloramine), as well as either sodium or potassium depending on whether your Campden tablet is sodium metabisulfite or potassium metabisulfite.

DREW: Second closest in my years as "Official Troubled Beer Taster" for the Maltose Falcons is the flavor of green garden hose. I'm utterly amazed at the number of brewers who will absorb by osmosis from homebrew knowledge floating in the area all this stuff about chlorine and utterly miss the fact that you shouldn't use a green plastic water hose! The vinyl phenols in those hoses easily leach into your beer and are utterly and ruinously distinctive. Use either food grade vinyl hose from your homebrew shop or a white "potable water/RV" hose.

DREW: I used to be really stressed out about chloramine removal from my water. I had an activated carbon filter setup in the brewery, did all the right things, etc. For the amount of brewing I was doing, the maintenance and replacement filter costs made the whole thing an expensive pain in the wallet. When I first learned of the Campden tablet trick, I didn't want to believe it would work, but since I had to get rid of the chloramine and was sick of dealing with my filter, I gave it a shot. Nowadays, I do nothing else. I fill my HLT with water straight from the tap (via a white potable water hose for RVs), stir in a pinch of metabisulfite powder, stir, and get ready to brew. What finally convinced me it was working was buying a set of chloramine test strips. Like pH papers, these paper strips get dipped into a sample of your water and will change color in the presence of chlorine or chloramine. It's so simple—a little paper and I saved myself a bunch of time, money, and pain. I think I buy a new thing of powder every two years or so for less than $10. Highly recommended!

Now, before you freak out about these new compounds, you need to know that the amounts are infinitesimal and will not affect the flavor of your water or beer. We could go into scary math here to show you how little, but this book is about simplicity. Just know that the theory is sound and that thousands of homebrewers have been doing this for years. We have empirical proof that it works!

Finally, you can use a granulated activated charcoal (GAC) filter system to remove both chlorine and chloramine. This is a more expensive solution, but many people already have these installed for their entire house. There are two things to keep in mind about GAC systems. First, remember to change the filter regularly to avoid bacterial contamination. Second, run the water slowly to ensure that the chlorine/chloramine is actually removed. Because of the amount of water you need for brewing and the slow recovery time of some GAC systems, you may need to draw your water in batches for a day or two before you brew.

You occasionally hear the question, "Since boiling removes chlorine and I'm going to be boiling my beer anyway, doesn't that remove the chlorine?" If only it was that easy! Unfortunately, by the time you start boiling the wort, the chlorine will have reacted with your grain or extract to form the dreaded plastic, medicinal-tasting chlorophenols. And once they're in your wort, there's no way to eliminate them. Your beer will have flavors and aromas reminiscent of plastic or Band-Aids. Take it from us, it's bad, it's disgusting…there is no way to save a beer with chlorophenols. So, take a few minutes to deal with chlorine/chloramine before you start brewing.

DISTILLED AND REVERSE OSMOSIS WATER: THE LEVEL PLAYING FIELD

Rather than trying to deal with stuff that's already in your water, you can take the opposite approach and start with water that has no minerals in it. That's the beauty of using distilled or reverse osmosis (RO) water. Distilled water is devoid of minerals and is a blank slate for water treatment. You know there's nothing there when you start! Although RO water has greatly reduced mineral levels, they're still only there to a small extent (less than 10 ppm). Reverse osmosis water can be a good base if the residual mineral content is low enough—the only way to know is to get an analysis of the RO water, or just brew with it and see what happens. Water put through a well-tuned RO/distillation process can be treated as a table full of zeros, an aqueous blank canvas for you to paint your beer on. And while you don't want to brew with water that has no minerals, starting with distilled or RO water means that you can add the proper amounts of just those minerals you want for the beer style you're brewing, rather than trying to compensate for what's already in your water.

You can find distilled or RO water in jugs or bottles in most grocery stores. Avoid water labeled as "drinking water" because it will likely have minerals in it. Most of the major brands have water profiles available online, so you can look and see the numbers, but it's not the same as starting from scratch.

We also recommend you avoid the bulk water dispensing machines. There have been many disturbing reports of the water from those machines not being free of minerals, even when they carry a recently dated seal assuring you of the water's purity. Some homebrewers even go as far as carrying a total dissolved solids (TDS) meter with them to check the water from those machines before purchasing it. In far too many cases, what they find is that it isn't as pure as claimed and should be avoided for brewing.

DREW: If you live in a big city like Los Angeles, you'll have witnessed the phenomenon of the "water store." Like it sounds, it's a store that sells nothing but water. They usually will have big banks of machines and the better ones will properly maintain their systems so you're getting proper water. If you're going to purchase RO/distilled water in bulk, these usually provide the best value.

You can also buy RO filter systems for your tap water. They work well but RO tap filters have their drawbacks: they waste a lot of water as they filter it; they require frequent maintenance in order to keep the filter in good working condition and free of bacteria; and they usually require you to draw the water slowly in order to filter it, which may mean you need to collect the water over the course of a few days before you brew. Since many RO filter systems produce a fair amount of wastewater (this is water that doesn't make it through all the membranes), you'll need to do something with it. If you live where water conservation is an ongoing concern, don't waste it! Water your plants, fill your laundry machine, make beans. Whatever! Just don't put it down the drain.

Despite these drawbacks, many people find RO filter systems to be just the ticket for their situation. If you think one of these might be solution for you, we encourage you to compare the various systems out there and determine which one best fits your needs.

Another benefit of using distilled water as a blank slate is that you can take advantage of the prepackaged mineral additions sold at local homebrew supply stores. Kind of like using the Bru'n Water software (which we look at below), pick a color and flavor profile, then add the prepackaged minerals to the water. There are several companies out there making these packets. We've had an opportunity to test the salts from ACCUmash™ (http://www.accu-mash .com/) and we were really impressed by how easy they were to use and how well they worked. The ACCUmash products simulate the type of additions you'd get from water profiling software and makes the water part of your brew day as easy as "get distilled water, drop packet in water, brew"! The same type

TRULY SIMPLE WATER

Distilled and reverse osmosis (RO) water can make the extract brewer's life even easier. Manufacturers produce extract by mashing grain, just like is done in an all-grain beer. And as in an all-grain beer, the extract manufacturers use the proper minerals for the type of extract they're producing. That means the basic minerals you need for a healthy fermentation and correct flavor are in the extract you buy, and by using mineral-free water you don't have to add anything else or worry about compensating for what's in your water supply. (You may want to add a bit of gypsum for additional dryness or some calcium chloride for sweetness.) Win-win if you ask us!

DREW: See my comment in the last section about my charcoal filter experience. Multiply that by tenfold and you've got the experience of owning your own RO system. Fun!

of product is available from other companies too. Beer Dust (https://beerdust .com) is one that has gotten very good reviews, but look around, try several, and determine which works best for you.

ADJUSTING YOUR WATER

So now you know what's in (or not in) your water and what kind of effect the various mineral salts will have on your beer. Where do you go from there?

First, we recommend you get some water treatment software. Some popular brewing software, like BeerSmith™, will have it built in. There are online water calculators like Brewer's Friend that you can use; there are also many standalone calculators like Bru'n Water (which Denny uses), Brewer's Friend (https://www.brewersfriend.com), or Palmer's Brewing Water Adjustment App that you can download. If you're really, deeply interested in being nerdy, then go forth and make your own spreadsheet (that's how Bru'n Water started), but we really do recommend going and finding a calculator that works for you because the math gets weird.

These are all basically spreadsheets that allow you to play "what if" games. You input the profile of the water you're using, select a target profile for the beer you're making, and start manipulating the various salt additions until you get close to the profile you want.

A word about target profiles before we get into how to make the chemistry happen. If you look through a lot of older brewing books, you'll see tables of famous brewing cities and what their water profiles look like. The old way of talking about water treatment was: "Oh, you're making a Scottish beer? You should make your water look like that from the Edinburgh rows in the table." This ignores the fact that Edinburgh water varies (drastically) from well to well. But it also ignores the fact that breweries worldwide treat their water, removing minerals and adding others all with the same goals in mind. Very few brewers just hew to their native water source. The newer means of targeting water is a sort of "color and intent" model. For instance, in Bru'n Water you have profiles for "golden, bitter" and "golden, malty". These profiles are modeled using mineral flavor impacts, pH, and residual alkalinity. We already walked you through the first one, so how about the latter two?

pH

When we build a water profile, we think of it as two distinct steps: how it will affect mash pH and how it will affect beer flavor. pH gets manipulated to affect the function of your mash and boil, and mineral salts get manipulated to affect the flavor of your beer. Sure, there's some crossover—pH will have an effect on flavor and the salts can have an effect on pH—but thinking of them as separate adjustments helps you get a handle on what you're doing and why.

pH is a measure of how acidic or basic something is—technically, it's a measure of the hydrogen ion activity in a solution, hence "power of hydrogen" or pH. Keep in mind that the pH of your source water makes little difference. The pH of the mash is what matters and the grain you use will affect that. The more dark grain you add, the more the mash pH will be pulled down. Enzyme activity in the mash is influenced by pH: beta-amylase has a pH optimum in the 5.0–5.5 range while alpha-amylase is in the 5.2–5.7 range. Note these ranges overlap, which is why pH 5.4–5.5 is the sweet spot many homebrewers aim for. You'll notice that some products on the market offer the ability to automatically dial in your pH to this magical pH zone, but neither of us have had much luck with them. Sometimes the hard way is the only way.

Alkalinity

Along with pH, we need to talk about alkalinity. Alkalinity is a measure of how resistant to pH change your water is. Water high in carbonate and bicarbonate will have a high alkalinity and require more acid to bring about a change in pH. Alkalinity is NOT the same as hardness, it's actually the opposite. Hardness comes from high levels of calcium and magnesium ions in your water. Some hardness in your water is not necessarily a problem and can actually be a good thing for some styles.

Alkalinity can be a big obstacle to you hitting your mash pH and usually needs to be neutralized by an addition of acid when brewing lighter-colored beers. Brewers use either lactic or phosphoric acid to neutralize alkalinity and adjust the pH of their mash (notice we said mash, not water). Too much alkalinity can result in a high pH and a muted flavor to the beer. Too little alkalinity can result in low mash pH and tart, almost wine-like flavors, as well as poor conversion. On the other hand, alkalinity is a good thing when you brew dark-colored beers. It balances the acidity from the dark malts and helps keep your mash pH from going below 5.2.

Residual alkalinity (RA) is a concept introduced by Paul Kolbach as a specific tool for brewers. It's the alkalinity that is not neutralized by the calcium and magnesium in your water. It's what's "left over" after the neutralization reactions, hence the "residual" part. It's the true measure of what a brewer needs to know about their water. Darker beers benefit from a higher RA and lighter beers from a lower RA. You can increase RA by adding calcium carbonate (chalk), sodium bicarbonate (baking soda), or calcium hydroxide (pickling lime). The easiest way to increase the alkalinity of your water is to use baking soda, because calcium carbonate is hard to dissolve. You can reduce RA by hardening the water with additions of calcium or magnesium, or by adding acid.

Function and Flavor

OK, does your head hurt yet? Yeah, we understand. But we think it's important to have at least a bit of an idea how and why things happen with your water. Here's the takeaway from all of this (i.e., the simple part):

WE DON'T ADJUST WATER PH

Brewers do not adjust water to adjust water pH. Water is adjusted to change the hardness and alkalinity concentrations, which in turn affect the pH of the mash. Mash pH is the equilibrium between water chemistry and malt chemistry. The only time brewers acidify water specifically to change the water pH is when they are acidifying sparge water to prevent wort pH from rising during lautering. However, it must be understood that the mechanism for preventing rising pH is the neutralization of the alkalinity in the water, which is gauged by measuring the pH of the water. We measure the water pH to know when we have neutralized all the alkalinity.

DREW: If this all seems a bit intimidating to you, go visit a commercial brewery and you'll see that they almost always fret the measurements when adjusting systems, grains, or water supplies. Once they've dialed it in for a particular recipe though, everything becomes rote for that recipe, for example, "400 mL of lactic acid in the HLT before we heat and add X grams of gypsum." In other words, the water recipe becomes part of the beer recipe.

- Start adjusting your water by adding mineral salts to build the flavor profile you want.
- Mineral salt additions will affect the RA of your water, so after you get your flavor profile built, use acid or bicarbonate to adjust the mash pH to the value you want it to be.
- In general (VERY general!), shoot for a pH on the slightly high side (5.4–5.8) for dark beers and on the lower side (5.2–5.4) for lighter, crisper beers. Amber colored beers should fall somewhere between those outside values.

Adjusting Your Water: An Example

Let's walk through a water adjustment for a beer. We'll be using the Bru'n Water spreadsheet, but other water calculators work similarly. Denny's Noti Brown Ale, an American brown, was the first beer that won a ribbon for Denny and it's always been a tasty, reliable recipe. But it had always struck him as coming off a bit harsher than he wanted it to be. Adjusting the water he used took care of that.

Denny started by entering the water profile he had gotten from Ward Labs into Bru'n Water (fig. 8.2). He then entered his grain bill (fig. 8.3). Remember, the grain will affect mash pH so the calculator has to know what grain you're using and how much of it. *Note:* It is important to understand that the predicted mash pH, such as that shown in figure 8.3, is just an estimate made by a numerical model. Every malt from every maltster will be slightly different. In other words, your mileage may vary.

Next, Denny moved on to the "Water Adjustment" page and chose the "Brown, Balanced" water profile. Bru'n Water lets you select your target profile based on beer color and desired flavor. It also has water profiles from some of the great brewing cities in the world, but we encourage you to not use those.

Bru'n Water — Denny Conn

Program Volume Setting	Gallons ▼		Enter Data into Light Blue cells

Water Report Input — Hover cursor over cells w/ red corner mark to display comments

Cations	Enter Ion Concentrations from Water Report (mg/L or ppm)		Anions
Calcium (Ca)	34.0	90.0	Bicarbonate (HCO$_3$)
Magnesium (Mg)	7.0	0.1	Carbonate (CO$_3$)
Sodium (Na)	11.0	57.0	Sulfate (SO$_4$)
Potassium (K)	2.0	3.0	Chloride (Cl)
Iron (Fe)	0.0	0.0	Nitrate (NO$_3$)
		0.0	Nitrite (NO$_2$)
		0.0	Fluoride (F)

If water report provides only Total Alkalinity or Temporary Hardness (as CaCO$_3$), use the calculator below to estimate the Bicarbonate and Carbonate concentrations. Insert the estimated Bicarbonate and Carbonate results in the table above.

Reported Total Alkalinity or Temporary Hardness (as CaCO3) (mg/L or ppm)	Reported or Measured Water pH	Estimated Bicarbonate Concentration (ppm)	Estimated Carbonate Concentration (ppm)
74.0	7.4	90.1	0.1

Ion Balance Results			
Total Cations (meq/L) or (mval)	2.80	0.05	Cation/Anion Difference (meq/L)
Total Anions (meq/L) or (mval)	2.75	158	Total Dissolved Solids (TDS) (ppm)

Hardness and Alkalinity Results			
Total Hardness, as CaCO$_3$, (ppm)	114	74	Alkalinity (ppm as CaCO$_3$)
Permanent Hardness, as CaCO$_3$, (ppm)	40	99	RA Effective Hardness, (ppm as CaCO$_3$)
Temporary Hardness, as CaCO$_3$, (ppm)	74	46	Residual Alkalinity (RA), (ppm as CaCO$_3$)

Figure 8.2. Denny's water profile in Bru'n Water. Image courtesy Martin Brungard.

Mash Acidification Calculator

Hover cursor over cells w/ red corner mark to display helpful comments

Enter Data into Light Blue cells

Grains	Grain Type		Quantity (lb)	Quantity (oz)	Color (L)	Percentage of Grain Bill
2 Row Pale Malt	Base Malt	▼	8.0	0.0	2	59.3
Munich	Base Malt	▼	3.8	0.0	10	27.8
Crystal 60L	Crystal Malt	▼	1.3	0.0	60	9.3
Chocolate	Roast Malt	▼	0.5	0.0	350	3.7
	Base Malt	▼	0.0	0.0	0	0.0
	Base Malt	▼	0.0	0.0	0	0.0
	Base Malt	▼	0.0	0.0	0	0.0
	Base Malt	▼	0.0	0.0	0	0.0
	Base Malt	▼	0.0	0.0	0	0.0
	Base Malt	▼	0.0	0.0	0	0.0
Enter grain names above to help	Base Malt	▼	0.0	0.0	0	0.0
verify that all the grist is entered	Base Malt	▼	0.0	0.0	0	0.0

Total Grist Weight (lbs)	13.50	Est. Beer Color (EBC)	46.0
Water to Grist Ratio (Qts/Lb)	1.63	Est. Beer Color (SRM)	23.4

| Malt Color Setting | Lovibond ▼ | Remove Crystal Malts from Main Mash? | ☐ |
| Water used for Mash | Adjusted Water ▼ | Remove Roast Malts from Main Mash? | ☐ |

Mash pH Result

Estimated Room-Temperature Mash pH	5.45

Mash pH Guidance

Suggested mash pH range for lighter colored beers is 5.3 to 5.4
Suggested mash pH range for darker colored beers is 5.4 to 5.5
Tart or crisp beer styles may benefit from a mash pH range of 5.2 to 5.3

Figure 8.3. Mash acidification estimate using Bru'n Water, based on Denny's well water composition and grain bill. Image courtesy of Martin Brungard.

For one thing, there's no guarantee that the city profile is indeed what the water there is really like. And you have no idea if or how the breweries there treat the water. You can be pretty certain that almost none use it as is, though. So, by using beer color and desired flavor you can tweak your water to give you a beer that might be brewed in these cities after they dealt with their water.

Denny entered the amount of mash and sparge water he was using, as well as the total batch volume (fig. 8.4). The more water you use, the more minerals and/or acids you'll have to use to adjust the profile to your liking. To start, Denny compared his existing water profile to the target profile, which let him see where he needed to add mineral salts and where the existing values were close enough (remember, you don't have to be exact).

Figure 8.4. Denny compared his existing water profile to see how it might be djusted to more closely match his desired water profile. Image courtesy of Martin Brungard.

By entering different values to the "Water Additions" table, the values in the line "Finished Water Profile" changed and could be compared to the target profile. If some minerals start out too high in the existing water, you can cut your water with distilled water to reduce those and then build back up any that were diluted too much. After experimenting with his additions, Denny finally took a look at the predicted pH and found it higher than he wanted, so he added some lactic acid to pull it down to 5.4. Here are the additions he ended up with:

Mash
- 0.6 g gypsum (calcium sulfate)
- 2.2 g calcium chloride
- 1.1 mL 88% lactic acid

Sparge
- 0.5 g gypsum (calcium sulfate)
- 1.9 g calcium chloride
- 1.6 mL 88% lactic acid

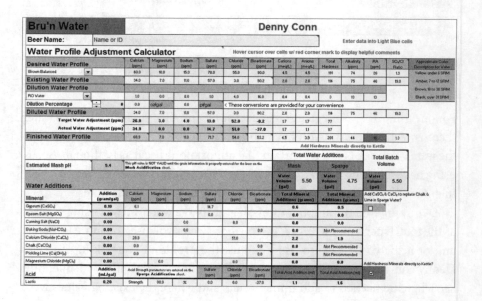

Figure 8.5. Denny adjusted his mineral amounts and added lactic acid to reach an estimated mash pH of 5.4. Image courtesy of Martin Brungard.

The mineral amounts are really close to the target profile and the mash pH ended up at 5.4 (fig. 8.5). Bingo! Not only did the intellectual exercise work out, but the beer had a much more rounded flavor and that was what Denny wanted all along.

IS THERE A SIMPLER WAY?

"My head hurts. Is there a simpler way?" Yes and no. The simplest answer is, don't worry about all the adjustments: clear your water of chlorine/chloramine and learn what your water is best at by brewing beer. It'll cost you some time and some batches of beer, but the math is a lot simpler! The next simplest is to start with distilled/RO water and use premeasured water salts—they can really up your game. If you decide you want some math after all, let's go back to our brief aside about the flavor impacts of sulfate and chloride.

Sulfate-to-Chloride Ratio

The impact of sulfate and chloride on flavor in the final beer is known to affect how the balance of malts and hops is perceived. Professional brewers don't necessarily want to go digging into water calculations every time they start designing a beer, and everyone loves an easy to understand rule of thumb to make them feel like they're in the ballpark. Calculating the sulfate-to-chloride ratio is a simple division: you take your sulfate level and divide it by the chloride level in your water.

- If the sulfate/chloride value is less than 1, your water favors malt perception in the final beer. You can think of this as full and mouthcoating.
- If the sulfate/chloride value is 1–1.5, your water favors a balanced malt and hop perception.
- If the sulfate/chloride value is above 1.5, your water favors hop perception. What's hop perception? Think of it in terms of dryness—the beer doesn't really become more bitter, but you perceive a dry finish to the beer.

The effect of the sulfate-to-chloride ratio increases as you move to the extremes, but we suggest you stay somewhat near the middle until you really understand the impact. Take a look at the "Brown, Balanced" profile Denny used for Noti Brown Ale in figure 8.5. The desired water profile calls for 70 ppm sulfate and 55 ppm chloride. That's 70/55 or 1.27, squarely in the "balanced" perception range.

Please note that this ratio only works when you're not pushing to the extremes or dealing with water that is naturally excessively low or high in minerals. A sulfate/chloride ratio of 3 when your numbers are 30 ppm sulfate and 10 ppm chloride will give you far different results than the same ratio when your numbers are 300 ppm sulfate and 100 ppm chloride. If you find your natural levels are in the extremes (e.g., >200 ppm), you'll want to dilute first.

It's Never Too Late

Sometimes a beer doesn't turn out exactly like what you had in mind. Maybe it's too bitter, too "thin," or too "flabby." Your choices are to suffer through it or dump it, neither of which we want to do! However, you can actually add some water treatments directly to a keg or glass of beer. It still might not be what you had in mind, but chances are it will be a lot closer!

There's no formula to determine how much to add to a glass or keg because there's no way to quantify flavor. It's a trial and error thing, with hopefully the emphasis on the trial! Denny just adds a bit to a glass and tastes until he decides the beer has been improved. You can carefully measure the amount you put in a glass (hint: it's not very much) and scale that up to the size of the whole batch you want to treat. Or you can add a bit, taste, and add more if needed. It's unlikely the beer will turn out to be the perfect pint you had in mind, but you'll undoubtedly end up with a beer that you can enjoy both for itself and for the simple reason that you saved it from a fate as drain cleaner.

We don't know about you, but after all this water talk, we need a drink!

DENNY: I get a lot of ingredients to test and many times I don't know much about them or how they'll act in a beer. I end up with thin-bodied beers, under- or overbittered beers, and beers that have a lack of flavor or "pop" to them. I've "saved" a number of these by adding gypsum or calcium chloride directly to a glass or keg of beer. For instance, a beer that could have used more malt for the amount of hops in it was made drinkable by adding some calcium chloride to the keg. A friend's Bo Pils was saved from a flabby fate by adding some gypsum to the glass. Similarly, you can add lactic acid to a finished beer to give it some "pop." So, like they say in the movie Galaxy Quest, "Never give up, never surrender!"

PROFILES IN SIMPLICITY: MARTIN BRUNGARD

Martin Brungard has been homebrewing since 2000. You can consider him a beer nerd with tools. He has applied his engineering education and homebrewing experience to solving brewing problems and dispelling brewing myths for the brewing community. Martin is author and presenter of numerous brewing articles, a professional brewing consultant, and author of the Bru'n Water software for brewing water chemistry that we have mentioned throughout chapter 8. Martin also served as a technical editor for the Brewers Publications book, *Water: A Comprehensive Guide for Brewers.*[3]

We asked Martin for his simple guidelines about adjusting your water:

> While there is plenty of discussion on mineral levels in brewing water, I find that brewers gain the most from water adjustments by focusing on getting their wort pH into the proper range. It doesn't take a pH meter to figure if your pH is too high or low. You can look at the relative success of your past brews to guide you. If you find that your pale colored beers tend to be dull or coarse tasting and your dark beers are decent, then it's likely that your water has high alkalinity. If your dark beers tend to be too acidic or sharp tasting, then it's likely that your water has low alkalinity. With just that assessment, you can start making meaningful changes to your brewing.
>
> The following are water adjustments that can be applied relatively safely simply from the assessment above. In the case of high alkalinity water, adding acid to the water does make a big difference. Try adding either 0.5 mL of 88% lactic acid or 5 mL of 10% phosphoric acid to each gallon of mashing and sparging water when brewing pale colored beers. Those additions should make the resulting beers brighter and crisper.
>
> In the case of low alkalinity water, adding alkalinity to your mashing water can help take the acidic or acrid edge off your dark beers. Adding about 1/16 tsp of baking soda per gallon of your mashing water (about 0.5 g/gal., which is equal to 75 ppm of bicarbonate alkalinity) should be a safe dose for dark beers. Do not add baking soda to sparging water.

---

[3]   John Palmer and Colin Kaminski, *Water: A Comprehensive Guide for Brewers* (Boulder: Brewers Publications, 2013).

If those beers are better with those simple water adjustments, then paying more attention to your water may be worthwhile. While pH adjustments hold the most bang for your buck, simple adjustments to chloride and sulfate levels in your brewing water can also improve your beer.

To make meaningful adjustments to chloride and sulfate in your brewing water, it's important that neither of those ions be at too high a level. Therefore, you'll either need to get into more complicated chemistry calculations or you can start with water that has low mineralization (RO or distilled water). With unmineralized water, it's easy to add minerals to alter beer flavor and perception.

Adding chloride to your brewing water helps with the perception of fullness or mouthcoating maltiness in beer. A safe dose for enhancing those perceptions is 1/8 tsp of calcium chloride per gallon (1.7 g/gal.) of brewing water (mashing and sparging water). Higher dosing can increase those perceptions, but this is a safe starting point. Don't be afraid of boosting that level in the future based on your prior results.

Adding sulfate to your brewing water helps to dry the finish of your beers. While it doesn't make beer more bitter, that dryness does improve the perception of hoppiness and bittering. If your beers end up with maltiness that lingers too long, adding sulfate can dry that finish out. A safe dose for drying your beer's finish is to add 1/4 tsp gypsum per gallon (3.35 g/gal.) of brewing water (mashing and sparging water). Again, don't be afraid to experiment with larger gypsum doses as your experience grows.

These simple water adjustments are based on your perceptions of your beer. They can be implemented without calculation. However, if you find that they make your beer better, you may want to investigate further trials at higher doses to see what your preferences are for different styles. Different beer styles do benefit from different levels of mineralization and acidification. While you can make good steps in improving your beers with these simple recommendations, the many brewing chemistry calculators available may make your job easier.

Want an example? Here's a simple recipe where the whole character changes based on the water. Please note, although this recipe is for a lager, you can substitute a clean, neutral ale yeast and see the same effect. ∎

Hobo BoHo Pilsner

Batch size: 5.5 gal. (21 L)
Original gravity: 1.051 (12.6°P)
Final gravity: 1.010 (2.6°P)

Color: 3.2 SRM
Bitterness: 40 IBU
ABV: 5.2%

Malt
- 11 lb. (5 kg) Bohemian Pilsner malt

Hops
- 2.25 oz. (64 g) Saaz 4.5% AA @ 60 min.
- 1.00 oz. (28 g) Saaz 4.5% AA @ 0 min.

Yeast
- Wyeast 2124 Bohemian Lager

Water
- Use water with minimum of 50 ppm calcium and minimal levels of other minerals.

Mash
- Strike with 4 gal. (15.1 L) of 134°F (57°C) water and rest at 122°F (50°C) for 20 minutes.
- Decoction #1: Pull 1/3 of the mash with minimal liquid. Raise to 152°F (67°C) for 20 minutes in a separate vessel and then bring to a boil, while stirring. Add back to the main pot to raise the mash to ~150°F (66°C).
- Decoction #2; Pull 1/3 of the mash volume with liquid. Bring to a boil. Add back to the main pot to raise temperature for mash-out.

Fermentation
- Ferment for 2 weeks at 48–50°F (9–10°C). Raise to 64°F (18°C) for 24 hours and then crash to 35°F (2°C) for 2 more weeks.

Variant

Johann's Pils

- Adjust water with gypsum (~1 tsp for a neutral water source).
- Use Wyeast 2206 Bavarian Lager.

DREW: The decoction schedule specified is traditional but, as noted repeatedly throughout the book, hardly necessary. For a simpler brew day, perform a single infusion mash at 150°F (66°C) before proceeding to mash out or straight to the lauter.

9

SIMPLE ADJUNCTS

> "Thankfully, if you're lazy, pragmatic, or just looking for the simplest way to do this adjunct thing, then we have the technology, we have the processes."

Many brewers and beer enthusiasts treat the German Beer Purity Law, the *Reinheitsgebot*, as the be-all and end-all codex of brewing. After all, water, malt, hops, and yeast[1] is simple, clean, and appeals to an orderly mind. A great case could be made that, really, when it comes to beer, those four things are all you need and all you should ever want. If that's not simplicity we don't know what is.

When you begin exploring humanity's continuously evolving relationship with alcoholic beverages you'll quickly notice that the preciousness around what ingredients belong in a particular drink—whether beer, mead, wine, cocktails, etc.—is a relatively new thing. Dig back into history and you'll see a long line of "beery" beverages based around cereal grains that mix a bunch of different ingredients: grapes, honey, fruits, rice, corn. Virtually anything

---

[1] Caveat: yeast wasn't part of the original, mystical 1516 *Reinheitsgebot*. Brewers didn't know enough about the stuff at the time to specifically call it out. Also, go read about the actual law—those simple "four" ingredients have so many exceptions it makes the English rule of "*i* before *e*, except after *c*" look consistent and clear.

starchy or sugary eventually found its way into the local beverage. Modern brewers would call these extras *adjuncts*, basically sugar/starch supplements that aren't barley. Historical brewers, including American stalwart lager brewers of the 1800s, would have called them "things we use."

We both started homebrewing in the late 1990s, when the craft brew scene was the Rebel Alliance to the macrobrewers' Galactic Empire. At that time, a ubiquitous rallying cry for the homebrewing community was, "We don't want your cheap corn and rice beers!"

Let's face it, these days we have other rallying cries and concerns and people have largely started to understand the purpose and utility of adjuncts. Seriously, adjuncts aren't just all about being cheap or easy. Heck, some of them even qualify as "brewing the hard way." Fortunately, we have a lot of options when it comes time to play in the field of other ingredients.

A LITTLE ADJUNCT HISTORY

Digging into brewing history, most of us know the story of beer. You don't? Well, OK, it starts at the dawn of civilization, at least in writing, with the Sumerian *Hymn to Ninkasi*, a quasi-brewing process and recipe encoded in a prayer chant. There's some debate about the legitimacy of this interpretation, because history is always up for debate. But look at the translation done by Miguel Civil, the world's leading Sumerian expert:

> Ninkasi, you are the one who spreads the cooked mash on large reed mats,
>
> Coolness overcomes...
>
> You are the one who holds with both hands the great sweet wort,
>
> Brewing [it] with honey [and] wine...
>
> (Miguel Civil, "A Hymn to the Beer Goddess and a Drinking Song," *Studies Presented to A. Leo Oppenheim, June 7, 1964* [Oriental Institute of the University of Chicago, 1964, 67-89])

The Ninkasi beer recipe starts with a baked bread called *bappir*, possibly made of unmalted barley and date syrup. Some loaves contained an early form of wheat called emmer. So here, in the beginning of history, we see beer made with multiple ingredients.

Research done by Dr. Patrick McGovern of the University of Pennsylvania takes us back even further to a beverage brewed around 9000 years ago in what is now modern day China. This Neolithic "beer" left chemical traces of rice, grapes, hawthorn berries (a relative of the apple), and honey. Examples discovered from other sites and time periods included grains like millet, wheat, and barley.[2]

What's the point of this brief history lesson? Basically this: in most of humanity's time as brewers, if you showed the level of assiduous preciousness about the base ingredients of beer as demonstrated by devoted adherents of the Rheinheitsgebot, you would have earned a lot of very strange looks for being so fussy.

HOW TO ADJUNCT

By now you're used to the relatively simple process of making beer from grain: mill it, mash it, drain the liquid, and boil. Piece of cake!

It's easy because our usual cereal players love to cooperate together. Barley begins to unleash its starches into liquid in the low 140s Fahrenheit (~60–61°C) in a process called gelatinization. Gelatinization occurs due to the combination of heat and water opening up the starch matrix, which allows the amylase enzymes to get to work transforming the complex carbohydrate chains into their simple, fermentable constituent sugars. Complete gelatinization does not occur until the temperature has reached 149°F (65°C), because some starch granules are harder to "loosen up" than others. The same process happens with wheat across a broad range of temperatures starting around 125°F (52°C); rye gets moving even lower at 120°F (49°C); and oats do their thing at 140°F (60°C).

The true difficulty lies in the fact that most other grains and starch sources aren't so cooperative. Most other cereals require temperatures higher than our normal mashes. If you simply added them to your standard mash you'd gain very little from your extra fodder. You have to coax those starches out into the open. You have a few choices of what to do.

Adjuncting the Hard Way: Cook 'Em

If you can't mash your starches into submission, then you'll need to cook them harder. You could very carefully raise the grains to a precise set of temperatures, but there's little call for that level of care here because we are all about making this simple. We're trying to swell, hydrate, and blow out the starch granules, not massage them lovingly. Basically, you're making gruel, porridge, the basic foodstuff of mankind and we're feeding it to our mash. Bear in mind that this process will work with any grain/adjunct. It's not the subtlest method, but it's as simple as boiling and using. You're not aiming for perfectly plump and separate fluffy grains of whatever, you're going for a fully exploded thing.

You start by milling the grain, say, rice or corn, into smaller particles. (Drew has an old Corona® Mill on hand for this purpose.) Bring 1–2 quarts of water per pound of grain (2.1–4.2 L/kg) to a boil and stir in the coarse ground grits.

---

2   Patrick E. McGovern et al., "Fermented Beverages of Pre- and Proto-Historic China," *Proceedings of the National Academy of Sciences* 101, no. 51 (December 21, 2004): 17593–17598, https://doi.org/10.1073/pnas.0407921102.

Boil for 15–20 minutes, stirring constantly. Let cool slightly and add to your mash to boost the temperature.

Want to be more traditional? Prepare to work for it, Sunny Jim! Cool the sticky boiled rice/corn glop with additional water to 150°F (66°C) and stir in 20% of your initial cereal weight in pale malt (e.g., if you mash 5 lb. of rice, add in 1 lb. of pale malt). After 20–30 minutes rest time, in which the enzymes are attacking the starch and helping prevent its retrogradation, hit the heat and start stirring to bring everything back to a boil. You'll add this lava goo to your main mash as a heat booster. (You can skip the boil if you're not trying to raise your mash between rests.)

Congratulations, you've just performed an American-style cereal mash. This standard, labor-intensive method is pretty much the way American lagers were brewed. Modifications and simplification to the method will work, just as long as you heat everything up and blow up the starch.

A caveat: if you try the above methods, don't let the mass cool all the way. Retrogradation of the starch will occur—basically, everything will get bound up again but it's slightly worse. You'll have to heat up the cereal even more the second time to blow out the starches. Think how crunchy your leftover rice gets when left in the fridge overnight. It may be perfect for making fried rice, but it's lousy for making beer.

We'll get into some easy methods in a moment, but why go through all the hard work of cooking grains? Maybe you want to do things traditionally. Others hold that the less processed an ingredient, the better/fresher it will be as well as being less expensive.

A final note: this basic process will work on any grain out there. Quinoa, millet, amaranth, spelt, wild rice (OK, technically that one's a grass, but still)—if you're in doubt about the temperatures at which their starches will unfurl, a basic porridge will always do the trick.

Adjuncting the Easy Way

Thankfully, if you're lazy, pragmatic, or just looking for the simplest way to do this adjunct thing, then we have the technology, we have the processes.

Flakes and puffs.

Remember, the whole purpose of that complicated cooking process above is to blow everything apart. It requires heat and water. If you take the grains, soften them with steam, and then flatten them between heavy heated steel rollers, you accomplish the same thing and make breakfast cereal or oatmeal in the process. Look around your homebrew shop and you'll see flaked variants of wheat, barley, oats, corn, rye, and even rice. One of Drew's favorites is flaked potatoes for their silkiness, but make sure you get the 100% flaked version because potatoes will usually come packaged with powdered dairy to make instant mash potatoes.

DREW: Oh, you let the adjunct porridge cool down? Didn't we just tell you not to? Sigh, fine. Add some boiling water, stir it up and gently heat to a near boil. Keep stirring unless you really love scrubbing burnt starch from a pan bottom (keep some Bar Keepers Friend and a stainless steel scrubby handy, just in case). If you're small-batching this, hey, use a microwave. No seriously, make rice porridge.

DREW: Actually, let's back that up—the process of making something into a hot slurry will work on just about anything starchy. I've had beers made with leftover stale bread, cake, tortillas, bagels, pretzels, cous cous, pasta, etc. Give people a plate of beans and they'll find a way to make a pint of beer.

Flakes require no prep work, no milling, no soaking, nothing. All that's needed is your mash to rehydrate and the enzymes of your barley to finish the conversion. It's that easy.

Flakes do have some disadvantages. They have no husk material, which means your mash could get gummy and resist lautering. Also, because the grain has been smashed and more surface area exposed, the flakes can go stale and any fats (like in corn and oats) can become rancid with time. Look for fresh ingredients before getting flakey.

The other choice is to find your grains "puffed" or if you want to sound more proper, *torrified*. Most commonly, wheat, rice, and sometimes oats can be found ready popped via high heat. Think any breakfast cereal with the name "puff" or "krispies" attached. This also includes your air-popped popcorn. No need to crush or smash, just drop it straight into your tun and go!

Extract solids/liquids.

A number of adjuncts have extract forms, just like malt extracts. Some are ubiquitous, such as corn syrup and corn sugar, while others are a little harder to find, like rice solids. But, like your malt extracts, these powders and syrups go straight into the kettle and dissolve with a good stir. (Turn off the heat first unless, once again, you're fond of scrubbing.)

When formulating recipes, remember that many of the wheat or rye extracts you find in the homebrew shop are mixed with barley extract as well. Wheat extract, for instance, is usually a 50/50 or 60/40 blend of wheat and barley.

One Final Tip: Hulls are Your Friend

Almost all of the adjuncts we use lack a hull. You know, that weird, tough, papery outer coating on our barley malt. The husk is incredibly important to the brewing process; it prevents our hot mass of water and starch from glomming into a giant ball of the world's worst dough. The tough curls of husk cut through the dough and give our starch and sugar-saturated liquid space to move.

With adjuncts adding 10%–50% of doughy goo to the mash tun without any husks, they can get a bad rap for making nightmare lauters. It doesn't help that many adjuncts get super gooey as well. It's all a recipe for a long brew day… unless you use rice hulls. Any well stocked homebrew shop will have rice hulls available. They're tasteless and are dirt cheap. Some brewers find that they absorb water and recommend pre-soaking them. If you're going big on your adjuncts, buy a pound of rice hulls and mix them into your mash to save your brew day!

MAJOR PLAYERS OF THE ADJUNCT WORLD

Wheat

Barley's more glamorous cousin, wheat has always gotten a pass from the beer snobs of the world. Barley and early versions of wheat grew up hand in

DREW: I love watching what happens when I add torrified grain to the mash. The giant pile of cereal just dissolves like the Wicked Witch, never to be seen again. It feels like a magic trick.

DENNY: Briess Rye Extract is made with pale malt, rye malt, and crystal malt in pretty much the exact proportions you need to make my Rye IPA recipe. One tip is to always substitute a bit of table sugar (another adjunct!) in place of the same amount of extract. One-quarter to one-half pound will put the body, flavor and final gravity in the same range as the all-grain version.

hand, even back in Sumerian times. Wheat, with its softer, sweeter nature has usually occupied the upper hand in humanity's estimation. After all, thanks to the bounty of gluten unleashed by kneading dough, wheat makes the oft-desired fluffy bread with light crumb and airy chew. By comparison, barley bread is a tough, flat, hearty biscuit. It'll keep you on your feet, but you'll grumble eating another flat cake. (Incidentally, bread is also the reason why wheat was kept out of the Reinheitsgebot. The Bavarian court needed bread to feed the army and the people.)

In terms of beer history, wheat's been there since things started with the Sumerians and has never truly left the beer pot. Before the rise of "styles," European beer was a simple affair. Towns had a few varieties of beer, usually named for colors like "red," "brown," or "white." The white ales—a broad style—were usually the beers for the richer classes and incorporated precious wheat. Though a number of historical examples have been lost over time, you still find the white ale tradition prevails in styles like Bavarian hefeweizen and Belgian witbier. Some of our more interesting wheat ales, like Gose and grisette, are extensions of this class as well.

Since wheat gelatinizes in the same range as barley mash temperatures, you really don't need to treat it any differently than your regular mashed grains. Your real choices are going to come down to variety (red vs. white), origin (mostly US or Canadian vs. German), and malted versus unmalted.

Although we're treating wheat like an adjunct here, it can also be a base malt, even as much as 100% of your grist, though you will want to add some rice hulls for that.

RECIPE

White Ale

Batch volume: 5.5 gal. (21 L)
Original gravity: 1.053 (13.1°P)
Final gravity: 1.009 (2.3°P)

Color: 4 SRM
Bitterness: 13.3 IBU
ABV: 5.5%

Malt
- 6.5 lb. (3 kg) Pilsner malt
- 4.5 lb. (2 kg) wheat malt

Mash
- Mash at 150°F (66°C) for 60 minutes.

Hops
- 0.25 oz. (7 g) Magnum 12% AA @ 60 min.
- 0.50 oz. (14 g) Hallertau (or something noble) @ 10 min.

Yeast
- Wyeast 3944 Belgian Witbier

Extras
- 0.25 oz. (7 g) bitter orange peel @ knockout
- 0.25 oz. (7 g) Indian coriander, crushed @ knockout (Indian coriander is different than the traditionally available Mexican coriander, but Drew thinks it makes a difference!)

Hefe

Batch volume: 5.5 gal. (21 L)
Original gravity: 1.055 (13.6°P)
Final gravity: 1.011 (2.8°P)

Color: 4 SRM
Bitterness: 19 IBU
ABV: 5.7%

Malt
- 10 lb. (4.54 kg) wheat malt
- 4.5 lb. (2 kg) Pilsner malt

Mash
- Single-infusion mash at 150°F (66°C) for 60 minutes. (This mash protocol is controversial because a number of homebrewers claim the beer must be decocted, but fie!)

Hops
- 0.45 oz. (13 g) Magnum 12% AA @ 60 min.
- 0.25 oz. (7 g) Tettnang @ 5 min.

Yeast
- WLP306 Hefe IV or Wyeast 3068 Weihenstephan

Chill after the boil
- Ferment in the mid 60s°F (63–66°F) to emphasize the spicy clove flavors, higher temps to push bubblegum and banana flavors.

Rye

Like wheat, rye comes in both malted and unmalted forms. Unmalted rye is usually found as flaked rye; its flavor is slightly subdued compared to malted rye. Malted rye has a spicy flavor to it and adds a smooth, almost slick, mouthfeel to your beer; it also brings a lovely orange color. You can get all of those characteristics from flaked rye, but to a lesser degree.

Denny feels that you need to use a minimum of around 18% rye in order to really get much from it. He's gone as high as 60% of the total grist, but that's only for real rye lovers! The beer gets very spicy and almost viscous at that level.

Unlike crystal malts, rye is as fermentable as your favorite barley malt, unless you use crystal rye. You can also find chocolate rye, which is the same color range as barley chocolate malt but made with rye. The beer may have a fuller mouthfeel, but the rye won't affect your final gravity in an adverse way.

Rye gelatinizes at mash temperatures, so you don't need to do anything special to use it. Many people need to use hulls in order to get rye beers to lauter properly, but that's not a given. Denny has made many rye beers and never needed to use hulls. As always, the key is to know your equipment and what it's capable of.

So, what do you do with rye in either form? It's a great addition to many styles of beer. Start by replacing 20% of the base malt in a recipe with rye malt: rye Pilsner, rye *bock* or *doppelbock*, rye saison, rye IPA (duh!), rye porter, rye hefeweizen… Think of your favorite beer style or recipe and put some rye in it! If you use a large amount of rye, you may want to consider its spiciness and how that could affect your perception of the hops in a hoppy beer.

Wry Smile Rye IPA

Batch volume: 5 gal. (19 L)
Original gravity: 1.073 (17.7°P)
Final gravity: 1.013 (3.3°P)

Color: 13 SRM
Bitterness: 74 IBU
ABV: 7.95%

Malt
- 11.0 lb. (5 kg) pale malt (two-row)
- 3.0 lb. (1.36 kg) rye malt
- 1.25 lb. (570 g) crystal 60°L
- 0.50 lb. (225 g) Carapils
- 0.50 lb. (225 g) wheat malt

Hops
- 1.00 oz. (28 g) Mt. Hood 6% AA @ first wort hop
- 1.25 oz. (35 g) Columbus 16% AA @ 60 min.
- 0.50 oz. (14 g) Mt. Hood 6% AA @ 30 min.
- 1.50 oz. (43 g) Mt. Hood 6% AA @ 0 min.
- 1.00 oz. (28 g) Columbus @ dry hop

Water
- Add 1 tsp. of gypsum to the boil.

Yeast
- WY1450 Denny's Favorite 50 Ale

Extras
- 1 tsp. Irish moss or 1/2 tablet Whirlfloc, added 5 minutes before end of boil

Brewing notes
- Mash at 152°F (67°C) for 60 minutes.
- Boil 60 minutes.
- Ferment at 63–65°F (17–18°C) until FG of around 1.013 (3.3°P) is reached.
- Transfer to secondary and dry hop for 1 week or longer.

Rye Barleywine

Note: This is a beefed up version of the Wry Smile Rye IPA recipe above. Be sure to make a big yeast starter, or make a 1.050 OG beer first and use the entire yeast slurry from that for this beer. See, it's the same thing we talked about on pp. 132–33 with our Template Pale Ale to Template DIPA recipes!

Batch volume: 5 gal. (19 L)
Original gravity: 1.110 (25.9°P)
Final gravity: 1.025 (6.3°P)

Malt
- 15.00 lb. (6.8 kg) pale malt (two-row)
- 5.00 lb. (2.27 kg) rye malt
- 1.75 lb. (0.8 kg) crystal 60°L
- 0.75 lb. (340 g) Carapils
- 0.75 lb. (340 g) wheat malt

Hops
- 1.50 oz. (43 g) Mt. Hood 6% AA @ first wort hop
- 2.00 oz. (57 g) Columbus 16% AA @ 60 min.
- 0.75 oz. (21 g) Mt. Hood 6% AA @ 30 min.
- 2.00 oz. (57 g) Mt. Hood 6% AA @ 0 min.
- 2.00 oz. (57 g) Columbus @ dry hop

Color: 15.6 SRM
Bitterness: 104 IBU
ABV: 11.4%

Water
- Add 1 tsp. of gypsum to the boil

Yeast
- WY1450 Denny's Favorite 50 Ale

Extras
- 1 tsp. Irish moss or 1/2 tablet Whirlfloc, added 5 minutes before end of boil

Brewing notes
- Mash at 152°F (67°C) for 60 minutes.
- Boil 60 minutes.
- Ferment at 63–65°F (17–18°C) until FG of around 1.013 (3.3°P) is reached.
- Transfer to secondary and dry hop for 1 week or longer.

Oats

The humble oat. *Avena sativa* (Latin for "cultivated oat," clever, eh?). It's never been mankind's favorite grain. It can't make bread (no gluten) and it can't make beer by itself (not enough enzymes—more on that in a moment). Oats are a sort of weird fatty thing that people find comforting in gruel or oat cakes, but otherwise, meh. Like non-malt quality barley, so much of the oat crop ends up being horse feed or in the slop of the poorhouse. Oats have been part of human history since roughly forever, although we didn't start trying to purposefully grow the stuff until the Bronze Age, well after the cultivation of wheat and barley.

But that doesn't stop us from using it in beer. Oats, for all their humbleness and associations with poverty, do have a place in brewing beer. They provide richness, an unctuous mouthfeel, silky, sweet, a little gritty and gummy in higher quantities. Oats are one of Drew's favorite ingredients because they soften roasted and harsher notes and the sweetness they provide rounds the profile without being cloying.

Oats come in several usable styles. The least processed is the groat or oat berry, which is just the whole oat dried. They're nutty and fatty, which is interesting but does present a challenge. The most common form of oats you'll find are either steel-cut or flaked. Steel-cut, sometimes sold as Irish or Scottish oats, are just the groats chopped up into several smaller pieces; same nuttiness and earthiness as your regular groats, just more usable. Flaked oats are, like other flaked cereals, just flattened and steamed grains; but, unlike other flaked grains, you have several options with oats, from "regular," to "quick," to "instant" (in order of decreasing size and increased processing).

We highly recommend using the least processed oat you can get your hands on. Groats will need to be crushed, but all will hydrate and release starch at mashing temperatures without additional processing from the brewer. (We tested it!) Part of the reason you should go with the less-processed versions is to avoid the rancid and stale fats that bad oats can carry. The more surface area exposed, the more rancidity can happen. It's a bad idea!

There are two unique brewing version of oats that we love, malted and Golden Naked Oats®. Like the term implies, malted oats are processed just like barley malt, that is, they are steeped, sprouted, and then kilned. Drew really loves the nuttiness of malted oats and their ease of use—just grind them up and take advantage of the extra husk material for less tricky lautering. Thomas Fawcett is the longtime maker of these beauties. Meanwhile, Simpson's Maltings have created Golden Naked Oats, which are the oat equivalent of crystal malt. They're nutty, sweet, almost caramel and brown sugar-esque—like a really good bowl of maple syrup and brown sugar oatmeal.

In general, with oats you'll want to use somewhere between 5%–10% (e.g., 0.5–1.5 lb. per 5-gallon batch). But with some of the oat-specific styles we'll discuss, you'll see that you can get away with even more, at the cost of clarity and lauterability.

These days we tend to think of oats as being an element of British brewing, but, truthfully, outside of oatmeal or malted oat stouts, oats were never a big part of British brewing. You know who was oat crazy though? The Dutch. In the times of white ales, the Dutch had several oat-based white ales with up to 50% oats in the mash. After all, throw enough oats into a beer and it becomes a cloud factory. If only American craft brewers could figure out a way to use the oat to make things cloudy…Oh wait.

The Haze Craze Oated Pale Ale

Batch volume: 5.5 gal. (21 L)
Original gravity: 1.050 (12.4°P)
Final gravity: 1.011 (2.8°P)

Color: 7.3 SRM
Bitterness: 20 IBU
ABV: 5.0%

Malt
- 8.5 lb. (3.9 kg) pale malt
- 1.3 lb. (590 g) malted oats (or flaked)
- 0.67 lb. (300 g) Simpson's Golden Naked Oats
- 0.33 lb. (150 g) crystal 50°L

Hops
- 0.75 oz. (21 g) Magnum/Warrior/something neutral 12% AA @ 60 min.
- 1.00 oz. (28 g) Mosaic @ knockout
- 1 oz. (28 g) hops of choice (choose something fruity) @ whirlpool
- 2 oz. (57 g) hops of choice @ dry hop (for 1 week, ideally just prior to end of primary fermentation)

Yeast
- Wyeast 1318 London III

Brewing notes
- Single infusion mash @ 150°F (66°C) for 60 min.
- Ferment in the mid 60s°F for 1 week. Add the dry hops around day 3 or 4 of active fermentation. Allow to rest for an additional week before packaging.

Corn

So common, so cheap, so ubiquitous, so misused, and so, so the enemy of "real" beer. Corn, or maize as it's often known outside North America, is an interesting case of human intervention. It's just about the most extreme example of agricultural manipulation that mankind has ever pulled off. It's also one of the world's largest crops, coming in second behind sugar cane.

If you came across the original plant that begat corn at a picnic, you'd be sorely disappointed at the weird, baby corn-looking, hard green thing you'd be expected to eat. In Central and South America, teosintes were selectively bred over time to yield modern maize. It took scads of human intervention to turn that weird grass into the big bountiful ears of summer goodness we slather in butter.

Of course, the corn that feeds the world's food industry (in the form of corn syrup) or fuel industry (in the form of corn ethanol) doesn't look a thing like those plump fresh delights we eat. Most corn is still ugly, but it's hardy and plentiful and yields a ton of cheap sugar. But, as we know, beauty doesn't matter when it comes to brewing, it's all about the end result.

The traditional form of brewing corn would have been coarse corn grits or cornmeal. Yes, we know you smell creamed corn in something like Rolling Rock, but it was grits, not the canned vegetable. The grits would be cooked in the traditional American-style cereal mash method outlined earlier.

Eventually, due to the cost of labor and energy needed to convert grits to usable corn starch, the big brewers outsourced that portion of their brew day. Many breweries switched to flaked corn or corn syrup to save time and money. In fact, it's not uncommon to pass by a big American brewery and see tankers from Cargill and ADM filled with corn syrup waiting for use.

For an unusual way to use corn in beer, try popcorn. Use 1–2 lb. of kernels (before popping) for a 5-gallon batch of beer; it will look like a huge amount, but once it gets wet in the mash it will reduce. Try a light lager made with popcorn to really let the flavor come through.

Rice

Rice is often overlooked by homebrewers for the same reason as corn, which is that it's used by the megabreweries. Remember the rallying cry of, "If it's good enough for Budweiser, it's terrible for me"? Only, unlike corn, rice's reputation as a cheap additive is largely undeserved. At least in the case of Budweiser, they use an expensive golden rice grown exclusively for them in Louisiana. It's not cheap. In fact, when Drew was doing research, the golden rice turned out to be the most exclusive and expensive ingredient in a batch of Budweiser.

So sometimes we do want to use rice, even if it's not for cheapness' sake. Even if you're not into brewing a light lager, as it's traditionally used in, rice is still a great way to lighten the body of your beer and bring in a bit of unique flavor. Not a lot, mind you, but it will add a little bit of a grainy, nutty character to your beer and a light, crisp sweetness to the finish. But remember, it will cut into your beer's body and the head, which can be a good thing if planned for.

Looking beyond our American shores, rice is important to the character of so many international lagers. No surprise, since rice is a fundamental and available foodstuff pretty much everywhere in the world.

To use rice, you'll need to choose a form and a type. If you want to go the easy route, just look for rice solids. Rice solids work just like any extract or sugar—dump them into the boil, stir, done. There's also puffed/torrified and flaked rice available, which you can just dump into the mash.

If you insist on starting with whole rice, and hey, we aren't going to blame you, you'll need to use the American-style cereal mash method we mentioned above (or one of the variants). Grind your rice up into coarse chunks and cook away!

Don't forget, you can always cheat and just use precooked rice, but you'll want to reheat the rice to re-break the starch matrices. It's a little less efficient and probably not as "good" a method, but hey, we're homebrewers, since when did we care about efficiency?

What about a par-cooked instant rice, like Minute® Rice? Like instant oats, they're chopped up and steamed to the point of really just needing to be hydrated. They too can go directly in the mash, although Drew is usually paranoid and cooks them up. Old habits and what not. (Denny isn't paranoid and experience has taught Denny that Drew is wasting his time.) A word of

DREW: To give you an idea, at least pre-merger, Budweiser's brewers required that they only use the unbroken whole grains of rice to avoid oxidation. It was a huge scandal when there were rumors that the new corporate owners were going to end that policy. No confirmation if they ever did. And there you go, I can say a few nice things about the making of Budweiser!

DREW: If you really want to tell the difference between rice and corn in a beer, go grab a Budweiser and a Busch. Same brewery, same basic concept for a beer, only Budweiser uses rice and Busch uses corn. The difference between the two should be readily apparent and a lot of that is down to the adjunct choice. I got intimately familiar with the cost factor in college because the bar near my room had both on draft. Budweiser was the premium beer and was $$. Busch was the daily special that never changed in my four years—$2.50 for a large schooner. Yeah, it was dirt cheap.

warning though, make sure your par-cooked rice doesn't come coated in oil. Some variants do and, boy, do you not want that in your beer!

All told you can expect around 32 PPG when you add rice to your mash and from 37 to 42 PPG from rice extract.

We haven't even touched on rice varieties, like the wonderfully aromatic basmati and jasmine rices that can add unique aromas to your beer. Some folks love playing around with short-grain rices, like the proper Japanese sushi rices or the more commonly available Calrose medium-grain sushi rice from California. Even wild rice, which is technically a whole other genus of grass species, can bring something interesting to your beer, including a fair amount of color. Denny loves a wild rice lager in the vein of a Pilsner. Remember, when playing with these other variations, you'll want to keep your beer fairly subtle because their contributions will be hard to sniff out at first. Play and learn!

So, remember it's not that rice deserves its bad reputation, just that some brewers use rice to a beer's detriment. Actually, the same could be said for all adjuncts, not just rice.

RECIPE

Cream Ale or Lager

Batch volume: 6.0 gal. (22.7 L)
Original gravity: 1.052 (12.9°P)
Final gravity: 1.010 (2.6°P)

Color: 3.4 SRM
Bitterness: 19 IBU
ABV: 5.5%

Malt
- 9.5 lb. (4.3 kg) Pilsner malt
- 2.75 lb. (1.25 kg) flaked rice or corn (brewer's choice)

Hops
- 1/8 oz. (3.5 g) Magnum 12% AA for 60 minutes

Yeast
- Wyeast 2035 American Lager / Wyeast 1056 American Ale / WLP001 Calfiornia Ale / SafAle US-05

Brewing notes
- Single infusion mash @ 150°F (66°C) for 60 min.
- Ferment cool – 55°F-60°F for 2 weeks until the krausen falls and the beer is done fermenting. Crash the beer to 35°F for 2 weeks before packaging

---

Potatoes

Even the humble and lowly *pomme de terre* wants in on the beer action. Since potatoes are cheap, they've frequently been used as a starch extender, particularly in times of privation and rationing. Turns out potatoes are a hardy crop that can be reliably counted on.

They're also mostly water. No, seriously, a potato is something like 70–80% water by weight. Contrast that to malted barley, which comes in around 3–6%. So, the first question any brewer must ask is, "Just how many potatoes am I going to need to bump my gravity?" The safe answer, if using raw potatoes, is five times as much as you think. We say this because a potato provides roughly 20% as much starch as the equivalent weight of barley. For example, if a pound of barley provides a maximum gravity of 1.038 in a gallon of water (assuming 100% efficiency) then a pound of potatoes would provide a gravity of 1.0076.

With whole potatoes, first you need to choose a variety; we recommend a starchier, less waxy variety like the classic russet from Idaho. You'll want to slice the potatoes into thin medallions and either boil or steam until tender, then process with your handy dandy food mill/potato ricer and mix the potatoes into the mash. No ricer? OK, smash them into a fine paste and mix that in.

Better yet, let's skip the whole potato thing and just use potato flakes. Make sure you find flakes that are 100% potato with no dairy or other additives. You want flaked potatoes not mashed potato flakes (a.k.a. instant mash potatoes). The flakes just mix right into the mash and go to work. If you can't find flakes, you can also try potato flour or potato starch from the grocery store. This was a big go-to for brewers under rationing, but we can't speak to how well it works because we've never done it.

What quality does potato give your beer? If we're being truthful, not much. It gives you sugar. It gives you water. But, depending on how you structure the beer, it can also give you an incredible silkiness.

RECIPE

Earl Grey Saison

Batch volume: 5.5 gal. (21 L)
Original gravity: 1.058 (14.3°P)
Final gravity: 1.006 (1.5°P)

Color: 4.5 SRM
Bitterness: 33 IBU
ABV: 6.5%

Malt
- 5 lb. (2.27 kg) pale malt
- 3.5 lb. (1.6 kg) Maris Otter
- 1.5 lb. (680 g) oat malt
- 1 lb. (450 g) wheat malt
- 1 lb. (450 g) flaked potato (no dairy!)

Mash
- Single infusion mash @ 150°F (66°C) for 60 minutes.

Hops
- 0.6 oz. (17 g) Magnum 12.9% AA @ 60 min.

Yeast
- Wyeast 3711 French Saison

Extras
- 4 fl. oz. (120 mL) Earl Grey tincture @ add to keg
- Make tincture by soaking 1 oz. [28 g] of Earl Grey tea in 4 fl. oz. [120 mL] of vodka for 1 week and strain.

Variations
If you want a different spin on the tuber, you can use sweet potatoes, yams, cassava, yucca, or other starchy tuber in the same fashion as a plain russet potato.

Sugar

It's almost unfair to include sugar as an adjunct, but sugar is a major ingredient in both English and Belgian inspired brews. Whether whole candi sugar, like that used by a few traditional Belgian brewers, or the invert sugars of the British brewhouse, sugar has a place. We would argue that it's near impossible to make a number of beer styles without reaching for the sugar. And if you want to get weird about it, remember all that fancy mashing we're doing is converting grain starches to a fair amount of the simple sugars you can add via your grocery store shelf.

Many brewers stress out over finding the exact ingredients for their beers, but for regular sugars we say don't sweat it. Seriously, when you really dig into the variations between corn, cane, and beet sugar (a source of constant angst amongst homebrewers because Belgians like beets while most American sugar is cane), there's no discernable taste or aroma difference. Heck, go wild and crazy and play with different sugars; the Latin and Asian sugars you can now find in the grocery store—those have flavor! Sugars like demerara or piloncillo add a distinct character to your beer.

The place where we do think sugar choice matters is when it comes to syrups. While we still don't have ready access to the dark British invert syrups, which are critical to many of the classic bitter characters, there is an easy way to fake it by combining an invert syrup with blackstrap molasses. Here's the trick: invert's are numbered and the higher the number, the darker the color and the more character the sugar imparts. If you're looking for a light invert syrup, the easy answer is to use Lyle's Golden Syrup.

The other syrups are the Belgian candi syrups, a by-product of the sugar making process and long used in the Belgian brewing industry. For years, we American homebrewers struggled to replicate that holy grail of Belgian brews, Westvleteren 12, that magnificent *quadruple* produced by the Saint Sixtus Abbey in Vleteren. We tried all sorts of recipes and malts; Drew had one from a friend that felt pretty close that used six malts and two sugar additions. Turns out that once you get your hands on Belgian candi syrup the answer is simply a bunch of Pilsner malt and a pound of midnight-dark candi syrup. Nowadays, we even have American companies making brewing syrups, so you have no excuse! Yeah, sometimes ingredients matter.

To use sugar syrups, treat them like extracts: turn the heat off and stir them in vigorously; stir until you're certain the syrup is dissolved and then stir some more; finally, bring back the heat (or, if you're being tricky, add them to the beer during fermentation). Speaking of which, let's talk timing—when does it go in? Depends on what you want. If you just want the gravity and don't care about hop utilization, get it in during the early part of the boil. If you want to preserve sugar character or increase the amount of hop bitterness you obtain, add it late to the boil. If you want to maximize yeast health, there are some who would argue for adding the sugar to the fermentor after primary is rocking at high krausen to

DREW: Fun tip I picked up from Dave Mathis, a long-time professional brewer: if you're dealing with a crystalline substance like sugar, instead of dumping the sugar into the boil, put it in a mesh bag, like the ones you use for hops. When it comes time to add your sugar, just suspend the bag in the boil from a dowel or a spoon and let it hang. The action of the boil will gradually dissolve the sugar. No mess, no fuss, no scorchies!

DREW: Having said all that, I don't quite see the call for some of the clear syrups. Those seem less useful to me. But the dark syrups? Those are a miracle. Use them!

avoid overstressing your yeast. If you're going for a fermentor addition, make sure you have the sugar in a syrup form—adding crystalline sugar to a fermentor will cause the CO_2 to rush out of solution due to the nucleation sites provided by the sugar. This causes a messy beer geyser. You don't want that!

AND NOW IT GETS WEIRD

All of the adjuncts we've talked about up to now are at least passingly common in the brewing world. But, if you're like Drew, you want to go farther. You want to use stuff that will make Denny go, "What ARE you thinking?" And when it's that time, you need to have at least some idea of where you're going and what to expect. Well, we're just the guys to help you with that.

What follows is a list of fruits and veggies you might want to use in your brew, if you're crazy—OK, make that creative—enough. Most of the fruits will add sugar, so if you add them post-primary fermentation, be sure to give them enough time to let the sugars ferment out. A good rule of thumb with most fruit is to add a 1–2 lb. of fruit for every gallon of beer (120–240 g/L). Adjust that amount based on your tastes and how flavorful the fruit is. We know it seems like a lot, but some fruits only really sing when you're closer to 2.5–3 lb./gal. (300–360 g/L) … looking at you, strawberries!

The PPG estimates are just that, estimates. If you use fruit juice, it's a simple matter of taking a direct gravity reading so you know what you're getting. This list below is not exhaustive, but covers many of the ingredients that home-brewers love to use.

Fruit

Apple juice. The specific gravity of apple juice averages about 1.045. It's a reasonably subtle flavor, so try it in a beer that doesn't have a lot of other stuff going on. Apple juice can be added after primary fermentation has taken place, but be sure to give it enough time to ferment out after you add it.

Apricots. Apricots have about 45 PPG. It's a delicate flavor and you might want to consider boosting it with a bit of quality apricot extract. You can add dried apricots to secondary (make sure they're not sulfured) or add apricot juice. Again, be sure to give it time to ferment after adding.

Blackberries. Considered a weed where Denny lives, you'll get around 40 PPG from blackberries. Again, they're a subtle flavor, so you'll want to use at least a pound per gallon of beer (120 g/L). We recommend adding blackberry juice to secondary.

Cherries. Cherries are a classic flavor in many Belgian and sour beers, but don't limit yourself to those styles. Cherries in a porter or stout recipe, for example, can be wonderful. To avoid blowing out your taste buds, use less sour cherries for a beer than if you were using something sweeter like Bing cherries. Expect around 79 PPG.

Cranberries. Cranberries are a popular addition in the winter holidays.

Remember, cranberries are tart and tannic, so take that into account when you design your recipes. You might want to cut back a bit on bittering hops when you use them. Expect about 44 PPG from cranberries.

Lemons. Lemons can add a bright acidic note to your beer. If you use the sweeter Meyer lemons, you can use more of them. You will get around 36 PPG.

Limes. Using limes can give you the same brightness as lemons. If you use key limes, you can use more than if you use the more acidic Persian lime. Expect 36 PPG.

Mangos. Mangos are tropical fruit that can make a great sweet/tart addition to your beer. Try a mango wit. Expect around 70 PPG.

Melons. There's a world of melons out there and pretty much all of them can make an interesting sweet, earthy addition. Try making a puree with several varieties for a more complex flavor and aroma. You'll get around 57 PPG.

Oranges. Oranges can go in various styles, from Belgians to IPAs. They can vary a lot in tartness and sweetness, so be sure to taste them before adding their juice. Expect to get 48 PPG.

Passion fruit. Passion fruit (along with guava) is pretty common in South American beers. It can be a flavor that you just can't put your finger on, but can make a definite contribution to your beer's flavor. As Drew says "deeply odd"... but in a good way! Expect to get 61 PPG.

Peaches. Peach is not an uncommon addition to find in beer. Peaches have a sweet, earthy flavor and aroma that complements many styles. But they can be subtle, so you'll need to use a lot of them and possibly boost the flavor with extract. You can expect to get 48 PPG.

Pineapple. Pineapple can be an interesting flavor addition. If you add it to the fermentor, be aware that it will drive the pH down, possibly enough to affect the yeast. We recommend adding pineapple post-primary fermentation. Give it some time after that to see if it's going to ferment more. You will get around 57 PPG.

Plums/prunes. Plums and prunes seem to be a natural for dark Belgian styles, since those have so much of that flavor from the ingredients already in the beer. Denny's favorite method is to wait until primary fermentation has finished, then heat a wok until it's red hot. Add the plums or prunes to caramelize them, then deglaze the wok with some of the beer. Add all of that to a secondary fermentor and rack the beer on top. Expect 57 PPG for plums, 70 PPG for prunes.

Pomegranates. Pomegranates add brightness and acidity. Pomegranate juice is the most common way to use this fruit in beer. You can also use pomegranate molasses for a more intense flavor (and higher PPG). Expect around 75 PPG from the juice.

Raspberries. Raspberries are a classic in sour beer, but can be added to just about any style. Raspberry may be the most popular fruit flavor in beers. Expect to get 44 PPG.

Strawberries. Strawberries are something homebrewers love to talk about using, but it can be very difficult to get strawberry flavor into beer. You need to use more than you ever thought would be enough, and you'll likely have to bump up the flavor with some extract. Expect to get 61 PPG.

Tamarind. Tamarind is a citrusy sweet, tart, sour fruit usually sold as a paste, although you can find tamarind seeds also. It's a very intense flavor so approach with care. Use it on the last minute in the boil, about ⅛–¼ lb./gal. (15–30 g/L).

Watermelon. Watermelon is best used by juicing and/or pureeing, but be careful not to get any of the rind in with the flesh, unless you like the flavor of jalapeño mixed with grass! Expect around 61 PPG.

Vegetables

OK, so fruit's not weird enough for ya? How about a veggie beer? Yeah, now that's weird! We dealt with the humble potato earlier in this chapter, but here are some options from the road less traveled.

We're not going to provide PPG estimates for vegetables because, other than carrots and corn, there just isn't a lot of sugar there (typically 0.08 PPG or less). But they still need to go into the mash because there's starch there that needs to be converted into the minimal amount of sugar they have. Unconverted starch can be a breeding ground for bacteria, so you need to deal with that.

Aloe vera juice. Aloe vera juice has a bitter bite that can be interesting in a beer. Use ⅛–½ lb./gal. (15–60 g/L).

Beans. We don't think we've ever seen a beer that uses beans, but that doesn't mean you can't do it! Dried or canned beans should be rinsed and added to a cereal mash (unfortunately, beans need to hit 185°F/85°C to be useable). Dried beans should be broken up or milled before mashing. Use 0.5–2.0 lb./gal. (60–240 g/L).

Beets. Beets can lend a purple color and a sweet earthy flavor to your beer. Steam the beets before adding them to the mash. Use ¼–½ lb./gal. (30–60 g/L).

Carrots. Carrots are best juiced or steamed and added to the mash. Peel them first to reduce the earthiness. Use 0.5–1.0 lb./gal. (60–120 g/L).

Celery. Using celery can provide an elusive aroma that adds an indescribable "something" to your beer. Use 0.5–1.0 lb./gal. (60–120 g/L).

Chili peppers. Chili peppers are one of those things that you see in beer frequently. Maybe too frequently. We prefer the more aromatic, earthy varieties rather than the "blow yer face off" hot ones. Be very careful when using peppers—less is more! We like them roasted and added to secondary or a keg. The amount is up to you!

Corn. Corn (maize) has a long history in brewing. Some homebrewers like to use fresh corn in place of flaked corn when making a cream ale, although it changes the character considerably from a light corny flavor with flakes to a more intense, sweet, vegetal flavor with fresh corn. There are even breweries using corn chips in their beer! About 0.25–2.0 lb./gal. (30–240 g/L) is a good place to start.

Cucumbers. Cucumbers can be a great addition to a refreshing summer beer. One of Denny's favorite beers is a Berliner weiss made with cucumber juice. Just the thing when it's 95 degrees and you're sitting on the deck! Juice them, skin and all. Use 0.25–1.0 lb./gal. (30–120 g/L).

Lettuce. Lettuce, lettuce … let that sink in for a moment. You can add lettuce to beer for a unique bitterness. It takes a lot, but hey, we're homebrewers, we can do weird stuff. But no iceberg lettuce! Chop or puree and add to secondary. Use 1–2 lb./gal. (120–240 g/L).

Peas. Peas are a traditional ingredient in beer. You can use fresh or dried peas. Before using fresh peas, smash them up (pods too) before adding them to your mash. Use 0.25–1.0 lb./gal. (30–120 g/L).

Pumpkin/squash. Pumpkin and other squash show up every fall in holiday-themed beers. Although it's usually the pie spices people think of when they imagine these beers, you can get flavor from the gourds themselves. The best way to do that is to roast them in an oven before adding to your mash. Use ¼–½ lb./gal. (30–60 g/L).

Spinach. Spinach and its kale and chard brethren have assertive flavors and add a mineral quality to the beer. Some people like that, others not so much. Puree them and taste before adding to secondary. 0.25–1.5 lb./gal. (30–180 g/L).

Not Weird Enough Yet?

For the ultimate in unusual adjuncts, try adding mushrooms to your beer. Sure, they'll bring a certain amount of earthiness to it, but mushrooms have some wonderful subtle flavors underneath that funk. Adding them to beer transforms them and brings out flavors that you didn't realize were there.

When the idea of adding mushrooms to beer comes up, Denny usually gets one of two reactions. The first is, "Eww, that sounds gross and disgusting." The other one isn't so positive! But mushrooms can add great flavor to certain beer styles, so get over your bad self and let's talk fungi!

So, what beers benefit from mushrooms? How about a wee heavy with chanterelle mushrooms? Chanterelle have a lovely apricot quality to them that really sings with the malt in the style. Or what about portabellas in a brown ale? The earthy richness of portabellas really complements the beer. Candy cap mushrooms, which have a distinctive sweetness, go great in a porter. Or, if you have the budget, the exotic matsutake mushrooms work beautifully in a Belgian golden strong ale. Matsutake have been described as being like "dirty socks and Red Hots," but once they go into the beer they're transformed into a slightly funky, slightly earthy flavor and aroma that adds another dimension to the beer.

So, if you decided you want to take a leap of faith and add fungus to your beer, here's how you do it…

WARNING:

Mushrooms can be expensive and you need to use a lot of them to get flavor in your beer. Denny scavenges some of his own and gets most of the rest from trained, experienced mushroom pickers. **DO NOT** pick your own mushrooms unless you know EXACTLY what you're looking for! It's not worth the extreme danger that can come from using the wrong mushroom.

DENNY: I went through a learning process when it came to using mushrooms. I tried the usual homebrew vodka tincture, but I didn't get a lot of flavor and I didn't care for what the added alcohol did to the beer. After deciding that the vodka soak just didn't get me what I was looking for, I started playing with other methods. One thing that had always worked for me with fruit was vacuum-sealing the fruit, then freezing and thawing it before I used it. That breaks down the cell walls of the fruit and lets the juice come out more readily.

Trying the freeze/thaw method with mushrooms worked pretty well. When I thawed the 'shrooms there was a bit of juice in the bottom of the vacuum seal bag, and a quick taste revealed that's where most of the flavor was. To get even more of that flavor elixir, I chopped up the next batch of mushrooms before vacuum-sealing and freezing them. That certainly got me more liquid but there was also a problem. I had washed the mushrooms and sprayed them pretty heavily with Star San in order to sanitize them. I mean, they had just come from the woods and were covered with dirt, pine needles, and who knows what kinds of microbes. What sane homebrewer wouldn't do that? Unfortunately, that diluted the flavor and all the liquid made it really hard to get the vacuum bag to seal.

PROCESSING THE MUSHROOMS: DENNY EXPERIMENTS

Figure 9.1. Fresh matsutake mushrooms.

Figure 9.2. Processed mushrooms ready for freezing.

DENNY: It was obviously time to do something insane, something that no homebrewer would ever do. I left the mushrooms unwashed and unsanitized! Blasphemy! I told myself that the alcohol content and low pH of the beer would protect it. I would simply wipe off the surface dirt and hope for the best. It was a wild bet, and I won! I have now used this method dozens of times and have never had an infected batch.

I realize that this is anathema to most homebrewers, so if you can't bring yourself to try it, here's an alternative. After you chop the mushrooms, spray them very lightly with Star San. Other sanitizers such as iodophor work great too, but require a longer contact time. While I love iodophor for fermentors and yeast starters, Star San is a better choice in this case. Just brush off the dirt (no washing!), chop, spray, and vacuum pack.

The other thing you'll have to decide is how much to use for a batch. For chanterelles in a wee heavy, I find that you want about half a pound per gallon of beer (60 g/L). Three-and-a-half pounds of matsutake in a 5-gallon batch of BGSA (1.6 kg in 19 L) will give you a subtle flavor; seven pounds (3.2 kg) will leave no doubt about the earthy, funky flavor. For both portabellas and candy caps, anywhere from 0.5 to 1 pound per gallon (60–120 g/L) works great.

Look, we could keep going in this vein for a good long while. There are so many starch and sugar sources we haven't even touched. You can be a purist, if you want. We think ignoring adjuncts not only skips over the majority of humanity's fermentation history, but misses out on a broad swath of interesting flavors.

Having said that, we still encourage you to avoid adding everything all at once. You're making beer, not stone soup!

PROFILES IN SIMPLICITY: MIKE WILLIAMS OF CANDI SYRUP, INC.

If you don't remember the pre-candi syrup days, you'll be forgiven for wondering why we're talking about sugar syrups at all. Belgian candi syrups were first imported into the US via Los Angeles and instantly made dark Belgian beers a breeze. The introduction of this traditional brewing adjunct transformed brewing of Belgian style beers in America overnight, replacing the overwrought grain bills of yore with a lot of Pilsner malt and a bit of syrup to achieve the same goal.

Candi syrups in Belgium are a traditional by-product of sugar production, but Mike Williams, of CSI Confections, took on the challenge of making candi syrups domestically in the US. Mike came to the adjunct realm after a couple of decades at Hewlett-Packard. Mike gave us a bit of the history of candi syrups from his perspective:

> Candi syrup originated in England during colonial expansion when sugar was a premium commodity. Candy making by-products were washed from copper basins and sold to brewers as residual syrup (thus its name to this day). It is interesting to note that the English used these "cooked" syrups in brewing, which exemplifies the frugal nature of brewing. Some of this tradition made it to the American colonies in the form of porter ales that incorporated sorghum and molasses into the fermentation bill. Ales using candi syrup were remarkably varied and complex. It was innovation from the simple conservation of resources. Candi syrup became such an integral part of ale production that it began to be produced specifically for brewing and ceased to be a by-product.

Now, if you're a home cook of any sort then probably at some point you've made your own caramel. So, it should be just as simple to get a pot of sugar and water and go to town with the heat to make your own syrups, right? Well, making caramel is a little simpler and safer than candi syrup. In this case, we suggest you think about the value of your time; after all, you're not going to make your own malt, right? Besides, the candi syrup process isn't that simple, and is a jealously guarded secret to boot! Here's Mike again:

> We thermally invert sugars then cook them under specific environmental controls. Some of our candi syrups take four days to produce from sugar to packaged product. We never use additives and never use pre-inverted sugars. It's done the old-fashioned way each time. No shortcuts and no fillers, ever. We think this makes a better product.

Mike reinforces this point:

> In the present day, making even a small amount of candi syrup requires patience. Heating and cooling over many cycles is time consuming, with each cycle taking as much as 1–2 hours depending on the microvolume. With as many as 3–6 cycles (depending on color desired) this can take the better part of an entire day. Buying candi syrup is also expensive at the retail level.
>
> However, the frugal home brewer might calculate the cost comparison of 10 to 12 dollars in candi syrup versus the cost of 6–8 hours making something similar. Making truly fine ale with the same ingredients used in Trappist ales is possible in our world market today. The option to buy a consistent product is available to make your brew day simple, precise, consistent, and straightforward. Color, flavor profiles, and fermentation will match prior brews of the same recipe each time. Our best wishes on your next brew!

Seriously, thanks to the introduction and development of candi syrups here in the US, we can finally capture the nature of both Belgian and British brewing styles, which routinely rely on candi and caramel syrups. Give one of our favorite recipes for a Belgian quadruple a try. It just needs 20 lb. of Pilsner malt, a pouch of Candi Syrups, Inc. D-180, a tiny bit of Magnum for ~20 IBUs of bitterness, plus your favorite Belgian yeast.

This is why we like adjuncts, they can simplify the heck out of everything! ∎

10
SIMPLE YEAST AND FERMENTATION

Y ou've collected your equipment, picked out a recipe, gotten your ingredients, and made a batch of wort. Congratulations! Now, there's just one more step to making beer: fermenting that wort into the magic elixir you've been thirsting for. How hard can this be? You just toss in the yeast and wait a couple weeks, right?

Well, kind of... Maybe it's because there's minimal effort involved, but we've run across too many brewers who don't take fermentation as seriously as it should be taken. It's not hard to ferment your beer properly. If you want an incentive to do it right, remember this: if you don't properly control your fermentation, all the time, effort, and money you've put in up till now could be wasted, and that's a serious bummer.

"Look, we said it at the start of this whole thing and we've said it several times since—your yeast health matters. It matters more than anything else you do in the brewery."

Simple rules for ensuring a good fermentation and great beer:

- Choose the right yeast strain for your beer.
- Add enough healthy yeast to your wort to get the job done.
- Maintain the proper fermentation environment for your chosen yeast and style.
- Give the yeast enough time to work.

Yeast was the last beer ingredient to be enumerated. We hesitate to say discovered, because really those little fungi have been around longer than we have, so it seems imperious to say we discovered them. If you look at the Reinheitsgebot, the purity law for beer drawn up in Bavaria in 1516, you see that the only ingredients listed are malt, hops, and water. Yeast wasn't isolated and identified as the cause of fermentation until Pasteur described it several hundred years later.

There are endless stories of families making beer and stirring it with a "magic stick" in order to get it to ferment. Since even Denny isn't old enough to have been around back then, we have to assume that the stick had previous yeast embedded in it and stirring with it transferred some of the yeast to the wort. Hey, it makes for a good story!

Once the yeast meets the sugar-rich wort, it begins fermenting immediately while also growing more yeast cells. It was once thought that there were distinct stages that occurred before the yeast's metabolism switched to fermentation, but it's now known that everything kind of happens at once.

Besides more yeast cells, two other very important things are created: alcohol and carbon dioxide (CO_2), which are by-products of yeast metabolism. That's what we're really interested in! As the beer ferments, the food for the yeast (the fermentable sugars in wort) runs out and the alcohol content increases to a point where the environment becomes hostile for the yeast. At that point, the yeast goes dormant. But it's not dead. You can harvest some of the yeast from the fermentor and reuse it in future beers.

Besides creating alcohol and CO_2, the yeast also creates flavors in the beer. What kind of flavors and how much of them are in your beer is primarily determined by two things: the particular strain of yeast you use and the temperature at which you ferment.

THE IMPORTANCE OF YEAST IN ONE RECIPE

Just to demonstrate how different a beer can be just from which yeast you choose, here's a perfect example of a beer that with one yeast is a fairly innocuous American blond ale, but with another becomes a punchy aromatic Belgian blonde. There are even more dramatic shifts you can make, but this is one of our favorites because one mash can please a wide variety of drinkers.

Trans-Atlantic Blonde

Batch size: 5.5 gal. (21 L)
Original gravity: 1.048 (11.9°P)
Final Gravity: 1.010 (2.6°P)

Color: 4 SRM
Bitterness: 24 IBU
ABV: 4.8%

Malt
- 9.0 lb. (4 kg) Pilsner malt
- 1.0 lb. (450 g) caramel 8°L

Hops
- 0.5 oz. (14 g) Magnum 12% AA @ 60 min.
- 0.5 oz. (14 g) Willamette 5.5% AA @ whirlpool for 20 min.

Yeast
- American variant: Wyeast 1272 American Ale or Wyeast 1450 Denny's Favorite 50 Ale
- Belgian variant: Wyeast 1214 Belgian Ale or White Labs WLP550 Belgian Ale

Brewing notes
- Single-infusion mash at 154°F (68°C) for 60 minutes.
- American variant: ferment between 65°F and 68°F (18–20°C).
- Belgian variant: ferment with an initial cool start at 63°F (17°C) for the first 2–3 days of fermentation and then allow to warm up to 70°F (21°C).

TYPES OF YEAST

Ale and Lager Yeast

In brewing we're primarily interested in two types of yeast: ale yeast, *Saccharomyces cerevisiae*; and lager yeast, *Saccharomyces pastorianus* (a.k.a. *S. carlsbergensis* after the Carlsberg Brewery where it was isolated). These two main types come in hundreds of strains (and some even weirder variants that we'll cover later).

Each strain of yeast will differ slightly in terms of *attenuation*, which is how much of the sugar in the wort it will ferment, and *flocculation*, which is how well a strain drops out of suspension in order to clarify your beer.

Additionally, each strain produces different by-products that provide the actual organoleptic sensations in beer that we know and love. There are a few simple rules. In general, fermenting at lower temperatures produces cleaner flavors with less flavor contribution from the yeast; fermenting at higher temperatures results in the yeast contributing more fruity esters to the beer. With strains that give off spice characters (a.k.a. phenols) like cinnamon, nutmeg, and cloves, cooler temperatures emphasize them, but not because there's a magical switch inside the yeast. It's simply because the higher temperatures will emphasize the fruitier characteristics of the yeast, which makes it harder for your palate to pick out the phenols.

But wait, there's more!

"Wild" Yeast and Bacteria

There are other *Saccharomyces* species out in the world, and it turns out more than one critter figured out that sugar is useful! *S. bayanus* is most commonly associated with wine and cider and does fun things when mixed with beer yeasts, including killing them dead. There's *S. eubayanus*, a strain first isolated in Argentina but also found in other places, that turns out to be one of the parents (along with *S. cerevisiae*) of our lager yeast, *S. pastorianus*. Scientists are still puzzling out how all that came about. There are many other species, but they aren't generally used in the world of brewing.

A genus of wild yeasts called *Brettanomyces* (which translates to "British fungus"!) can be used in conjunction with other yeasts to impart characters to the beer ranging from fruit to a funky barnyard character. *Brettanomyces* was once thought to be a bacteria, but subsequent DNA analysis has shown it to be another variant of yeast.

But that doesn't mean that bacteria can't be useful in brewing. As weird a thought as that might be, things like enteric or lactic bacteria can add layers of complex flavor to some styles. Many Belgian styles owe their existence to these bacteria. That's enough of that for now. Join us in chapter 11 for even more bacterial weirdly goodness.

Top versus Bottom Fermenting

You may be wondering about some other terms thrown around about yeast like "top fermenting" and "bottom fermenting." Those terms came from the really old tests for separating ales and lagers. Ale yeasts were said to be top fermenting—the yeast rose to the top on a big rocky kräusen in the fermentor, perfect for capturing and reusing the yeast. Lager yeasts typically don't throw a big kräusen so the yeast settles to the bottom without ever really rising up, hence lager yeasts were said to be bottom fermenting. Later testing determined that rule of thumb was insufficient. Lager and ale strains were then identified based on their ability to ferment some of the longer chain sugars, such as raffinose. And then, because of the way of the world, even that turned out to be insufficient. Nowadays, for proper classification, scientists are increasingly turning to genetic testing to fixedly determine which way is north.

YEAST FLAVORS

In chapter 6, we divided yeast by flavor into the categories of clean, estery and fruity, phenolic, and sulfury. Let's see how those characteristics relate to the particular species of yeast. There are two yeast genera that are intentionally used for brewing beer: *Saccharomyces* and *Brettanomyces*. There are several species within these genera that are used, and then various strains of those species besides.

DREW: It's the way of the modern world—as we look closer, the less "whole truth" lies in simple black and white tests and rules of thumb. This is important if you're dealing with big issues, like say a commercial brewery, or running a big enterprise, but for us dweeby little homebrewers, the rules of thumb usually will work just fine.

Ale Yeast: *Saccharomyces cerevisiae*

In terms of flavor, ale yeast exhibits the largest variation of any of the yeast types used for brewing. Ale yeast can be squeaky clean, imparting no flavor of its own, to dramatically fruity, with distinct flavors and aromas like apple or berries, to phenolic, with notes of smoke or clove.

With such a wide range of flavors available, choice of yeast becomes as important as the choice of any other ingredient in your beer. Sometimes you want a very clean yeast that will impart no flavors of its own in order to let your malt and hops shine through. Other times the entire character of the beer can be defined by the yeast flavors. German hefeweizen, for example, would simply be a relatively flavorless wheat beer without hefeweizen yeast imparting the distinctive banana and clove flavors the beer is noted for. And if you ever want to be trapped in a discussion for hours (or days), ask Drew about the various saison yeast strains that exist. Bring provisions, you'll need them.

Most ale yeasts will perform best in the temperature range 60–70°F (15.5–21°C). Some will work at lower temperatures and produce even cleaner profiles, which is great for "pseudo lagers," ales with the low ester character of a lager.

DREW: I'd disagree, but why disagree with the truth?

Lager Yeast: *Saccharomyces pastorianus*

Lager yeasts have a lot less obvious variance than ale yeasts. They're a little more subtle, which for homebrewers may be beyond our typical scale of exploration. Lager yeasts are almost always very clean yeasts, although some tend to throw more sulfur or diacetyl characters than others. They are meant to be fermented at lower temperatures (48–55°F/9–13°C) than most ale yeasts. Some lager yeasts perform well at higher temperatures, but the general belief (and tradition) is that high fermentation temperatures should be avoided with lager yeast. Of course, as with all things dogmatic, these views have been challenged. There are even strains that produce amazing results at increased pressures, but that requires a bit of technology. (Check out our Experimental Homebrewing podcast for instructions on building a "spunding valve."[1])

DENNY: When has that ever stopped you?

The reason lager yeast have come to rule the world (if you look outside the world of specialty craft and microbrewing, it really has) comes down to its ability to more completely ferment the complex sugars found in barley wort. Earlier, we mentioned that the old technique of classifying strains used raffinose. If grown in media containing raffinose, a typical ale yeast cannot completely break it down, leaving behind a residual sugar, melibiose. Lager strains, however, do have the ability to completely ferment raffinose, breaking it down to melibiose and then degrading the melibiose to glucose and galactose. Although raffinose is not usually present in beer wort, a small amount of melibiose is, which lager yeast can consume. The end result in the beer is something a bit drier and crisper, part of that mystical refreshing character that lagers have.

---

[1] Episode 24 - We Answer Many Of Your Questions," September 28, 2016, *Experimental Brewing*, podcast, 1:40:44, https://www.experimentalbrew.com/podcast/episode-24-we-answer-many-your-questions.

Lager strains do produce a few funnier things in excess of their ale counterparts (or at least the aromas are more prominent in lagers), namely, sulfurous characters. Some lager strains straight up throw hydrogen sulfide, a.k.a. the smell of rotten eggs. Other strains are prone to producing dimethyl sulfide (DMS) in the right conditions, which gives a cooked corn or cabbage aroma. Both of these results are avoidable via strain selection and proper wort handling. (Follow the basic guidelines of brewing and you're fine!)

Why has homebrewing and craft brewing been so largely ale-focused when there are the mighty lagers? The first reason is that typical lager fermentations require temperatures in the 50–55°F (10–13°C) range, which is not as easily achieved as the ale range of 64–70°F (18–21°C). The second reason is the long, cold storage necessary for maturation—the "lagering" of lager beer. Lagering requires more temperature control, more time, and more space to keep fermentations moving along.

WHAT'S IN A NAME?

The more we started looking into the differences between ale and lager yeasts, the more we came to realize that maybe there wasn't as much difference as there appears to be. Looking at several dry lager yeasts, we noticed that they were labeled as *S. cerevisiae.* To help clear up the mystery, or confuse us even further, we talked to Dr. Bryan Heit, the author of the *Sui Generis Brewing* blog (http://suigenerisbrewing.com/) and an associate professor of microbiology and immunology. He was able to help answer the questions we had. Here's what Dr. Heit had to say:

A lot of the confusion of what lager yeasts should be called is due to the disastrous state that fungal taxonomy (naming of fungal species) has slid to over the past two decades. Back in the day when lager yeast was first identified, it was identified using classical microbiological techniques, which identify species based on characteristics such as the sugars an organism can consume, whether it reproduces sexually, and other characteristics. Based on this classification, lager yeast was clearly different from ale yeasts, and was first assigned the species name *Saccharomyces carlsbergensis* (after the brewery it was isolated from), and later *Saccharomyces pastorianus* (after Louis Pasteur, who developed the methods to allow the species to be isolated).

This naming began falling apart in 1985 when modern genetic techniques were invented. It very quickly became apparent that at least a part of the lager species' genome was derived from *Saccharomyces cerevisiae* (ale yeast), and the other part from a then unknown species of yeast. It took nearly 20 years, but eventually it was shown that lager yeasts contain two sets of chromosomes, one from *S. cerevisiae*, and the other set from *S. eubayanus*. The discovery that the non-*S. cerevisiae* portion was from *S. eubayanus* was only made in 2014, and so if you look back, there are other *Saccharomyces* species that were proposed as the source of the *S. eubayanus* part of the lager yeast's genome, which makes it even more difficult for people reading through the literature to figure out what is going on. To make things even more complicated, depending on the strain of lager yeast you are looking at, the amount of *S. eubayanus* genomic material can differ because some of the strains have lost differing amounts of the DNA they originally inherited from *S. eubayanus.*

In terms of whether a yeast company has misnamed the yeast, the answer is "technically no." There is no set way to name interspecies hybrids, but one convention is to use the name of the species that provided the largest portion of the hybrid's DNA, which for lager yeast is *S. cerevisiae.* But it is confusing when labs do this and, in my opinion, using *S. carlsbergensis* or *S. pastorianus* is less confusing even if those names are no longer official.

Wild Yeast: *Brettanomyces* Species

Brettanomyces (or "Brett") produces flavors that at first may make you think, "Why the heck would I want my beer to taste like that?" The flavors Brett produces are often described as barnyard, horse blanket, smoky, Band-Aid, foot odor, and putrid cheese…yum! Why would you want those in your beer? Because in the right amount mixed with the other flavors in your beer, they can create a depth and complexity that's not only intriguing but also delicious. And to be fair, there are some strains of Brett that create pleasant fruity flavors, like orange and pineapple. As a brewer, you will generally be working with one (or more) of three species of Brett: *Brettanomyces bruxellensis*, *B. claussenii*, and *B. lambicus*.

Brettanomyces bruxellensis (available as White Labs WLP650 and Wyeast 5112) is probably the most common species of Brett used in beer. Named for the city of Brussels, this is the strain that Orval uses to dose bottles of its beer. Anyone who's ever had an Orval knows that you chose your bottle by the age. Younger bottles will have a pleasantly fruity quality to them. As the bottles age, the Brett gets more aggressive and funky, getting into the classic sweaty, horse blanket flavors.

Brettanomyces claussenii (White Labs WLP 645) is at the opposite end of the Brett spectrum. It has a fruity pineapple-like flavor and can often be tasted in classic barrel-aged British ales.

Brettanomyces lambicus (White Labs WLP653 and Wyeast 5526) is associated with Flanders ales. It is intensely funky and sour. Just the thing for those styles!

Brett is usually used after fermentation with an ale yeast, although there are beers made with 100% Brett. Once fermentation is complete, or nearly so, you add the Brett along with something else (usually fruit) to provide sugar for the Brett to work on. Brett is occasionally used on its own, but not often.

So, now you have choices to make: clean, fruity, or funky; high temperature or low temperature? But you're not done yet…you have one more choice to make.

DRY OR LIQUID?

When we started homebrewing, liquid yeast was just starting to appear on the market. Before that, all yeast was only available as dry yeast, similar to bread yeast. In fact, bread yeast and beer yeast are the same genus. The difference is that beer yeast strains have been selected to produce alcohol while bread yeast strains have been selected to produce CO_2 to make bread rise.

In years past, dry yeast was kind of looked down on as being inferior to liquid yeast. Due to imperfect manufacturing processes, brewers would often get dry yeast packages that were contaminated.

The other disadvantage with dry yeast, historically, has been strain selection. Until the past few years, you had basic choices like "here's an ale strain and another ale strain that's like a lager." Slowly, the yeast manufacturers have been introducing new strains for our variety loving brewing ways. Today there

DREW: In the archive of Maltose Falcons newsletters, there were plenty of articles where microbiologists-turned-homebrewers took a close look at the available dried yeasts and invariably found contamination, primarily from spoilage bacteria like *Pediococcus* and *Lactobacillus*. These days the dried cultures are far more reliable.

are genuine lager strains available dry, like Fermentis' Saflager W-34/70 and Lallemand's Diamond Lager yeast.

Dry yeast does have its advantages though. It tends to cost less per package and it stores for longer periods of time. Packs have years-long shelf lives as long as you keep them refrigerated.

Liquid yeast gives you a lot more variety when it comes to selecting just the right yeast for your beer. This is especially helpful when you want to make a beer, such as a hefeweizen or a Belgian style, that gets a large part of its flavor from the yeast. The trade-off is that using liquid yeast takes a little more effort than using dry yeast. In most cases you'll want to increase the cell count of the liquid yeast you're pitching into your beer. Liquid yeast manufacturers claim that there are sufficient cells in their packages to ferment 5 gallons of a 1.060 OG beer. And we don't doubt them … It's just that the viability of the yeast starts decreasing the moment it's packaged, so when you get the yeast you may not have much of an idea how much happy yeast is left in the package.

GETTING THE YEAST READY TO WORK

Rehydrating Dry Yeast

The biggest advantage of dry yeast is that it's easy to use. Simply open a pack and pour it into your wort. Many people prefer to rehydrate the yeast in lukewarm water for a few minutes before adding it to the wort. Rehydrating means that you'll be pitching a larger amount of viable cells than if you just dumped the yeast in. But is that really necessary?

A package of dry yeast contains many more yeast cells than a pack of liquid yeast, but it still may not contain enough cells for the beer you want to brew. By rehydrating the yeast in water before putting it in your beer, the nutrients dissolve and become available to the yeast in order to grow more cells. If you simply pour the pack into your freshly brewed wort, the sugar in the wort causes an increase in osmotic pressure on the cells compared to using water. That increased pressure will kill a number of your yeast cells, but there will likely still be plenty to get your beer off to a good fermentation. At least, maybe, depending on the beer you're making.

There seems to be disagreement about how many cells are in a pack of dry yeast. Some people claim that there are as many as 18 billion cells per gram of dry yeast. Fermentis, a major manufacturer of dry yeast, says that there are 6 billion cells per gram in their packs. Lallemand, another major manufacturer, puts theirs closer to 5 billion cells per gram. But both companies say that an 11 g pack of their dry yeast is more than enough for 5 gal. (19 L) of 1.060 (14.7°P) wort. Both companies also used to recommend on their websites that you rehydrate the yeast before pitching it into your beer, but now there are conflicting opinions.

You want to make sure when rehydrating not to use water that's too warm. Yeast can be killed if the water is over about 114°F (45°C), so you need to be careful to keep your rehydration water around 95–100°F (35–38°C).

The biggest downside of dry yeast is the lack of variety. There are some strains of yeast that just don't take to drying as well as others. The number of different dry yeasts is always expanding though, so hopefully one day there will be nearly as much variety as there is for liquid yeast.

Liquid Yeast Starter

With liquid yeast you generally need to make a *starter* to increase the number of healthy yeast cells. A starter is basically a very small batch of beer. There's no need to use hops in it because you're not going to drink it! You're growing yeast, not making beer. Yeast grows best in a lower gravity environment, so you want to keep the specific gravity of your starter around 1.035 (8.8°P). Also, yeast grows better at warmer temperatures than beer is usually fermented at.

Starter by the Numbers

So, how many yeast cells do you need and how do you figure out how to get them? For an ale, you need 6–18 million cells per milliliter, depending on the original gravity (OG) of your beer. For a lager, the top end increases to at least 24 million cells per milliliter, again depending on OG. The higher the gravity, the more yeast you need.

Wyeast and White Labs, the two major producers of liquid yeast, both say that their packages contain about 100 billion yeast cells. Their websites claim one package is sufficient for 5 gallons of beer with an OG of 1.060.

DENNY: I've pitched yeast rehydrated and unrehydrated and haven't seen any difference. And some dry yeast manufacturers say to rehydrate while others don't. Being driven by laziness, my current practice is to not rehydrate. I'll continue to do that until I have good personal evidence that it makes a difference. I'm not telling you not to rehydrate, though. Try it and make your own decision.

DREW: Hate to admit it, but unless I'm trying to go big I usually pitch dry yeast directly. If I'm going to go big, sometimes I might be lazy and pitch two packs (bad brewer!), but usually I'll do "proper" rehydration and even add a pinch of a special rehydration nutrient called Go-Ferm Protect®.

DENNY: My experience has led me to make a starter for any beer over 1.040 OG. It just works better for me that way.

DREW: And I just make a starter every time out of flat paranoia. Also, if I always make a starter, I know my yeast is somewhat healthy. I tend to have a lot of older yeast packs laying around anyway, so it's pretty straightforward.

One way to figure out how much yeast to pitch is to use a yeast calculator. Calculators are often available as part of brewing software, as well as on several websites. A calculator will generally ask you for the date the yeast was manufactured so it can make an educated guess at how many viable cells might be in the pack. It will ask you for the amount of beer you're intending to make and what the original gravity will be. It will probably ask you if you're making a simple starter (simply putting the yeast in and letting it sit), or if you're using a stir plate or aeration with your starter. All of those things factor into how big a starter you'll make and how long it will take.

DREW: Or, better yet, until you have a real desire to dig deep into the weeds of flavor manipulation by pitch control, make a quart or two of starter for your beer. It's pretty much what I do.

DENNY: When it comes to flavors created by the amount of yeast you pitch, there are two schools of thought. One says that if you want more ester character from your yeast, you should pitch fewer yeast cells than you would otherwise. How much less? You'll need to experiment to see what you like. That's what makes this such an uncertain way to control ester production. The idea is that the stress from underpitching will lead the yeast to produce more esters.

On the other side of the debate is the theory of acetyl coenzyme A. Acetyl CoA is necessary for both cell growth and ester production. When acetyl CoA is mostly being used for one of those things, it cannot be used for the other. When you increase the rate of yeast cell growth through methods like aeration, less acetyl CoA is available for ester production. Conversely, low nutrient and/or oxygen levels slow cell growth and increase ester production. Dr. Clayton Cone of Lallemand has found that dropping oxygen levels in wort from 8 ppm to 3 ppm can cause an eightfold increase in ester production.

So, which theory is correct? If we were microbiologists we might be able to give you a definitive answer. But we're not, so we can't. The main thing is to know about both of these theories—we suspect that results will vary depending on the strain of yeast you use, but try it and decide for yourself. But be aware that trying to control beer flavor through the amount of yeast you pitch can be a pretty uncertain way to do things. We think you're much better off by careful selection of yeast strain and fermentation temperature than trying to guess at and control the amount of yeast you pitch.

Simplifying the Starter: The Vitality Starter

DREW: Who said beer couldn't be a religious experience?

Denny did starters by the numbers for many years, the whole sciency, stir-plate-and-flask kind of thing. Yeah, it was effective, but it was also a pain. You had to make the starter several days to a week in advance of brewing, then refrigerate it for a day or two in order to help the yeast settle on the bottom. On the day of brewing you decant the spent wort, leaving just the yeast slurry behind and that slurry gets pitched into your new wort. And then, one day there was a revelation.

A commenter appeared on the AHA discussion forum, "S. Cerevisiae."[2] It was obvious that this commenter knew more about yeast than most people think there is to know. He pointed out that the calculators were doing nothing more than making a wild guess at the starting yeast viability and the amount of growth that would occur. He also mentioned there was a potential problem with using a stir plate that could damage the cells as it stirred them, pointing out that the yeast manufacturers didn't use stir plates because of that.

The commenter advocated a yeast starter method called "Shaken, Not Stirred." His ideas were resisted at first because they didn't sound appropriately sciency. But when you look at it, you see that what this commenter was talking

2   S. cerevisiae, January 14, 2015, comment on Philbrew, "Right RPM for stir plate?" https://www.homebrewersassociation.org/forum/index.php?topic=21705.msg275578#msg275578.

about was the same method that Denny used in the late 1990s when he first started making yeast starters. Science might advance with every passing year, but sometimes the old ways are still valid.

The idea is to make what's called a "vitality starter." Unlike the starters based on calculated cell count (called a viability starter), the idea with a vitality starter is to pitch actively working yeast already fermenting strongly and ready to do its business in your wort. You use the starter to somewhat increase the cell count, but less so than in a viability starter. The real beauty of a vitality starter is that it's working before it even goes into your beer!

Vitality Starter Procedure

A vitality starter for 5 gallons of average strength (1.050–1.075 OG) wort starts with a quart of 1.035 wort in a gallon container (Denny uses a glass apple juice jug, Drew uses a large, oversized chemical reagent jug). The day before you brew, bring a quart (~1 L) of water to a boil. Remove it from the heat and stir in 3 oz. (85 g) of light dry malt extract and a pinch (⅛ tsp or less) of yeast nutrient. You can get by without the nutrient, but it's cheap insurance so we prefer to use it. Return to the heat and boil for 5 minutes or so. Cool the wort under 80°F (27°C). Denny cools his by putting it in a sink of ice water and monitoring the temperature.

Once the wort has cooled down, pour it into a sanitized starter container. After putting your cooled wort into the container, shake it until the container is filled with foam. The foam contains oxygen that the yeast will use to synthesize sterols, which will keep cell walls flexible and encourage budding (cell division and growth). The more foam, the more oxygen in your wort and the more subsequent cell growth. Now pour in your liquid yeast. Set the container in a place where it can stay between 60–80°F (16–27°C).

The next day, your starter will be ready to go. When you pitch it, the entire actively fermenting starter goes in. No refrigerating and decanting like you would do with a starter made on a stir plate. In fact, no stir plate! All in all, it's a much more straightforward, dare we say simple, process.

But the best part is that it works at least as well as the calculator and stir plate method. Yeah, it's cool to feel like a real scientist when you make a starter in a flask on a stir plate. But it's also a waste of time and effort. And those are two things that we don't want to waste.

High-Gravity Fermentations

If you're wondering about the world of bigger fermentations—say, above 1.080 OG or so—we actually recommend the simplest way to deal with the yeast is fermenting a lower gravity batch of beer and then using the yeast cake from that to drive the ferment of the "monster" batch. Drew does this all the time. His high gravity Falconsclaws lager, which starts at 1.140 OG and uses a lager yeast that traditionally requires more yeast cells to begin with, is fermented with half a cake of Zurich lager yeast from a 5 gal. batch of a modest gravity *schwarzbier* or traditional bock.

DREW: Don't believe us that it works? We'd say trust us, but that's boring. We've done trials on it and found that it works at least as well as making a full-fledged stir plate starter with less fuss. Put off by all that starter wort going into your beer? Nobody says you can't chill and decant like you normally do (we're assuming you make a starter, because of course you do).

CANNED STARTER WORT

This is Drew's canned starter method that simplifies getting going with your brewing. All it takes is malt extract, a pressure canner (a larger version of a pressure cooker), and a mess of mason jars. It's a simple recipe and a simple process. Just a few hours and you have starter material for multiple batches.

- Per quart jar, add 3.2 oz. of DME and a pinch of yeast nutrient and fill with water. Close the jar with a canning lid and a ring; close it finger tight.
- Put the jars in the pressure canner with an inch of water. Operate the canner according to the instructions.
- Allow the jars to cool, remove the rings and store.
- To use, sanitize the outside of the jar, pop the lid, and pour the wort into your sanitized starter vessel and pitch the yeast.

FERMENTATION

You've got your yeast and it's raring to go. Those little unicellular fungi are champing at the bit to gorge themselves on a buffet of sugary goodness, like a rabid pack of six-year-olds at Halloween. Our challenge as brewers is to keep the partygoers happy, the mess to a minimum, and the level of energy controlled and somewhat calmer than an explosion.

If yeast health is job number 1 for brewers, fermentation temperature control is number 2. (For the record, sanitation is really job number 1.5, but why ruin a perfectly cromulent list?)

If we were running a professional brewery, this is where we'd tell you to break out the glycol-jacketed fermentors and just punch in a temperature. (And hey, big surprise, some homebrewers have these types of gadgets—you crazy loons!) While you don't need a gleaming super-cooled stainless steel fermenting vessel, you do need to control your temperature!

Why Control Fermentation Temperature?

Temperature is what controls the growth rate of the yeast and that growth rate in turn controls what by-products the yeast produce and in what amounts. Keep in mind, in order to know how to control the temperature you have to know what the temperature is. The stick-on thermometers that go on the outside of your fermentor are remarkably accurate. We recommend that you put one on every fermentor you have.

Before we start talking about why fermentation temperature control is important and how you do it, we need to define a couple of terms you'll often hear used to describe flavors and aromas created by yeast.

Esters are chemical compounds that usually manifest themselves as fruity. Apple, banana, pear, honey, and roses are examples of esters that may be found in beer. Sometimes esters are unwanted, but other times yeast strains are specifically selected for the esters they impart to beer. For example, German hefeweizen yeast produces a banana flavor and aroma due to an ester known as isoamyl acetate.

Phenols tend to show themselves as clove-like, medicinal, or smoky. Generally, phenols are considered undesirable in beer. An example is cholorophenols, created by using water than has chlorine or chloramine in it. If you've ever tasted a homebrew that reminded you of Band-Aids, you've had the unfortunate experience of tasting chlorophenols. But sometimes phenols are desirable. The smokiness of a *rauchbier* or the clove notes of a good hefeweizen are examples of desirable phenols.

The thing to be aware of for beer fermentation temperatures is that cooler temperatures lead to cleaner, less estery beers, while higher temperatures produce more fruity esters. So, fermentation temperature gets manipulated depending on what type of beer you make. A British ale, where those fruity notes are desirable, benefits from a bit higher fermentation temperature than an American ale, which in general should get less of its character from the yeast.

Easy Methods for Controlling Temperature

Short of getting yourself a glycol jacket or a big walk-in cold box (so jealous of the people with those), there are really only a few ways of getting your beer to stay at the right temperature. But first…

Primary rule for controlling fermentation: Short of supercharged cooling mechanisms, you will not be able to force a beer's temperature down once fermentation starts kicking into high gear. In other words, don't cool your wort in the kettle to 75°F, pitch a bunch of yeast, and then try and lower it to 50°F for lager fermentation. Fermentation is exothermic (heat generating)—once it kicks off, your fridge isn't going to budge that wort mass down any.

OK, so we've got that out of the way. Chill your wort to fermentation temperature prior to pitching your yeast. If your kettle chilling can only get you down to 75°F (24°C), it would be best to offer a quick prayer to the beer gods, trust in your sanitation, and put the fermentor somewhere chilly until it's cool enough.

There are three primary ways of controlling your fermentation: ambient air, a water bath, or a fridge/freezer. The first method, ambient air, is the "trust in your weather forecast/air conditioning" method. In other words, you stick your fermentor somewhere cool and leave it be. While achingly simple, the big disadvantage with relying on ambient air is that fermentation can raise the temperature of your wort in the neighborhood of 10–15°F (5–8°C), which means for an ale you want your fermentation space to be, say, 50–55°F (10–13°C). That's a little cooler than most of us can manage.

The second method is using a water bath along with ice and/or a heater. Placing your fermentor in a water bath and using ice or a heater to stabilize

DREW: I go one step further—I almost always advocate for chilling below your desired fermentation target. Say 63°F if you want to ferment at 65°F. I think it results in cleaner better beers.

DENNY: And don't worry if you're a little below the recommended temperature range for the yeast. First, that's only approximate. Second, the heat created by fermentation will quickly raise the wort temperature up to where you want it. That's why you pitch at a temperature just a little bit lower than your fermentation temperature.

DREW: In an effort to emulate our professional cousins, some homebrewers use thermowells, which are sealed tubes that are suspended in the wort. The tube is open to the outside and made for slipping a temperature probe into. The idea is you get a better contactless reading of the wort temp. In my experience they're not worth the extra hassle of cleaning and sanitation risk. Just tape the probe to your fermentor or figure out a pattern of control that works for you.

the water bath temperature is the cheapest, easiest, and least accurate way of managing your temperatures. But, boy, is it attractive from a cost standpoint—really, as a fan of cheap and easy it's hard to beat. For many years, Denny used the tub of water method. He put a large plastic garden bucket in a spare closet (dark, right?), filled the bucket with water, and then put his fermentor in the water. To cool things down, Denny used frozen ice packs that he dropped into the water in the bucket. To warm things up, he had an aquarium heater in the water in the bucket. Denny also used (and still does) Fermometer strips on his fermentors to monitor the temperature. His tests have found these strips to be very accurate, or good enough for beer at the very least!

The fridge/freezer method also requires a thermostat and probe set-up, but this method affords you more control over your fermentation temperatures. Air is a lousy cooling mechanism. It has no thermal capacity, which makes it really difficult for it to move the temperature of the wort. In other words, get your wort near/at the temperature you want it to ferment at before the yeast takes off. Don't think you can pitch yeast into wort at 75°F, stick it in a fridge set to 65°F and expect it to cool the wort that low before the yeast is generating a ton of heat.

These days, Denny has a 15 cu. ft. chest freezer that he uses as a fermentation chamber. It is plugged into a temperature controller that has its probe taped to the side of his bucket fermentor. Also plugged into the controller is a reptile heater bulb. Denny sets the minimum and maximum temperatures he wants the freezer to get to using the controller. If it gets too warm, the freezer comes on until it hits the preset temperature. If it gets too cool, the heater bulb comes on. A reptile heater bulb is a great way to warm up a fermentation chamber that's too cold. They're easy to use, relatively inexpensive, and because they're ultraviolet they give off no beer-spoiling light.

The kind of set-up above that Denny has is very effective and simple, but it's not the cheapest way to go. Another trade-off of money for simplicity.

BEER AND LIGHT

Wait, is your beer a vampire? Yep, light levels need to be controlled also. There is a long-standing beer myth that repeated heating and cooling of beer causes it to turn "skunky." But that's not it! It is actually certain ultraviolet wavelengths of light that can cause a beer to turn skunky. If you've ever had certain light lagers, you know that aroma. Turns out that sunlight or fluorescent light will cause some hop-derived molecules (isomerized alpha acids, if you want to be geeky about it) in the beer to break apart and recombine with sulfuric compounds. The resulting compound is called mercaptan and is the same thing that's in skunk spray! So, while you look to control your fermentation temperature, keep your fermentor in a darkish place too. Don't look for a blackout environment—it's more about reducing the amount of ambient light your beer receives.

One of the reasons that beer is usually packaged in brown bottles is that they block the ultraviolet light better than clear bottles. Green bottles are a little better than clear, but not much. And as you might suspect, the hoppier the beer, the more susceptible it is to skunking. For example, a very hoppy IPA in a clear glass in direct sunlight can skunk in as little as a few minutes.

Temperature Manipulation

One of the great advantages of setting up a fermentation chamber in a refrigerator or chest freezer is being able to easily and accurately manipulate the temperature of your fermenting beer. Manipulating the fermentation temperature allows you to get your beer ready to drink faster than if you simply let it sit at one temperature for a couple of weeks. The idea is based on the fact that the majority of esters are produced in the first few days of fermentation. After that, you can safely raise the temperature in order to get the beer to ferment more quickly. And once it's done fermenting, you can easily drop the temperature to near freezing to help clear the beer. Although the concept is the same for both ales and lagers, the specifics vary a bit.

For ales, start off in the 63–65°F (17–18°C) range. This might seem low based on yeast manufacturers' recommendations, but it will be fine for just about any ale yeast out there. Leave it at that temperature for 4–5 days, which will get you through the bulk of the fermentation. On day 5 or 6, raise the temperature to 70–72°F (21–22°C) and leave it there until the fermentation is done. Depending on the beer, that can be anywhere from two to five more days. Use the tips below to determine when fermentation is done.

For lagers, start the beer in the range of 50–55°F (10–13°C). After about four days, check the gravity of the beer. You want it to be at about 50% toward your expected (or guesstimated) final gravity (FG). At that point, raise the temperature by 3 degrees Fahrenheit (~1–1.5°C) and leave it there until the beer is about 75% of the way to your expected FG. At that point, raise the temperature to 62°F (17°C) and hold that until the beer is 90% of the way toward your expected FG. At that point, raise the temperature to 66°F (19°C) until the beer reaches your expected FG. Using this method, 75% of your fermentation will be done at 58°F or less.

With either an ale or lager, once you hit FG, drop the temperature to 33°F (0.5°C). An ale should spend anywhere from 3–7 days at this temperature. A lager will take anywhere from a week to several months, depending on how long you can wait!

WHEN IS FERMENTATION DONE?

Probably the biggest question people have about fermentation is how to tell when it's done. Denny likes to say, "The beer makes the schedule, not the calendar," but that's pretty lame (although he thinks it's clever).

In truth, the only way to be certain fermentation is finished is to take a specific gravity reading. When you get the same result three days in a row, the beer is done and ready for the next step. But how do you know when to take a reading? So many questions, but there are answers…

You can almost never go wrong in anything related to brewing by just waiting a little longer. If you're not sure the beer is done, wait a few more days. In most cases, for most beers, two weeks should be enough time for fermentation to finish.

There are visual indicators that can help you guess when it may be done. One of the most common things people look for are bubbles (or lack thereof) coming from the airlock. That's a good indication, but it's only an indication. Because cold liquid holds more CO_2 than warm liquid, bubbles coming from the airlock could mean nothing more than the temperature has gone up and the CO_2 that dissolved into the beer as it was fermenting is now coming out of solution. A lack of bubbles can also be caused by a bucket fermentor lid that isn't tightly sealed, in which case CO_2 will escape from the lid rather than the airlock. An absence of bubbles isn't meaningless, but you need to look at other things to be certain it means what you think it means.

Another sign fermentation might be over is the lack of kräusen. Kräusen is the foam that forms on top of the beer as it ferments. As fermentation proceeds, you'll see the kräusen build up and then slowly recede. So, if it's been two weeks, the kräusen has fallen, and there are no bubbles coming from the airlock, there's a good chance your fermentation is finished and you should take a specific gravity reading.

Some software will try to predict what your FG should be. It's only a semi-educated guess on the part of the software since there are so many things that can influence your FG, but it does give you a target to shoot for. Don't get hung up if you're a few points under or over the predicted target. Given what the software is trying to do, that's darn good!

The next thing you have to decide is whether you want to do a "secondary fermentation." This used to be the norm for homebrewers, but not so much anymore. The idea is that you transfer the beer to another fermentor (the secondary) and let it sit for a while to clarify and "clean up." In truth, any clean up should happen during active fermentation while there's food for the yeast. Clarifying is directly related to time, so if you simply let the beer stay in the primary fermentor for longer, it will clear as well as if you had moved it to a secondary fermentor.

Whether or not you do a secondary, you want to make sure to give the beer time for maturation. A few extra days in primary will give time for the reduction of diacetyl and acetaldehyde levels, which will be done by the yeast.

It's also been thought that you need a secondary to get the beer off the yeast in order to prevent off-flavors. This idea comes from the world of commercial brewing and has little applicability to most homebrewers. In a commercial brewery, tall narrow cylindroconical fermentors (CCFs) are used. This means that there is a large column of liquid (which is heavy) sitting on top of the yeast. The pressure from this column of liquid could theoretically cause yeast cells to rupture and off-flavors to form. In order to prevent this, CCFs have valves on the bottom that allow yeast to be discharged. The homebrew version of this concept (unless you're one of the people who has a CCF at home) is to simply remove the beer from the yeast by transferring to a different fermentor.

Except… we don't use tall, narrow fermentors that apply thousands of pounds of pressure to the yeast. We generally use buckets or carboys, which are short and wide in comparison to a CCF. So, the need to transfer to get the beer off the yeast is lessened. (Although we do still recommend not leaving the beer on the yeast for more than a month or two – your beer needs to be enjoyed after all!) In addition, perhaps most importantly, yeast health these days is far superior to what homebrewers used in the "olden days" and strains are far less susceptible to ill effects, not in small part due to the improved quality of packaging. As we stated above, good yeast health and all the work we do to maintain it allows brewers to focus on making beer instead of never-ending minutiae.

So, the general rule of thumb is you shouldn't bother transferring to a secondary fermentor for most beers. Simply leaving the beer in the primary will provide the clarification you're looking for. (Doesn't that sound Zen?) If you transfer the beer, you not only waste your time and effort, you run the risk of picking up oxygen, which can shorten the life of the beer, or even contamination. Sure, we know you're gonna be careful and minimize those risks, but why take a chance with something that's pretty much unnecessary? And aren't we trying to make things simpler?

But there are a few times when a secondary might be appropriate. The main one is when you're adding fermentables, which can restart fermentation due to the sugars they contain. For instance, if you want to use fruit in your beer, the best way to do it is to put the fruit into an empty, sanitized fermentor and rack the beer onto it. Another case where a secondary might be useful is when dry hopping. Certain strains of yeast will interact with hops to create flavors that don't come from either one alone. This is commonly called "biotransformation," but that's a specific term that we can't use for all of these interactions. There is also evidence that biotransformation doesn't really exist! Sometimes, these interactions are exactly what the brewer is looking for, like the "juicy" New England IPA style, where much of its unique character comes from the interaction between hops and yeast. (Although even then it seems most of the beneficial interactions arise when the yeast is actively fermenting, not falling out.) For other styles, the interaction between yeast and dry hops is undesirable, so getting the beer off the yeast before dry hopping provides a different, maybe sharper, character of hoppiness that more accurately represents the hop itself.

But if you do or don't go to secondary, there's one final step that we think is key to getting the best bang for your buck and it's as simple as getting your beer ice cold and letting it sit. This is the vaunted "cold crash" and it's really not that dramatic. Reduce your beer in temperature to, say, 35°F (1.7°C) or thereabouts, and let it sit. Drew does this in a keg with CO_2 on top of it to avoid the vacuum factor that the cold crash will cause. (A decrease in temperature means a decrease in pressure in the headspace behind the airlock, which leads to a low vacuum/suck back of the sanitizer in your airlock/blowoff.) The cold crash punches down all the remaining yeast, trub, hop matter, and big gloppy protein strands and forces it all to settle out. Once down at the bottom, assuming you're careful with your transfers, it will never bother you again! We like it as a gentle clarifying and finishing step. Just turn your fridge/freezer/chamber down as close as you can get to 35°F and leave the beer there for a few days. You'll be surprised!

Look, we said it at the start of this whole thing and we've said it several times since—your yeast health matters. It matters more than anything else you do in the brewery. Even if you have the world's worst sanitation, temperature control, recipe formulation, and bottling practices, good yeast health can at least get you something drinkable (maybe in the loosest possible sense of the word). If you take nothing else away from all of our blatherings, remember this:

- Use healthy yeast. Do everything you can to insure that your critters are happy and plentiful. Make a starter, use more packs, whatever you need to get everything raring to go.
- Use good sanitation. But you know this, of course. You want your yeast to have a playground unfairly slanted their way. Clean, sanitize, and then hit the wort with a ton of yeast for the cleanest fermentations possible.
- Control your temperatures. At least for a little while. If you can keep the chill on your beer for the first few days, you'll be a much happier camper when your final product is ready. Keep in mind, this doesn't mean let your beer run amok in the 90s Fahrenheit for the rest of the ferment, but starting low and cool (63–65°F/17–18°C) for 3–4 days before rising to the 70s Fahrenheit (low 20s Celsius) is almost as effective as perfect control the whole way through!

And if all else fails, remember that—almost always—yeast just want to do their job. Let them.

PROFILE: MARK VAN DITTA

Mark Van Ditta first appeared on the American Homebrewers Association discussion forum under the *nom de web* "S. Cerevisiae." It soon became apparent that Mark had a wealth of information about yeast strains and how to use them. But some of the information was controversial because it flew in the face of conventional homebrewing wisdom. Probably the biggest brouhaha came when Mark introduced his advice for making yeast starters. He called it "Shaken, Not Stirred," also referred to as the "James Bond method" and "SNS." Rather than using a yeast calculator to figure out how much yeast you needed, putting the starter on a stir plate, crashing the yeast, and decanting the wort (the popular method at the time), Mark advocated for putting a quart of 1.035 wort in a gallon container and shaking it to fill the container with foam. You then pitch your liquid yeast into that and pitch the entire thing at high kräusen the next day.

It sounded like heresy to Denny. Where was all the sciency stuff? But somewhere in the recesses of Denny's brain, something clicked for him. This was a lot like the starter method Denny had used when he first began using liquid yeast, before yeast calculators and stir plates. And he recalled how effective that method had been.

Denny gave the SNS method a try. The first thing he noticed is how fast and easy it was compared to the stir plate method he had been using. And wonder of wonders, the beer was every bit as good as when he used the more laborious starter method! Denny has now been doing it this way for so long that he doesn't even know where his stir plate is anymore!

We asked Mark to give us his thoughts on yeast. Here they are, in his own words:

> I taught myself most of what I know about yeast. Quality brewing yeast was difficult to obtain when I started to brew in early 1993. I caught the bug after culturing yeast from a bottle of Sierra Nevada Pale Ale. Brewing with that culture was a light-bulb moment for me. I learned how to plate and prepare sterile media in high school, so it was merely a matter of gaining access to glass petri dishes, screw cap culture tubes, and agar. From that point forward, I brewed with cultured yeast that I maintained on agar slants. While a lot of my early yeast strains were isolated from brewery samples, it helped that Jeff Mellem and Maribeth Raines started BrewTek around the same time. BrewTek was a fantastic resource during the early days of the home brewing revolution. Working with their mini-slants improved my yeast culture transfer technique. BrewTek's mini-slants

were so small that subculturing new slants and propagating stepped starters from 16 x 100 mm glass culture tubes was a breeze.

After I mastered maintaining a yeast bank in a home brewery environment, I decided to delve into microbiology and biochemistry. Interest in yeast genetics and molecular biology came later. I basically had to teach myself all of these disciplines. My ex-wife was a laboratory biologist when she first started her career. She was amazed that I was able to teach myself these subjects, especially organic chemistry. However, I have always found it to be easier to learn challenging subjects that have practical applications. Surviving graduate school in a STEM discipline also helped. One of the things that one learns in graduate school is how to read and decipher scientific publications. Writing about yeast reinforced what I knew. One needs to truly understand a topic in order to present it in a way that most people can grasp. The problem with scientific publications is that they are written by PhDs for PhDs, and most people are not PhDs.

In my humble opinion, amateur brewers tend to overthink yeast, especially when it comes to starter size. Yeast cultures grow exponentially; therefore, they are a like nuclear weapons in that close is good enough. The yeast cell population doubles every ninety minutes until the medium is exhausted or maximum cell density is obtained. After reaching maximum cell density (approximately two hundred billion cells per liter), additional cell production is for replacement only.

What is important when creating a starter is that the cells that end up being pitched into the fermentation have good ergosterol and unsaturated fatty acid (UFA) reserves, because the pitched cells will share these compounds with every one of their descendants. We need to remember that ergosterol and UFAs are produced in the presence of dissolved oxygen (O_2) during the lag phase; therefore, it is important to saturate the starter medium with O_2 when the culture is pitched. The SNS starter method is little more than a low-tech way of maximizing dissolved O_2 when the culture is pitched due to the fact that foam provides a large surface area for O_2 pickup.

A lot of brewers wait until a starter ferments out, but that is too long from my experience. A culture should be pitched at high kräusen. That is when the culture is making the transition from the exponential growth phase to the stationary phase. The quality of the cells declines after a culture transitions into the stationary phase due to mother cells being replaced by daughter cells with lower ergosterol and UFA reserves. Allowing a culture to ferment out and enter quiescence can result in pitching cells with significantly lower ergosterol and UFA reserves. Pitching the cells at high kräusen into freshly aerated wort shortens the lag phase and maximizes the use of dissolved O_2. Ergosterol is the plant equivalent of cholesterol, and while we only hear negative things about cholesterol, it is needed for things like brain health and hormone production. Ergosterol and UFAs keep the plasma membrane in a yeast cell pliable, which, in turn, makes it easier for a yeast cell to take in nutrients and expel waste.

Sanitation is the most critical thing to remember when starting yeast. Most infections are pitched with the yeast culture. A brewer wants the pitched yeast to be the dominant organism in the fermentation. That is why viable yeast cell counts are emphasized in brewing texts. Bacteria cells double in one-third the amount of time that it takes for yeast cells to double, which means that a bacteria culture grows by a factor of eight every time a yeast culture doubles. The yeast cultures available to brewers today contain so many yeast cells that a culture usually only has to double one or two times before reaching maximum cell density in a one-liter solution; therefore, the purpose of a starter is to bring the cells out of quiescence and allow them to build ergosterol and UFA reserves. Most of the time that elapses between pitching a culture and a starter reaching high kräusen is spent in the lag phase where the culture is adjusting to the medium and using dissolved O_2 to produce ergosterol and UFAs.

If a brewer keeps things clean, resists the urge to tamper with a starter while the culture is growing, and pitches at high kräusen into well-aerated wort while being mindful of sanitation, they will be rewarded with a healthy fermentation almost every time. We have to remember that we are dealing with biological organisms that convert wort to beer. Some yeast strains are more temperamental than others, so things do go wrong from time to time. It helps to keep notes about the progression of fermentation when working with a new strain. While I am currently on an indefinite hiatus from brewing, I always keep a handwritten log of all of my culturing and brewing-related activities. ∎

11

SIMPLE WILD

The last thing we want to simplify, before we get back on our journey to complicating everything, is the ultimate return to basics. You see, everything else in this book has been about how to make the best beer as simply and cleanly as possible, but that has only been the story of beer for the last briefest blip of history.

Before we got all clean and selective with our fermentations, many of our beers were fermented with a mélange of yeasts and bacteria. Some of these traditions are still alive, most notably in the *lambic* of Belgium, but as science has increased our understanding about what's responsible for the various weird and funky flavors and aromas, brewers have exerted more and more control over what ends up in their wild beers.

Wild fermented beers can be, and usually are, an acquired taste. In Denny's case, and for many other people, you don't get it at first sip, but there's something there that's intriguing enough to keep you coming back. It's a quest. You want to find out how you can hate it at the same time you're starting to love

"Just because you're going funky doesn't mean you shouldn't be just as careful as you would with a 'clean' beer."

DENNY: I got kind of a late start in homebrewing. When I was in my mid-40s, my business partner showed me how he was doing it and I decided to try it for myself. I dove in wholeheartedly, brewing and learning about different styles of beer. I had read online about Belgian styles, and people I respected raved about how delicious they were. I think the first one I tasted was a Celis White. Although it wasn't a sour beer, the flavor was unlike anything I'd ever tasted before and frankly I found it challenging. Yeah, now we all know that it's a pretty low-key (but delicious) beer, but at that point in my beer drinking it was...interesting. Then I heard that Rodenbach Grand Cru was the "best beer in the world," so I got my hands on a bottle. I still recall wondering why it tasted like vinegar. I kept choking it down, telling myself that I really should like it, but I ended up pouring out half the bottle. When I told my business partner/brewing mentor about it, his reply was, "That's what I try to get my beer to NOT taste like."

it. And then one day it happens—you get past the sourness and funkiness to the underlying complexity. And the next thing you know, that's exactly what you're trying to get your beer to taste like.

Before we get into this chapter, we just want to point out this is going to be a fingernail-thin overview of a very complex subject. We're here to get you started. You may find yourself saying, "Wait, I know there's more." Buddy, you don't know the half of it. Fortunately, Brewers Publications has you covered with Michael Tonsmeire's encyclopedic *American Sour Beers*.[1]

WILD DONE SAFELY

The first and, to our mind, most important rule about "wild brewing" is don't get lazy! A number of homebrewers tend to treat their funky beers with a more lax and carefree approach to sanitation, cleanliness, and fermentation control. Trust us when we say that's a bad idea.

Just because you're going funky doesn't mean you shouldn't be just as careful as you would with a "clean" beer. Remember, most critters that would love to take up residence in your sweet, sugary pool of wort make for bad flavors. Even the good funkmeister-type yeast will go wrong if their health and environment isn't cared for. In many ways, these less brew-savvy organisms need even more of our help to make sure they do what we'd like!

In other words, keep clean, keep sanitary, and keep your temperatures in check. Just like you would when making a clean beer.

There's also the flip side to this—your equipment aftercare. The microorganisms we're using to funkify the beer, namely members of the *Lactobacillus* and *Brettanomyces* genera, are incredibly impactful at even low levels of dosing. Allowing a few cells to slip into your next batch of beer (whether into the fermentor or keg) can, over time, lead to replication and the production of funky beer in what was supposed to be your IPA. It's great if that's what you want, but not so much if you're hoping to serve a bright, hoppy, clean-tasting beer. We recommend going full scorched-earth on your gear and hit it with iodophor after a thorough cleaning. We also dedicate anything plastic, like tubing or bucket fermentors, specifically to sour/funky stuff to reduce a chance of cross contamination.

The final thing to do for "safe" wilds is to shop around. There are a number of suppliers of pure cultures of bacteria and wild yeasts. When we first started brewing there were so few funky cultures on the market you could easily count them on one hand. You could have been forgiven for thinking that there was only one *Lactobacillus* and a few *Brettanomyces* species in the world. Nowadays, with microbiologists (turned brewers) deciding to help the rest of us out and suppliers like The Yeast Bay and Bootleg Biology cropping up all the time, there's no end to your options. Play with them, you'll be surprised!

---

[1] Michael Tonsmeire, *American Sour Beers: Innovative Techniques for Mixed Fermentations* (Boulder: Brewers Publications, 2014).

WILD INOCULATION

OK, fine, you want to really go au naturel, to go really, truly wild. Let's talk about this. We want you to be safe and have fun. Probably the most famous wild brewing tradition is lambic brewing, so let's start there.

Lambic is produced from a fairly complex "turbid" mash scheme that, traditionally, helped deal with the less than perfect malt and grains of the time; it also has the benefit of generating extra starchy wort. The starch ends up being extra food for the various critters in a wild inoculation. (Remember our friendly neighborhood brewer's yeast can usually only consume simple sugars and not the more complex carbohydrates like starches, but that doesn't stop the other microbes from chowing down!)

In traditional lambic production, the beer is pumped out of the boil kettle into a wide, shallow tray (roughly a foot deep, maybe a bit more), which is allowed to cool overnight while exposed to the air. During this time, as the wort drops below pasteurization temperatures, dust settles onto the surface of the wort along with its attendant load of bacteria, yeast, and other microbes. Once the wort is cooled, it's transferred into barrels for fermentation. While all the focus is usually on the magic of the coolship, there's a fair amount of speculation that the majority of the fermenting cultures actually come from the barrels that the cooled wort ends up in. Wood, it turns out, provides a stable residence for most of our fermenting friends. (Remember, "beer history" is often just good sounding stories told by beer drinkers to other beer drinkers. Tall tales make for easy drinking.)

If you want to recreate the coolship experience, the easiest thing is just hold your wort in your boil kettle overnight exposed to the air, ideally with airflow over the top from a fan and some rough cheesecloth covering the kettle. So, finish boiling in the afternoon of your brew day, wait until the next afternoon, and run the cooled wort into your fermentors and prepare to wait. Over time, the various free-roaming microbes (known colloquially as "bugs") that your wort collected will get down to business. Slowly, over the course of months, these bugs ferment the beer and alter its flavor characteristics. Each microbe rises to preeminence and falls away, leaving a wake of new experiences for the palate. It's a fascinating process, fraught with nervous waiting!

Want to make your process more like the big boys? Buy stainless steel hotel pans, like the ones you've seen at every mediocre catered buffet meal you've ever had. Hotel pans are the shallow stainless steel pans designed to fit into a chafing dish or steam table to hold warm food. The standard size, at 2.5 inches deep, holds ~8.75 quarts and can be had super cheap (outside the US, this equates to the 65 mm deep, 9 L pans). Three of those and you could hold a five-gallon batch of beer overnight, easily. Just pour your cooled, inoculated wort into a fermentor and go! For the record, hotel pans come in many sizes and depths—Drew can recommend going for the slightly deeper 4-inch (100 mm) pans to simplify life.

The same rules apply for using hotel pans as for using your boil kettle. Get a (clean) fan blowing over the top to aid both in cooling and preventing flies and other animated life-forms from settling in the wort.

Getting Safer with Booze and Acid

In an ideal world, when we let our wort rest for wild inoculation it would only be visited by friendly yeasts and bacteria. You know, the things that make flavors we enjoy and love. Sadly, that's just not the case. There are whole swaths of things longing for a wort bath that produce disagreeable flavors and worse. As Mike Tonsmeire reports in *American Sour Beers*, there is a chance of pathogenic enteric bacteria, like *Escherichia coli* (*E. coli*), subsisting in your wort during the first few weeks of fermentation.[2] Such bacteria can also produce "undesirable metabolites such as biogenic amines" that can cause a reaction in sensitive people, not to mention causing really nasty seweresque experiences for your palate. There are other spoilage microorganisms out there with similar characteristics.

To discourage these bad bugs from attending our pool party, we need to make the scene a little less attractive. The good thing for us is that many suspect organisms are relatively weak and cannot handle a mildly acidic and alcoholic environment. This means you can get the jump on them by adding acid or alcohol to the wort yourself. For adding acid, you'll need a way to measure pH (like a pH meter or pH strips) and some lactic acid. Drop the pH below 5 to around 4.5 with lactic acid (88%)—it doesn't take much, a few milliliters. For extra protection, you can add some hops during the wort production.

You can add some alcohol to your wort. Choose your poison, but 325 mL of a 151 proof neutral grain spirit (e.g., Everclear®) will do the job nicely for five gallons. You want to end up at around 1% ABV; even 650 mL of standard 80 proof vodka will put you over the mark. This might seem like a lot to do for a full batch, but it gives you a safe head start. This method becomes even easier with our next approach, which is making a wild starter!

Even Safer with Wild Starters

Even with all the precautions you can take when doing wild inoculations, you just don't know what's going to arrive in your wort. That's a lot of work to take a risk with, so our preferred way to do a wild inoculation for beer is to cheat and make a wild starter. Why take a chance on producing five or more gallons of drain cleaner?

The process for a wild starter is simple. Take some leftover mash runnings from a brew day (runnings in the 1.020-1.030 range) and briefly boil them to kill off any lactobacilli from the grain (you want to start clean here). Sanitize quart or half-gallon (1–2 L) sized mason jars and pour the newly boiled wort into the jars. Cover with cheesecloth that you secure with a rubber band and place the jars overnight in your target collection zone.

DREW: I came across an interesting fact when doing some lambic research a while back. We always tend to think, "Oh lambics used aged hops to avoid bitterness and flavor while still getting some antimicrobial effects." Turns out, not always! Fresh hops were used back in the day. Granted, even fresh hops back then weren't as potent as we get today, but it's nice to see a change of pace from the usual stories.

---

2   Tonsmeire, *American Sour Beers*, 163.

Once the overnight exposure is done, cover the wort jars tightly with foil and let them ferment. After a few days of fermentation, you should be able to smell and taste the new beer. Just grab a small sample with a sanitized beer thief or tube to prove your culture viability by tasting. If the taste is horribly off, throw out that starter. If you got lucky and got an interesting culture, add fresh wort to a sanitized vessel and pitch it with your new bug collection. Grow that up to at least half a gallon (~2 L) and use that starter to pitch a full batch of beer.

A few additional tips:

- Areas with lots of fruiting or blossoming plants, in our experience, produce the most interesting cultures.
- Place several jars in the areas you want to collect to give you multiple chances of getting a good sample.
- Don't want to use leftovers from a brew day or just want to make it simple? No worries! Use extract and just make your wort that way. We just like saving on ingredient costs.

Another approach we've played with is flipping the script. Instead of inoculating the wort with stuff coming off of plants, why not add the plants directly to the wort. In particular, taking washed organic fruit (or fruit from the garden, lightly scrubbed) and putting the fruit into a starter wort works like magic. Another idea is to play around with infusions of various trees, herbs, and flowers. The same rules apply: let fermentation happen, smell and taste, and, if magic has happened, grow!

A traditional, extraordinarily cheap way to get your sour on is to pitch some grain into your fresh wort. This isn't as far-fetched as it might seem. Barley is covered in *Lactobacillus* so you're guaranteed to get sour. While cheap though, there are a lot of other critters on your grain, so we still recommend making a starter first!

The Cultured Wild

You can use cultured "wild" microbes like you can use cultured yeast. Let's say that rolling the dice isn't your thing and you want to get a little more science behind you. That's fine, plenty of people are ready and waiting to help you. First, let's go over the main microbes you to need to know about (at least, if you're trying to perfectly recreate the main odd ducks you get in a lambic).

Lactobacillus (a.k.a. Lacto)

Lactobacillus is our fast acting, lean, mean, lactic acid-making machine. These bacteria bring the quick hit of tart, tangy acidity. We'll talk more about Lacto shortly, but safe to say it's an acid producer.

Saccharomyces (brewer's yeast)

We've covered *Saccharomyces* throughout this book, especially chapter 10. It's our good friend, brewer's yeast.

DREW: By the way, using blends doesn't just have to apply to truly wild beers. My favorite style in the world is saison. The classic saisons of Belgium, like the ones from Brasserie Dupont, have a blend of *Saccharomyces* and Brett playing in them. The trick is to get the Brett at the right "low" level of impact. My main beef with many American saisons is that they are really Brett beers, not saisons, because the Brett is so overpowering. OK, that's not my main beef, my main beef is that so many of them are underfermented. But as for the subject of this chapter my beef is, I want saison with Brett, not Brett with saison.

DENNY: Where I live there are breweries using yogurt to sour their beers. A local dairy produces a yogurt with live *Lactobacillus* in it, and breweries use it to sour their beers. As weird as it sounds, it works! To try this, make 1 qt. (~1 L) of unhopped 1.035 starter wort. When it's cooled, add 2-4 tsp. of live yogurt and let it ferment at 100–110°F (38–43°C) for 24 hours before adding it to your batch of wort for your beer. Hold that at 100–110°F for 24 hours. Then boil the wort to kill the lactobacilli.

Pediococcus (a.k.a. Pedio)

Pediococcus is one of our favorite names to say for a creature we hope to never unintentionally see in our breweries. These bacteria produce weird, deeply funky flavors, along with diacetyl (butter) and ropiness (long snotty strands of polysaccharides chained together that gave rise to calling the beer "sick").

Brettanomyces (a.k.a. Brett)

Brettanomyces is our cleanup hitter. No seriously, in a fully wild inoculation these warriors go to town on the leftovers from the other players. Brett destroys polysaccharides and take up off-flavors. These wild yeasts make the beer well again, while also imparting a whole raft of funky, hay, barnyard, leather, pine-apple, and citrus flavors and aromas.

An important note here, we tend to talk about a lot of these bugs as single species, but the reality is, like our good friend *S. cerevisiae*, there are countless species and strains under each genus. (OK, the exception is maybe *Pediococcus*, where the only one we seem to give a damn about it *P. damnosus* since that's the main player in lambic.) This distinction has become more important over the years as more brewers have discovered new strains to play with.

Let's start with the easy approach first. Get yourself a blend. These days there are so many fantastic blends available straight from talented microbiologists. Each blend will give you something different, but they've all been selected to be interesting and fun. Just pitch and wait for the magic to happen (give it at least six months).

If you don't want to go the blend way, a number of brewers have been taking advantage of the advent of probiotic drinks. Taking a step back, "probiotics" is a term used to describe various microorganisms that are believed to help promote digestive health. Various pills and drinks have arrived in the grocery store proclaiming their positive impact on our guts. Probiotics are independent of traditional foods like sauerkraut and buttermilk. In fact, most take their cue from yogurt and kefir. Go pick up a bottle of GoodBelly® or a similar probiotic aid and look at the back—it will list the active cultures found in them, including numerous variants of *Lactobacillus*. Using probiotics is as simple as adding them to your wort. (See the "Kettle Souring" segment below for the best way to encourage sourness from these critters.)

If you want to go for the real deal and use individual pure cultures, you can do a lot with just some simple scheduling of your pitches. In Drew's experience, which has been mostly Brett based, the prime difference is in when you pitch the Brett. If you pitch at knockout, along with or in lieu of your regular yeast, the Brett becomes very soft tasting and more subdued. If you pitch it in a secondary situation, after primary fermentation has stripped most of the sugar away, the earthy characters of Brett seem to pop more.

The Ultimate "Pure Pitch" Wild Method

(adapted from M.B. Raines, the microbiologist who taught Drew about yeast)

1. Brew the beer with a turbid mash to generate extra starch.
2. Pitch with your *Saccharomyces* strain and ferment as normal (2–3 weeks).
3. As the primary wraps up, add Pedio along with "food" (e.g., starter wort, fruit, etc.). The Pedio should finish in roughly 1–2 weeks.
4. When the beer smells buttery or looks ropy and "sick," pitch the Brett and Lacto, again with a bit more food. The Brett and Lacto usually finish in roughly 1–4 months.
5. Wait for the beer to become clean again and then wait a little longer for your flavors to meld. The whole process—from mash to clean beer—should be about 8–12 months.

KETTLE SOURING: THE ULTIMATE SIMPLE SOUR

No chapter talking about simple approaches to wild beer would be complete without a discussion of kettle souring. Besides the chances of getting a bad fermentation character from wild inoculation, the main problems with wild brewing are the risk of contaminating your equipment with something undesirable in your non-funky beers and the sheer amount of time a wild ferment (even a "cultured wild" ferment) takes to produce the final product. Traditional lambics take one to three years to mature into a drinkable product and most of us don't have the time and patience for that!

Here's the thing though, it doesn't take that long to produce sourness in beer. *Lactobacillus*, our main producer of tangy lactic acid, can drop a beer from sweet to mouth-puckeringly sour in as little as a few hours or days. It's rather impressive.

Traditional lactic-heavy styles like Berliner weiss would be simmered instead of boiled, inoculated with a *Lactobacillus* culture like *L. debrueckii*, and allowed to sour while warm. The resulting beer after a regular fermentation was brisk and bracingly sour. Sure, a Berliner weiss lacks the deep exotic funk of a lambic, but the zippiness of the clean acid was as refreshing as a glass of cold lemonade on a warm summer's day.

But you still have the problem of lactobacilli running around your brewery, so, just like flipping the script on wild inoculations, brewers have flipped the script on the whole souring thing. Instead of mashing, boiling, and pitching, they mash, pitch, and then boil. Because *Lactobacillus* works relatively quickly, you can mash and lauter into your boil kettle, then add bugs to the warm wort and let it to sit for 24–72 hours before bringing it to a boil, killing the bugs dead. Voilà, sour wort and no worries about your equipment getting infected!

Kettle souring has some disadvantages. It ties up your boil kettle and requires you to keep it warm (roughly 110°F/43°C) for the period of acid fermentation. By its quick nature, the process doesn't build up the deep earthy funk of traditional souring methods.

The major advantage of kettle souring is it keeps fermentation equipment safe from contamination thanks to the boil killing everything off. It also has the benefit of speed of production (no more waiting months) and the focused, clean acidity that results.

Traditionalists tend to look down on the whole kettle souring notion, but as long as you know what it can and can't do, we just consider it another tool in the brewer's toolbox. You'll notice this is a lot easier in many ways than the traditional methods looked at earlier.

Kettle Souring Step by Step

1. Mash your beer as normal. Raise to mash-out and lauter into your boil kettle.
2. Boil the wort for 15 minutes to kill any residual bugs from the grain. (Some treat this as an optional step.)
3. Cool the wort to 110–120°F. (43–49°C)
4. Pitch the wort with souring agents (*Lactobacillus* cultures, wild starters, etc.).
5. Purge the kettle with CO_2 (Another step that is optional, but some believe reduced oxygen levels in the kettle results in less off-flavors; the science around this is iffy, but it makes brewers feel good.)
6. Wrap the top of the kettle with foil or plastic wrap. Wrap the kettle in insulation and hold warm for 24–72 hours with the lid on. Downward drifting temperatures are OK, just don't let the wort get cold. If you're using a temperature-controlled brew rig, set it to keep the wort over 100°F (38°C).

RECIPE

The Sour Cat

Catharina Sour
As we write this, Catharina sour is one of a handful of newer styles involving heavily fruited sour beers. This example from Santa Catarina, Brazil, is a stronger take on a Berliner weiss with an explosion of fresh fruits. Local favorites included strawberries, citrus, guava, and more! The key here is to follow the kettle souring procedure above and hit this with whatever fruit you want!

Batch volume: 5.5 gal. (21 L)
Original gravity: 1.045 (11.2°P)
Final gravity: 1.005 (1.3°P)

Bitterness: 5 IBU
ABV: 5.9%
Boil: 20 minutes

Malt
- 6.0 lb. (2.7 kg) Pilsner malt
- 5.5 lb. (2.5 kg) wheat malt

Mash
- Single infusion at 150°F (66°C) for 60 minutes.

Hops
- 0.5 oz. (14 g) Magnum 12% AA @ 20 minutes

Yeast/Bacteria
- Any *Lactobacillus* culture you'd like for the kettle souring
- Wyeast 1056, WLP001, or Safale US-05 for primary fermentation

Extras
- 1.0 lb. (450 g) fruit puree, added post primary fermentation
  or
- 3–5 lb. (1.4–2.3 kg) fresh fruit, ideally pureed, added post primary fermentation

Notes
- Follow the kettle sour procedure to make the base sour, then proceed with boil, hop additions, and primary yeast fermentation as per a regular beer.

7. Remove the lid and wrapping and pull a sample of the wort to test the pH and taste. If acidity is at the desired level, proceed.

8. Remove wrappings, bring kettle to a boil and proceed as if the beer is a regular batch. (We recommend adding extra nutrient and a healthy yeast pitch since your acidulated wort is now a more hostile environment for the yeast.)

BLENDING AND FLAVORING

One last bit of voodoo in the world of sour and funky ales. Here's where we have to include notes from our friendly neighborhood winemakers and embrace the art of blending. Remember, we can't depend on always getting the same flavors from our varied bugs.

The smart play when blending is to run multiple batches of beer, ferment them, and taste each batch. You'll see that some are sourer, some earthier, some sweeter or funkier. Set up a few glasses and measure different proportions of finished beer into each to see what makes the ultimate beer. Many breweries will hold onto exceptionally sour wort in order to boost the newly fermented beer's acidity into acceptable and pleasant realms. (Think of it like adding a splash of vinegar to a finished stew for acidity and brightness.)

What are you looking for in this mix of glasses? Let's say you have three or four different beers. What you want to find is the proportions of beers A, B, C, and D you need to mix to achieve your "perfect" flavor. If you're a big sour candy fan, for instance, you might aim for a very punchy, sweet-tart blend. If you're more of an earthy funk fan, you'll tweak the blend to be more Brett-forward with just a touch of acid to perk up the proceedings.

Regardless of what you're going for, what you'll discover is the blending ratio (e.g., 10% beer A, 40% B, 50% C, and 0% D) that is perfect for you. When you scale up, just blend the appropriate volumes using that ratio into one big batch and you should be groovy.

Seems intimidating? It is, but blending is a special art that offers infinite possibilities. It doesn't just stop at different beers, you can do this same blending technique with liqueurs, wines, fruits, and other flavors as well. Play! It's only beer!

PROFILES IN SIMPLICITY: GARRET GARFIELD

When Garrett Garfield moved to Chile, he had never brewed a batch of beer before. In fact, he drank his first beer on the way to Chile in a Canadian airport! But by the time he got to Chile, he had become a beer lover. Unfortunately, at that time in Chile there was little to no craft beer and very few good beers of any kind. So, Garret decided it was time to learn to brew his own. Like most Chilean homebrewers, he went straight to all-grain because those were the ingredients he could get. But he also did something a little different.

Garrett married a Chilean woman whose father worked at an agricultural school, where a wide variety of fruits were grown. Garret thought that would make a great place to capture wild yeast, so he set out six jars of wort (1.035-ish gravity) covered with cheesecloth in various locations around the farm. He was about 50% successful in capturing usable yeast. Garrett advises that if you try this, be prepared to toss any samples that just don't seem "right." After all, you don't want to make subpar beer, so evaluate every sample carefully as to its suitability for brewing. When you have some samples that you think will be interesting, step them up to a useable pitch quantity. Interestingly, not all of the wild yeasts are funky or sour like you might expect. When Denny was in Chile, he had a chance to try several beers Garrett had made with his yeast. Some had a delightfully fruity sourness, and some were so clean that Denny thought they have been made with an American ale yeast! Not at all what he'd expected. If you're an adventurous person, give capturing your own yeast a try.

Denny also had an opportunity to try an earlier version of the beer that's given in the Purple Profundo recipe below. If you have access to the right kind of corn (fig. 11.1), we pretty much guarantee you that it will be a one-of-a-kind brewing experience. ■

Figure 11.1. Blue corn that Denny used to make chicha.

Purple Profundo by Garrett Garfield

Garrett plays around a lot with unique ingredients available to him in Chile, including red, blue, and purple corn. This is Garret's spin on a modernized version of *chicha*, or corn beer, produced all over Central and South America. When used with certain varieties of colored corn, the beer takes on a stronger earthy flavor as well as a profound color.

Batch volume: 5.5 gal. (21 L)
Original gravity: 1.053 (13.1°P)
Final gravity: 1.007 (1.8°P)

Malt/Grain
- 3 lb. (1.36 kg) pale malt
- 3 lb. (1.36 kg) Vienna malt
- 2 lb. (0.91 kg) wheat malt
- 3 lb. (1.36 kg) purple corn, cooked

Mash
- Single infusion at 154°F (68°C) for 60 minutes.

Hops
- 0.4 oz. (11 g) Mosaic 12.25% AA @ 30 min.
- 0.4 oz. (11 g) Mosaic 12.25% AA @ 15 min.

Color: will depend on corn choice
Bitterness: 43 IBU
ABV: 5.3%

- 0.4 oz. (11 g) Amarillo 7.9% AA @ 15 min.
- 0.4 oz. (11 g) Cascade 9.8% AA @ 15 min.s
- 0.4 oz. (11 g) Mosaic 12.25% AA @ whirlpool for 15 min.
- 0.4 oz. (11 g) Amarillo 7.9% AA @ whirlpool for 15 min.
- 0.4 oz. (11 g) Cascade 9.8% AA @ whirlpool for 15 min.

Yeast
- Safale US-05 or WLP838 Southern German Lager or your wild culture

INDEX

Entries in **boldface** refer to photos and illustrations.

rehydration, 196-97

Reinheitsgebot, 17, 22, 157, 165, 167, 190

Renner, Jeff, 36

residual alkalinity (RA), 155, 156

retronasal olfaction, 117

Revere, Paul, 6

reverse osmosis (RO), 109, 148, 152-54, 158, 161

rice, 22, 65, 165, 166; basmati, 177; Calrose medium-grain sushi, 177; flaked, 16; instant, 176-77; Japanese sushi, 177; jasmine, 177; wild, 168, 177

RoboBrew, 90

Rochefort, 116

Rodenbach Grand Cru, 214

Rolling Rock, 175

roses, 200

rye, 122, 169; chocolate, 171; flaked, 171; malted, 171; unmalted, 171

Rye Barleywine, recipe for, 173

Rye IPA, 124, 127, 128, 169

Saccharomyces, 192, 194, 217, 218, 219

Saccharomyces bayanus, 192

Saccharomyces carlsbergensis, 191, 194

Saccharomyces cerevisiae, 191, 192, 193, 194, 198, 207

Saccharomyces eubayanus, 192, 194

Saccharomyces pastorianus, 191, 192, 193-94

Safale S-04 English ale yeast, 115

Safale US-05 yeast, 114

Safale WB-06 yeast, 115

Saint-Exupéry, Antoine de, 145

Saint Sixtus Abbey, 179

saison, 26, 30, 60, 108, 125, 128, 135, 178, 192, 193; rye, 171

Saison Guacamole, 128

salt additions, 147, 154, 158; RA and, 156

sanitation, 29, 55, 58, 206, 209, 210, 217; proper, 49; wild brewing and, 214

Santa Catarina, 100, 101

Sasquatch Homebrew Competition, 81

sauerkraut, 218

Schneider, Bob, 94

Schutzen Lite Lager, recipe for, 17

Schwartz, Ken, 66

schwarzbier, 199

SenSafe iDip kits, 148

"Shaken, Not Stirred" method, 198, 207, 208

sherry, 107

Sierra Nevada Brewing Company, 112, 138

Sierra Nevada Pale Ale, 207

sieves, 51, 92

Simpler Times, recipe for, 119

simplicity, 7, 24-29, 34, 65, 165; efficiency and, 8-10, 13; key to, 13-14; money for, 202; returning to, 213

Simpsons Double Roasted Crystal, 109

Simpsons Maltings, 174

single malt and single hops (SMASH), 108, 112, 129-32, 130

sinks, plastic utility, 52

skunkiness, 202

slurry, 168, 198

small batches, 24, 45, 50-56, 57, 59; BIAB, 56; brewing, 46-50, 61; fermentation and, 47; shortcoming for, 49-50

SMASH. *See* single malt and single hops

smelling, 107, 217

smoke, 115, 116, 193, 195

Smythe, John, 136

soda, 36, 58

soda kegs, 11, 29

sodium, 146, 147, 148; described, 150

sodium bicarbonate, 155

sodium hypochlorite, 151

sodium metabisulfate, 151

software, 30, 71, 88, 92, 197; open-source, 98; water treatment, 153, 154

sorghum, 185

Sour Cat, The: recipe for, 220

sourcing, local, 140

souring: kettle, 34, 35, 220; pitching, 220; traditional, 219

sourness, 214, 218

sous vide circulator, described, 54

sparge water, 34, 157, 160

sparging, 34, 51, **51**, 72, 73, 77, 81, 91, 92, 157, 158, 160, 215; batch, 8, 66; BIAB and, 60; continuous/fly, 8; dunk, 60

specific gravity, 14, 28, 30, 55, 72, 197, 204

Speed Brewing (Izett), 32, 59

Speidel Braumeister, **91**, 91-92, 100, 101

spelt, 168

spice, 58, 111, 112, 191

spinach, 183

spoons, 25, 29, 53

Spudweiser, 15

squash, 183

Star San, 184

starches, 22, 65, 71, 108, 168, 185, 215; corn, 176; mashing, 167; potato, 178

starters: canned, 200; simplifying, 198-99; viability, 199; vitality, 198-99; wild, 216-17; yeast, 9, 34, 197, 198, 209